Prayer, Middle Knowledge, and Divine-Human Interaction

Prayer, Middle Knowledge, and Divine-Human Interaction

Kyle D. DiRoberts

FOREWORD BY
Glenn R. Kreider

WIPF & STOCK · Eugene, Oregon

PRAYER, MIDDLE KNOWLEDGE, AND DIVINE-HUMAN INTERACTION

Copyright © 2018 Kyle D. DiRoberts. All rights reserved. Except for brief quotations in critical publications or reviews, no part of this book may be reproduced in any manner without prior written permission from the publisher. Write: Permissions, Wipf and Stock Publishers, 199 W. 8th Ave., Suite 3, Eugene, OR 97401.

Wipf & Stock
An Imprint of Wipf and Stock Publishers
199 W. 8th Ave., Suite 3
Eugene, OR 97401

www.wipfandstock.com

PAPERBACK ISBN: 978-1-5326-5352-0
HARDCOVER ISBN: 978-1-5326-5353-7
EBOOK ISBN: 978-1-5326-5354-4

Manufactured in the U.S.A.

To Kaden and Oliver,
May you grow into men of prayer.
To Alanna,
I love praying with you. May we never stop.

Contents

Foreword | xi

Preface | xv

Acknowledgments | xvii

Introduction | xix
    Introduction   xix
    Compatibilism and Libertariansim   xix
    Middle Knowledge   xxi
    Summary of Remaining Chapters   xxii

1 **Theories of Providence** | 1
    Compatibilism   1
        God's Providence   2
            Preservation   3
            Government   3
        Biblical Evidence of Compatiblism   6
    Hard Determinism   7
        Human Freedom and Hard Determinism   9
        Theological Evidence of Hard Determinism   11
    Compatibilism vs. Hard Determinism   14
    Open Theism   26
        Introduction   26
        Open Theism Defined   27
        Biblical Example for Open Theism   28
        Theological Characteristics of Open Theism   29
            Sovereignty of God   29
            Dynamic Love, Knowledge, and Reactions   30
    Middle Knowledge   33
        Molina, Hubmaier, and Arminius   33
        Middle Knowledge Defined   35
        Logical Priority   35
        Logical Moments in God's Knowledge   37

Natural Knowledge   37
Free Knowledge   39
Middle Knowledge   40
Libertarian Freedom   43
Conclusion   45

2 **Petitionary Prayer and Theology** | 46
Introduction   46
Petitionary Prayer Defined   47
Biblical Examples of Petitionary Prayer   48
Petitionary Prayer and Theology   55
Petitionary Prayer, Inspiration of Scripture, and Hypostatic Union   56
Petitionary Prayer and Systematic Theology   57
Pastoral Theology   59
"Ask and You Will Receive"   60
Petitionary Prayer as Genuine Worship   62
Repentance and Confession   64
Conclusion   66

3 **Compatibilism, Hard Deteriminism, and Petitionary Prayer** | 67
Introduction   67
Sovereignty, Compatibilism, and Petitionary Prayer   68
John Calvin   68
Necessity of Petitionary Prayer   69
Humility and Prayer   69
Jonathan Edwards   71
Knowing God Correctly Is Paramount to Prayer   71
Petitionary Prayer and Worship   73
Edwards, Prayer, and the Omniscience of God   73
Edwards's Compatibilism   74
Compatibilism, Petitionary Prayer, and Theology   76
God's Sovereignty and Human Freedom Are Not Mutually Exclusive   77
Petitions Should Align with God's Purposes   80
Compatibilism, Petitionary Prayer, and Systematic Theology   84
Compatibilism, Petitionary Prayer, and Pastoral Theology   86
Hard Determinism   88
Introduction   88
Petitionary Prayer and Cancer   89
Hard Determinism and Petitionary Prayer   90
Sovereignty and Petitionary Prayer Defined   92
God Does Not Need Our Petitionary Prayer   94
God Uses Prayer to Enlist Participation in His Work   96
Conclusion   99

4 **Open Theism and Petitionary Prayer** | 100
   Introduction   100
   Sovereignty, Petitionary Prayer, and Open Theism   103
      Petitionary Prayer and Spiritual "Say-So"   104
      Open Theism, Compatibilism, and Petitionary Prayer   107
   Open Theism, Petitionary Prayer, and Theology   109
      Knowing God Correctly is Paramount to Prayer   109
      Petitionary Prayer and the Logical Moments of God's Knowledge   110
      Petitionary Prayers Toward an Open Future   113
   Open Theism, Petitionary Prayer, and Systematic Theology   115
      The Trinity and Petitionary Prayer   115
      Jesus as Priest and the Priesthood of All Believers   118
      Petitionary Prayer, God's Immutability, and Two-Way Contingency   120
   Open Theism, Petitionary Prayer, and Pastoral Theology   123
   Conclusion   125

5 **Middle Knowledge and Petitionary Prayer** | 128
   Introduction   128
   Sovereignty, Petitionary Prayer, Middle Knowledge   129
      Omniscience   129
      Libertarian Freedom as Expressed through Love   132
   Compatibilism or Middle Knowledge?   136
   Middle Knowledge, Petitionary Prayer, and Theology   139
      Middle Knowledge, Humility, and Petitionary Prayer   139
      Logical Moments of God's Knowledge and Petitionary Prayer   145
      Petitionary Prayer Is Meant to Change Us   148
      Divine-Human Friendship   152
   Middle Knowledge, Petitionary Prayer, and Systematic Theology   154
   Middle Knowledge, Petitionary Prayer, and Pastoral Theology   156
      Petitionary Prayer as Confession and Repentance   156
      Unanswered Petitionary Prayer   160
   Conclusion   164

6 **Conclusion** | 166

   Bibliography | 169

Foreword

"Rejoice always, pray without ceasing, give thanks in all circumstances; for this is the will of God in Christ Jesus for you" (1 Thess 5:6-18).[1]

THE PROBLEM OF EVIL is undoubtedly the most difficult of theological issues. How could a good and omnibenevolent God allow evil? How could the God revealed in the Scriptures not react to the evil that occurs in his world? Surely a good God would stop horrific evil before it occurs. Surely a good God would punish evildoers and would defend the cause of the oppressed and the abused. Since evil exists, and much of it is horrific, some conclude, God is not good, not powerful, or does not know what is happening in the world. Or, as a last resort, some conclude that there is no God. Many attempts have been offered to defend the character of God in the face of evil, to present a theodicy. This work builds upon those discussions, because any interaction with prayer and divine sovereignty will, inevitably, come face to face with the problem of evil.

How can we meaningfully confess that God is sovereign over his world, how can his providence be comprehensive, how can everything that happens in his world be part of a plan known to God before the creation of the world, and that plan be contingent upon the prayers of his people? And if the plan is not contingent, then is petitionary prayer really effectual? How should we understand the divine-human tension, the apparent inconsistency between a God who knows the end from the beginning and has ordained everything that comes to pass and a God who seems to encourage his people to pray and promises to act in response to those prayers? That is the question this work sets out to answer.

In short, if God is sovereign, if he knows what I will choose before I choose it, and if his knowledge of my choice makes my choice certain to

---

1. Scripture quotations are from The ESV® Bible (The Holy Bible, English Standard Version®), copyright © 2001 by Crossway, a publishing ministry of Good News Publishers. Used by permission. All rights reserved.

occur, then am I really free? And if I am not free, then what difference does prayer make? Why pray, if my prayers cannot impact God's will or actions in the world? Is prayer merely for my sake, to make my will correspond to God's will? What is the purpose and value of prayer—particularly petitionary prayer? Some people ignore questions like these or dismiss them without much consideration. Yet these are the kinds of questions that keep some people up at night, that drive them to wrestle with deep and mysterious concepts, to attempt to understand better, even if an answer is not found. From my introduction to Kyle DiRoberts when he moved to Dallas to start coursework, he was wrestling with petitionary prayer and sovereignty. In discussions over poached eggs at breakfast, while enjoying a cup of bold coffee, infrequently even relishing a well-marbled steak, or just hanging out and talking, our conversations almost always came back around to this theological dilemma. He worked long and hard on this question. The result of his work is this book, which is based upon his PhD dissertation.

As an evangelical theologian, DiRoberts begins with several presuppositions; among them are that there is a God and he is good, that the Scripture is God's verbal revelation and thus is consistent and non-contradictory but not comprehensive, that God's revelation in creation and providence is complementary to his revelation in Scripture, that there are a lot of things we cannot know about God and his world but we should continue to wrestle with our unanswered questions, and that ultimately God's desire for us is to trust and worship him whether or not we understand.

"God is good, all the time. All the time, God is good." Some of us were nurtured in traditions where this call and response was part of the church liturgy. I did not grow up in such a church; in fact, the first time I said, "God is good" in a classroom, and a student responded, "all the time," I was caught off guard. I stopped and asked her to explain it to me. When I did so, she was caught off guard. She thought EVERYBODY knew that God is good. She thought EVERYBODY knew to respond to "God is good" with "all the time." It led to a healthy discussion of tradition and theological method, as well as the importance of affirming the consistency of God's character and his actions. Although that incident was several decades ago, I seldom talk about God's goodness without remembering. And, in the midst of life in a fallen world, surrounded by death, decay, and devastation, remembering that God is good provides stability, security, and safety. Otherwise, if God cannot be trusted to act consistently with his omnibenevolent character, we have no hope.

If God is good, then God can never be the cause of something that is not good. Evil exists—it is somehow part of God's plan, but it is never the result of God's actions. He allows evil; he never causes it. How does this fundamental conviction impact petitionary prayer? One way of responding to the tension between sovereignty and prayer, sometimes called determinism, asserts that God has decreed everything that happens in his world. Some versions of determinism seem to make God the cause of evil. DiRoberts demonstrates this tendency and argues that determinism also denies libertarian freedom, a view of freedom he believes is important to affirm. Compatibilism, or soft determinism, in DiRoberts's view, affirms both freedom and sovereignty, but fails to explain adequately how the two fit together. Finally, open theism maintains a robust view of human libertarian freedom but denies comprehensive divine omniscience. Having surveyed these approaches, DiRoberts then affirms that middle knowledge, in the Molinist tradition, provides a better account of petitionary prayer. He argues that middle knowledge preserves both libertarian freedom and comprehensive divine omniscience in petitionary prayer. In short, he believes that middle knowledge handles the tension outlined above better than other responses, even though no theological position resolves it completely.

Most readers of this work will not agree with the author completely. But anyone who is interested in the theological foundation for petitionary prayer will find this work helpful. Further, as DiRoberts argues, it is not enough to provide a theology of prayer; the goal should be a more active practice of prayer, a more persistent habit of prayer, a more deliberate engagement with God in prayer, a more faithful wrestling with God in prayer. If the will of God is that we pray without ceasing (1 Thess 5:16), if we lack because we have not asked (James 4:3), if we are commanded to knock until the door is opened (Matt 7:7), and if we are to be persistent in prayer (Col 4:2), then anything that leads to such obedience is God's will for us.

Jesus told a parable encouraging his disciples to persevere in prayer, because "they ought always to pray and not lose heart" (Luke 18:1–8).[2] It is a parable about a widow who is petitioning a judge for justice against her adversary. The judge refused to respond but, because of her persistence, he eventually agreed to grant her justice, "Though I neither fear God nor respect man, yet because this widow keeps bothering me, I will give her justice, so that she will not beat me down by her continual coming." Jesus concludes, "Hear what the unrighteous judge says. And will not God give justice to his elect, who cry to him day and night? Will he delay long over them? I tell you, he will give justice to them speedily. Nevertheless, when the Son of Man comes, will he find faith on earth?" Persistence in prayer, perseverance in petition, brings results. One can only wonder what we lack because we give up too soon. One can only wonder what God might do in

---

2.. The parable is in Luke 18:1–8.

response to the prayers of his people. If this work encourages Christians to persevere in prayer, to petition the God of heaven on behalf of their needs and the needs of others, to demonstrate faith in God's goodness by pleading with him to act in mercy and compassion in response to pain and suffering, and to persist in this pursuit until God answers, the author will have achieved his goal. This is an academic work which has ministerial and deeply practical implications and applications. After all, the apostle Paul exhorts us: "Rejoice in the Lord always; again I will say, rejoice. Let your reasonableness be known to everyone. The Lord is at hand; do not be anxious about anything, but in everything by prayer and supplication with thanksgiving let your requests be made known to God. And the peace of God, which surpasses all understanding, will guard your hearts and your minds in Christ Jesus" (Phil 4:4–7).

Glenn R. Kreider

Professor of Theological Studies
Dallas Theological Seminary
1 April 2018
Resurrection Sunday

Preface

THIS STUDY RESULTS FROM my desire to understand the divine-human relationship in petitionary prayer. Christians generally believe that in prayer they are free in their act to petition God. Christians also believe that they pray to a God that is sovereign and omniscient. Explanation as to how one affirms these two truths is dependent upon one's account of divine providence, which determines how motivated the person is to offer petitionary prayer in the divine-human relationship. I will argue that middle knowledge is the preferred theory of providence as it relates to petitionary prayer, because it argues that God's sovereignty includes both his omniscience and libertarian human freedom.

The introduction of this book states the need for the study and provides definitions for key terms. The first chapter surveys middle knowledge in addition to its primary competitors, which include compatibilism, hard determinism, and open theism. The second chapter defines petitionary prayer and examines its biblical and theological characteristics. Chapters 1 and 2 serve as the foundation upon which this dissertation builds. Chapter 3 examines compatibilism and hard determinism and their attempts to explain the divine-human relationship in petitionary prayer. Chapter 4 examines open theism and its understanding of the divine-human relationship in prayer. Chapter 5 proposes a middle knowledge account of petitionary prayer, which is preferred over that of compatibilism, hard determinism, and open theism with respect to the divine-human relationship in prayer.

Acknowledgments

I am left humbled at the end of this project. While the writing and research were largely done in isolation, God providentially surrounded me with a community of people who gave up their own interests to make it possible for me to accomplish this work. To these individuals, I owe a debt that cannot be repaid.

I would like to thank Wes Roberts. You consistently measured my spiritual wellbeing throughout this journey so that at each point in the process my focus was upon loving God and those around me. Also, I appreciate Fred Chay, who would call or email frequently, not expecting anything in return. His intent was merely to make sure that I was giving my time to Alanna, the kids, and my relationship with God in the midst of writing. In addition, I want to thank Jenae Edwards. From start to finish you walked alongside me, providing outstanding suggestions regarding the content and structure of this book. I could not have asked for a wiser or more encouraging editor.

I also owe a debt of gratitude to my readers. Nathan Holsteen tirelessly helped me narrow my claim and refine my ability to make an argument. I am indebted to you for this work. Also, I am grateful to John Laing as he helped in my understanding of the various nuances of middle knowledge. In addition, thank you for providing invaluable insight into the direction of this project in its early stages. Richard Taylor, thank you for providing your keen eye to the form of this book so that it remained clean and consistent. Finally, a special thank you to Glenn Kreider. You are a hard person to introduce to people because you play so many important roles in my life. You are the supervisor for this project, and you led me with kindness, patience, and grace to completion. You are a theological mentor in that you have taught me how to think, listen, speak, read, and see theologically. Often, my intention was not to produce great work. Instead, I just wanted to make you proud. Finally, you are a good friend. You and Jan have walked through lots of life with me since my entrance exam into the doctoral program at Dallas Theological Seminary. Thank you.

Mom and Dad: Thank you for your commitment to see me succeed. You sacrificed so much to see me through to this day. Please know that I do not take that for granted and will be forever grateful that you are my parents.

Finally, thank you, Alanna. You gave up so much for me to pursue this work. Your belief in God's call upon my life fueled us through this long journey. You were patient with me during those long days of writing. You encouraged me and kindly pushed me through those moments of doubt. For us, finishing was always the only option. Thank you for embodying what it means to be faithful, compassionate, self-sacrificing, and loving. Honestly, I could not have done this without you. I love you so much.

Introduction

Introduction

THIS BOOK PROVIDES AN exposition of petitionary prayer in light of compatibilism, hard determinism, open theism, and middle knowledge. The relationship between one's theory of providence and the action of offering petitionary prayer is essential as it will determine how motivated the person is to offer petitionary prayer. I will argue that a theologically sophisticated understanding of petitionary prayer will include a number of features which are best explained by middle knowledge over against its primary competitors. What differentiates middle knowledge is its ability to preserve divine omniscience and libertarian freedom in petitionary prayer. Thus, human beings with libertarian freedom offer their prayers while God retains his absolute, divine sovereignty concerning the content of the prayer.

Compatibilism and Libertarianism

Compatibilism and libertarianism provide their own explanations for how petitionary prayer works.[1] *Libertarianism* is a term used to describe those theories of providence that include libertarian human freedom within their system, which means that the human could have chosen from at least two possible alternatives, and events outside his control did not cause the human's decision.[2] Philosophically, *compatibilism* includes libertarian freedom within its framework; however, this book employs the term *compatibilism* as it is understood theologically, which does not include libertarian freedom.[3]

---

1. In a 1992 article on providence and evil, William Hasker employs these same theories of providence. Hasker, "Providence and Evil: Three Theories," 91–105.

2. Laing, "The Compatibility of Calvinism and Middle Knowledge," 455.

3. Tiessen, *Providence and Prayer*, 290. Philosophically compatibilism is employed when one desires to discuss how God's sovereignty is compatible with libertarian freedom (van Inwagen, *An Essay on Free Will*, 13).

Thus, compatibilism should be understood as referring to an alternative view of freedom to libertarian freedom. For this book, middle knowledge and open theism provide theological examples of libertarianism. The term *compatibilism* is variegated in its meaning theologically. Some hard determinists might subscribe to compatibilism. For example, John Feinberg notes, "Hard determinists might understand free will as soft determinists [compatibilists] do, but still hold that causal conditions are sufficiently strong that no one can actually exercise such freedom."[4] In this book, Francis Turretin, John Flavel, John Piper, and John Frame represent hard determinism and will be discussed in chapters 1 and 3; however, this book distinguishes hard determinism from compatibilism due to the hard determinist's rejection in praxis of human freedom as evidenced by petitionary prayer (discussed in chapter 3). Another example of the variegated nature of compatibilism is displayed in John Feinberg, who writes that compatibilists agree that everything that happens is causally determined, "but they also believe that some actions are free."[5] That being said, a compatibilist could also be labeled a soft determinist.[6] Feinberg describes *compatibilism* as

> According to a form of determinism known as compatibilism, an action is free so long as there are antecedent conditions which decisively incline the agent's will in one way or another without constraining it. To act without constraint means to act in accord with one's desires. If one adopts this notion of free will, then God can have power to causally determine the free (compatabilistically) actions of others.[7]

In this book, the term *compatibilism* will be employed instead of *soft determinism* due to the frequent use of *compatibilism* in the literature surveyed.[8]

The unique challenge compatibilism poses to the topic of this project is that by definition the compatibilist position could be interpreted to mean something similar to that of middle knowledge.[9] However, compatibilism

---

4. Feinberg, *No One Like Him*, 635.

5. Ibid.

6. Ibid., 637. Wayne Grudem also notes that at times compatibilists are described as soft determinists (Grudem, *Systematic Theology*, 315–16).

7. Feinberg, *No One Like Him*, 290.

8. Grudem, *Systematic Theology*, 316; Feinberg, *No One Like Him*, 635–36; Helm, *The Providence of God*, 197.

9. For more on the discussion between compatibilism and middle knowledge, read Perszyk, "Molinism and Compatibilism," 11–33; Laing, "The Compatibility of Calvinism and Middle Knowledge," 462–63; Flint, "Hasker's 'God, Time, and Knowledge,'" 103–15; See also Craig, "Hasker on Divine Knowledge," 89–110.

is different from middle knowledge, because middle knowledge affirms libertarian free will. Conversely, compatibilists lack consensus in their definition of human freedom, which makes it difficult to understand what the term *free will* means. For example, Feinberg writes, "The truth of the matter, however, is that Scripture does not say what sort of freedom we have; it only teaches that we are free."[10] Furthermore, Feinberg notes that (1) libertarian free will and (2) compatibilism are contrary notions of freedom and also logically contradictory.[11] However, compatibilism and middle knowledge are unified in that God's sovereignty is, in a mysterious way, compatible with human freedom. Thus, middle knowledge is clear as to the extent of human freedom, which is libertarian freedom, and compatibilism is not. For this reason, having the distinction between middle knowledge and compatibilism is necessary.

Middle Knowledge

The theory of middle knowledge proposes that

> God's omniscience extends beyond mere knowledge of the past and the future to include knowledge of conditional future contingents (or propositions which refer to how free creatures will choose if circumstances turn out a particular way) and knowledge of counterfactuals (or propositions which refer to how things would actually be if circumstances were different).[12]

Middle knowledge is distinguishable from open theism (discussed in chapter 4) because middle knowledge affirms a "strong" view of God's sovereignty while also maintaining libertarian human freedom.[13] Open theism proposes that God's "goal is to make possible relationships of mutual love between God and creatures and therefore set up a dynamic give and take situation in which God can even be said to risk failure to the degree permitted by the overall plan."[14] Open theism asserts that in order to uphold libertarian freedom, God relinquishes some of his sovereignty and extends it to the human so that they are able to make genuine choices.[15] The result of this transmission of divine sovereignty from God to the human being

---

10. Feinberg, *No One Like Him*, 679.
11. Ibid., 637.
12. Laing, "The Compatibility of Calvinism and Middle Knowledge," 457.
13. Hasker, "Response to Thomas Flint," 117–18.
14. Pinnock, "Open Theism," 237.
15. Pinnock and Brow, *Unbounded Love*, 143.

brings about a future that is partly open (discussed in chapters 1 and 4). Middle knowledge is preferred over open theism because God's sovereignty is not limited in its defense of libertarian freedom. Instead, I will argue that God's sovereignty expands within the framework of middle knowledge. Middle knowledge is also distinguished from compatibilism, because human freedom is not "causally determined by events outside the control of the agent."[16] In other words, in compatibilism, the human could not have chosen otherwise regarding the decision made (discussed in chapter 3). By limiting human freedom to something other than libertarian freedom, the compatibilist feels that in terms of its ability to uphold the sovereignty of God, it is more reliable than middle knowledge. However, this book argues that compatibilism has unnecessarily limited human freedom as an attempt to affirm God's omniscience concerning petitionary prayer (discussed in chapters 3 and 5). Thus, middle knowledge is better suited to handle petitionary prayer, because, in contrast to compatibilism and open theism, middle knowledge maintains the sovereignty of God by including both God's omniscience and libertarian human freedom.

Summary of Chapters

Chapter 1 will focus on and define middle knowledge along with its primary challengers, which include compatibilism, hard determinism, and open theism. These theories of providence will be in question throughout the entire book as far as how they employ petitionary prayer. Chapter 2 looks at petitionary prayer and theology and provides a definition of petitionary prayer as well as the various theological questions that petitionary prayer poses to both systematic and pastoral theology. Thus, chapters 1 through 2 serve as the theological foundation for exploring which theory of providence best explains petitionary prayer. Chapters 3 through 5 deal with each of the aforementioned theories of providence independently and examine how each theory treats petitionary prayer as defined in chapter 2.

---

16. Laing, "The Compatibility of Calvinism and Middle Knowledge," 455.

1

Theories of Providence

IN THIS CHAPTER, I examine four theological systems concerning divine providence: compatibilism, hard determinism, open theism, and middle knowledge. Within evangelical literature, these four systems most commonly appear in the discussion concerning divine providence. This chapter will define each of the aforementioned terms and address their biblical and theological characteristics. Once the examination of each of these theories of providence is complete, I will define petitionary prayer (chapter 2). Each of these systems and their understanding of petitionary prayer will be treated individually in later chapters.

Compatibilism

John Feinberg offers the following definition of compatibilism: "An action is free so long as there are antecedent conditions which decisively incline the agent's will in one way or another without constraining it."[1] The key phrase in Feinberg's definition is, "without constraining," which entails, "to act in accord with one's desires."[2] For the compatibilist, God then has the power within his providence to determine causally a human's free will without compromising that human's freedom. D. A. Carson defines *compatibilism* as

> God is absolutely sovereign, but his sovereignty never functions in such a way that human responsibility is curtailed, minimized, or mitigated. Human beings are morally responsible creatures—they significantly choose, rebel, obey, believe, defy, make decisions, and so forth, and they are rightly held accountable for such actions; but this characteristic never functions so as to make God absolutely contingent.[3]

---

1. Feinberg, *No One Like Him*, 290.
2. Feinberg, *No One Like Him*, 290. See also Helm, *The Providence of God*, 174–77.
3. Carson, *How Long, O Lord?* 179.

Carson adds to Feinberg's definition by emphasizing the mystery involved in affirming the sovereignty of God and human freedom. Carson believes too many "unknowns" exist concerning (1) the sovereignty of God and (2) human freedom when each of these truths are treated independently from one another. Furthermore, the mystery compounds when one tries to understand them working together.[4] How God's sovereignty and human freedom are compatible is truly a mystery, and compatibilism is the belief that human free will (non-libertarian) is compatible with the sovereignty of God, which is why Carson and Feinberg would be considered compatibilists.

God's Providence

The providence of God speaks to the way in which he graciously works out his will within the created order, and compatibilism offers its own way of resolving the question of how God relates to his created order with the intent of bringing about his desired end. Open theism, middle knowledge, and hard determinism will present different ideas about how God's outworking of his divine purpose is fulfilled.

Wayne Grudem describes his view of divine providence as "compatibilism," because the word *determinism* can be confusing to contemporary English speakers.[5] Grudem explains that compatibilism holds that "absolute divine sovereignty is compatible with human significance and real human choices."[6] Also, he prefers compatibilism because determinism suggests that God governs the universe in a mechanistic sense rather than as a wise and personal God.[7] Similar to Grudem, Millard Erickson, a compatibilist, provides another helpful definition of *providence*. He writes, "The continuing action of God by which he preserves in existence the creation he has brought into being, and guides it to his intended purposes for it."[8] Due to God's preserving work, the relationship that God shares with

---

4. Carson, *How Long, O Lord?* 189. David Basinger provides a less favorable perspective of compatibilism from the open theist perspective: "If I possess the power of the God of theological compatibilism, I can simply irresistibly influence her will in such a way that she will decide freely to read the pages in question." Basinger, "Divine Control and Human Freedom," 60.

5. Grudem, *Systematic Theology*, 316. See also, Perszyk's definition of compatibilism as it relates to determinism in Perszyk, "Molinism and Compatibilism," 12.

6. Grudem, *Systematic Theology*, 316.

7. Ibid., 316.

8. Erickson, *Christian Theology*, 359. Paul Helm discusses the advantages of compatibilism in *The Providence of God*, 66–68.

his creation has implications for one's conduct as a Christian. In *Christian Theology*, Erickson emphasizes two implications for the relationship God shares with his creation: (1) God maintains and sustains his creation through the work of preservation; (2) God guides and directs his creation through God's governmental work.[9]

Preservation

A key aspect of divine providence is that God maintains and sustains his creation through the work of preservation. Grudem supports Erickson's first claim that God preserves his creation. Grudem explains that "God is continually involved with all created things in such a way that he (1) keeps them existing and maintaining the properties with which he created them; (2) cooperates with created things in every action, directing their distinctive properties to cause them to act as they do; and (3) directs them to fulfill his purposes."[10] Grudem posits that God's sovereignty emphasizes God's ultimate control over all things. For example, he cites Ps 104 as depicting God's preserving nature as he set the earth on its foundation (Ps 104:5); he sends springs into the valleys between the hills (Ps 104:10).[11] God also sets the darkness in so that the young lions might prey upon their meal for sustenance (Ps 104:20–22). In short, Erickson and Grudem describe God's providential work, which includes his preservation of creation. Thus, the work of preservation in petitionary prayer includes God's work whereby he cooperates with humans in order to bring about his purposes through human prayer.

Government

Along with God's preservation of his creation, Erickson claims that God guides and directs his creation to fulfill his purposes. He uses the term *God's government* for this second idea of providence. This term carries with it the connotation set forth in Ps 135:6–7 that God's creation does whatever the Lord pleases. Louis Berkhof describes God's government "as that continued activity of God whereby He rules all things teleologically so as to secure the accomplishment of the divine purpose."[12] In other words, not only is the

---

9. Erickson, *Christian Theology*, 360.
10. Grudem, *Systematic Theology*, 315.
11. Ibid., 315.
12. Berkhof, *Systematic Theology*, 175.

world properly ordered, but due to its structure, God is demonstrating that he is bringing about his divine purpose in an organized fashion. While Berkhof illustrates the orderliness of God's governmental work, Erickson claims that the difference between providence as government and preservation is quite nuanced. The focus on government deals with the "directing of the whole of reality and the course of history to God's end. It is the actual execution, within time, of his plans devised in eternity."[13] Erickson explains that the emphasis on God's government is that he is now executing the course of history, in real time, toward his end. Similar to Erickson's description, Herman Bavinck argues that the concepts of preservation and government "are not parts or segments in which the work of providence is divided and which, being materially and temporally separate, succeed one another."[14] Instead, Bavinck concludes that God's preservation and government are "always integrally connected; they intermesh at all times."[15] For both of these scholars, God guides and directs his creation to fulfill his purposes through the governmental work of his providence. Erickson illustrates God's government within the Bible.[16] First, Dan 2:21 describes God's providential government as: God "removes kings and sets up kings; he gives wisdom to the wise and knowledge to those who have understanding." Furthermore, in the New Testament, Paul at the Areopagus proclaims that God is working the course of history towards his end in that God "made from one man every nation of mankind to live on all the face of the earth, having determined allotted periods and the boundaries of their dwelling place" (Acts 17:26).[17]

In addition to the work of God's governance affecting whole nations, he also governs individual people to bring about his plan. For example, David finds comfort in this providential government. He writes, "But I trust in you, O Lord; I say, 'You are my God.' My times are in your hand; rescue me from the hand of my enemies and from my persecutors!" (Ps 31:14–15).[18] God's providence is so specific that he even governs those moments that appear to be accidental. Proverbs 16:33 says, "The lot is cast into the lap, but its every decision is from the Lord."[19] In compatibilism, God's governmental

---

13. Erickson, *Christian Theology*, 365. For God's government in nature see Mark 4:39; 1 Kgs 18:42, 45; Jas 5:17; Luke 8:25; Job 9:5–9; Ps 104:14; Ps 147:8–15; Matt 6:25–30. For God's government of animals see Ps 104:21–29; 1 Kgs 17:4.

14. Bavinck, *Reformed Dogmatics*, 605.

15. Ibid., 2:605.

16. Erickson, *Christian Theology*, 366.

17. See also Dan 4:24–25; Isa 10:5–12; Job 12:23; Ps 47:7–8; Ps 66:7.

18. See also 1 Sam 2:6–7; Luke 1:52; Gal 1:15–16; 1 Cor 4:6–7; Rom 12:3–6; 1 Cor 12:4–11.

19. See also Jonah 1:7; Acts 1:23–26; Exod 21:13; Esth 4:14.

work includes his effect upon those petitionary prayers offered to him. To further illustrate this, Bavinck concludes that God's providential knowledge is evident as he governs humanity with great detail.[20] For Bavinck, God's governance is over individual lives as well as broader communities.

Essential to a compatibilist view of providence is the idea that God's work of preservation and government are also compatible with human freedom. A hard determinist would also affirm this section on God's providence, which will become evident below. However, what distinguishes compatibilism from hard determinism is that compatibilism upholds that human freedom is compatible with divine sovereignty. Erickson notes that the sovereignty of God is compatible with human freedom. He illustrates this with Israel's departure from Egypt. They left not because they were coerced into it, nor did the Egyptians release them because they were forced. Instead, the Israelites exercised their freedom by requesting to leave, and the Egyptians freely decided to release them.[21] This biblical example illustrates that God was sovereign over the circumstance at hand; however, the actors involved were not coerced into their actions. In addition to Erickson, Thomas Oden warns that it would be inconsistent to claim that God does not influence creation in its continued sustenance and development. He warns of the "inconsistency in God creating beings with moral sensitivities only to restrict human development to chance or fate."[22] In other words, Oden is warning against any notion that God's sovereignty is not compatible with human freedom. Hard determinism provides an example whereby God's sovereignty is not compatible with human freedom. For example, Berkhof rejects the compatibility between the sovereignty of God and human freedom while still affirming God's preservation and government. Berkhof says that it is an error to assert "that it is of such a nature that man does part of the work and God a part."[23] Furthermore, he argues that it is an error to affirm "that the work of God and that of the creature in concurrence are co-ordinate."[24] Berkhof's belief in a lack of human ability displays a key difference between compatibilism and hard determinism.

In compatibilism, God's providence through his work of preservation and government is compatible with human freedom. God's government and preservation form the theological foundation to understanding God's

---

20. Bavinck, *Reformed Dogmatics*, 2:592.

21. Erickson, *Christian Theology*, 368. See also Van Horn, "On Incorporating Middle Knowledge into Calvinism," 807; Flint, "In Defense of Theological Compatibilism," 237.

22. Oden, *Classic Christianity*, 146.

23. Berkhof, *Systematic Theology*, 172.

24. Ibid., 173.

providence. Furthermore, God's government and preservation are important because they reveal how God relates to the world that he created. The relationship God shares with his creation affirms his preservation, which brings his creation to his desired end. In addition, God governs human beings so that their freedom and responsibility is maintained while still compatible with his sovereignty, thus the name "compatibilism."

Biblical Evidence of Compatibilism

An important passage to which many compatibilists appeal is Gen 50:20, "As for you, you meant evil against me, but God meant it for good, to bring it about that many people should be kept alive, as they are today." The story begins in Gen 37 and proceeds for the next thirteen chapters. In this account, Joseph has a dream whereby he has great power and authority, and he shares this dream with his brothers (Gen 37:5). Fearful of Joseph and his dream, the brothers sell him into slavery (Gen 37:28). Throughout the remainder of Genesis, Joseph is granted favor with Pharaoh and ascends to a great position of power within Pharaoh's empire (Gen 39:2; 41:41). This rise to power and authority is beneficial but not necessarily merciful; Joseph has to face many difficult circumstances. When a famine comes to the land, Joseph's brothers are forced to go to Egypt to seek help and food (Gen 42:3). There, they realize that their brother is alive and that he has great authority over Egypt (Gen 45:1–3). In the end, Joseph provides for his family, and they settle in the best of the land in Goshen (Gen 47:6), and this happened because Joseph's brothers sold him into slavery. At the end of the narrative, God receives the glory, honor, and praise because what these brothers meant for evil, God meant for good (Gen 50:20).

Wayne Grudem, John Feinberg, and Jonathan Edwards use this passage to support compatibilism by showing that God governs and is sovereign over individual situations while also maintaining the compatibility of human freedom with God's sovereignty. However, the human freedom that is compatible with God's sovereignty is not libertarian freedom. Thus, the characters in the story did not have the freedom to refrain from how they acted. Grudem, for example, observes that sinful men bring about their evil deeds and are responsible for their actions. However, these evil actions are mysteriously compatible with God's providential control as his purposes are accomplished even in the difficult circumstances that Joseph faces.[25] Feinberg, another compatibilist, uses this passage to affirm "that evil acts of human beings are under God's plan and that God can bring good even out

---

25. Grudem, *Systematic Theology*, 323.

of a horrible situation."[26] Jonathan Edwards uses this passage to explain how God's sovereignty and man's freedom of choice are not mutually exclusive.[27] Edwards believes that it is consistent to uphold the actions of Joseph's brothers as evil while also maintaining that God's plan was such that he permitted the event to take place.

John Calvin applauds Joseph for his ability not to dwell upon the evil works of his brothers, but instead, "he turned his thoughts to the Lord, forgetting the injustice, he inclined to gentleness and kindness, even to the point of comforting his brother."[28]

D. A. Carson also observes that the brothers' actions were compatible with the sovereignty of God. The brothers were responsible and free in their actions while God, from the beginning, had only good intentions.[29] On a grander scale, this story is to bring about the greater good, the preservation of Joseph's family, which preserves the line of the Messiah. For the compatibilist, it is imperative when interpreting Gen 37–50 to affirm the freedom of the human beings involved, which is not libertarian freedom while at the same time displaying agreement that those free actions were always compatible with the sovereignty of God.[30]

Hard Determinism

Most theologians would not desire to be called hard determinists. They do not openly accept the label. James Daane observes that hard determinism rejects the claim that God is the author of evil.[31] However, in hard determinism, God is the ultimate cause and source of sin as man does not have the freedom to refrain from any sin committed.[32] Daane asserts that God being the ultimate cause and source of sin but not its author is illogical.[33] Therefore, my explanation of hard determinism will focus on men who, although they might not claim the title, explain their view of God's providence in the same way a hard determinist would, which is: (1) a high view of divine sovereignty, and (2) a lack of human free will. Displaying that various

---

26. Feinberg, *No One Like Him*, 518.

27. Edwards, *Freedom of the Will*, 406. See also Berkouwer's use of this passage in *The Providence of God*, 90–91.

28. Calvin *Institutes* 1.17.8.

29. Carson, *How Long, O Lord?* 183.

30. Tiessen, *Providence and Prayer*, 290.

31. Daane, *The Freedom of God*, 80.

32. Hoeksema, *Reformed Dogmatics*, 1:226.

33. Daane, *The Freedom of God*, 80.

theologians tend toward hard determinism is important work for this book because I believe that petitionary prayer is only genuine when the human being is offering prayer freely. If hard determinism removes human freedom in order to affirm God's sovereignty, then God's desired end will take place irrespective of any human freedom in prayer. John Feinberg (not a hard determinist) also gives a helpful and gracious introduction to hard determinism in *No One Like Him*.[34] He describes hard determinism as a theology that involves God's control over human free will in such a way that it "removes not only human free will but also [man's] moral responsibility."[35] Feinberg also explains that although humans cannot be free in this framework, the hard determinist asserts that "Humans are still held morally responsible," even though their actions are causally determined.[36] If one were to claim that God holding humans responsible in this framework is unfair, a hard determinist would typically answer in this way: "God as sovereign has the right to set up any scheme or moral governance he wants, and there is no room for us to debate him about that or to accuse him of wrongdoing."[37] Furthermore, Feinberg explains, "Defenders of this view often add that sinners, though their acts are causally determined, sin very willingly; no one forces them to commit sin against their will. Hence, they are justly guilty before God."[38] The assertion that God removes not only human free will but also man's moral responsibility is a risky argument, because it calls into question man's responsibility with respect to a potential petitionary prayer.

In part, hard determinists hold a position that is similar to that of compatibilism in that they affirm divine sovereignty; however, these two views have a foundational difference in that, according to Feinberg, the proponent of hard determinism asserts that acts are "causally determined," and as a result "there is no human free will of any sort."[39] For the hard determinist, "everything that happens is decreed in advance by God. His decree is unconditional, based solely on his will and desires. Of course, if God has such con-

---

34. Feinberg, *No One Like Him*, 635.

35. Ibid., 649. Ben Vilhauer also asserts the lack of moral responsibility in determinism in "Hard Determinism, Humeanism, and Virtue Ethics," 121. However, Vilhauer asserts that " . . . most hard determinists do not wish to reject morality altogether" (Vilhauer, "Hard Determinism," 121).

36. Feinberg, *No One Like Him*, 649.

37. Ibid., 649. Although Feinberg defines hard determinism, he never cites an example of a hard determinist.

38. Ibid., 649.

39. Ibid., 635. Jeremy Randel Koons argues for something different as he philosophically believes that hard determinism is a form of compatibilism. He rejects libertarianism, which leaves compatibilism as the only account of freedom that one can endorse, "Is Hard Determinism a Form of Compatibilism?" 99.

trol over all things, there is really no room for human free will."[40] Since hard determinism restricts human freedom, Feinberg writes, "We cannot adopt [many hard deterministic systems], because Scripture also teaches human freedom, and hard determinism rules out all sense of freedom."[41] In other words, the hard determinist's view on human freedom cannot be accepted. Similar to Feinberg, Saul Smilansky argues against hard determinism due to its dismissal of human freedom.[42] Smilansky opposes hard determinism on the basis that it rejects free will and moral responsibility and concludes, "Any theology that rules out human freedom and/or moral responsibility is deficient biblically."[43] Feinberg and Smilansky demonstrate that hard determinism is not to be rejected because of its views regarding the sovereignty of God. Instead, due to the lack of support for human freedom (compatibilist or libertarian), hard determinism should be rejected.[44]

Human Freedom and Hard Determinism

Since the hard determinist omits human freedom, God then is responsible for the actions that take place in the world. Whether or not human beings are free is important for the purposes of this book because the amount of human freedom is essential to one's view of the necessity of petitionary prayer. Their belief in a lack of human freedom forces the hard determinist to describe how God is not the author of human prayer.[45] In terms of dealing with the accusation that God is the author of evil, Berkhof writes,

---

40. Feinberg, *No One Like Him*, 649.

41. Ibid., 682. According to compatibilism Scripture teaches human freedom and responsibility. However, hard determinism rejects that Scripture teaches such human freedom. See Pink, *The Sovereignty of God*, 115.

42. Smilansky, "Free Will and Moral Responsibility," 211.

43. Ibid.

44. Concerning the relationship between open theism and hard determinism, many scholars I have identified as proponents of hard determinism also share the common feature of writing against open theism (Pinnock, Rice, Sanders, Hasker, and Basinger, *The Openness of God*). For example, Schreiner and Ware note that a primary reason for their work is to oppose Pinnock's theology (Schreiner and Ware, eds., *The Grace of God*, 12). For more on Ware and open theism see "Prayer and the Sovereignty of God," 129. In addition, Mark Talbot also identifies open theism as a primary competitor (Talbot, "All the Good That is Ours in Christ," 36). Perhaps this should cause one to consider if the extreme nature (denial of human freedom) of hard determinism is largely a movement in reaction to open theism as it places a strong emphasis upon libertarian freedom.

45. This is discussed in detail in chapter 3.

> They [Reformed theologians] frankly admit that they cannot solve the difficulty, but at the same time make some valuable distinctions that prove helpful. Most of them insist on it that God's will with respect to sin is simply a will to permit sin and not a will to effectuate it, as He does the moral good.[46]

Herman Hoeksema goes even further and argues that God not only permits but also determines the sinful deeds of men and devils. He writes, "With regards to the sinful deeds of men and devils, we must not speak only of God's permission but also of his determination."[47] Hoeksema argues that man is responsible in an attempt to eliminate God as the author of sin.[48] However, he also asserts that man is not free in his actions. He writes, "[Scripture] knows of no sovereign rational, moral creature apart from or next to God. The almighty and omnipresent power of God controls the whole life and all the deeds of his rational, moral creatures."[49] This includes man's thinking, will, and sin.[50] Arthur Pink describes man's deficient freedom as well. He writes, "Nowhere does Scripture speak of the freedom or moral ability of the sinner, on the contrary, it insists on his moral and spiritual inability."[51] Thus, according to these scholars, as a result of God's sovereignty, man had no choice but to sin.

Turretin argues that God directly brings about good things while leaving bad things up to human freedom.[52] But if God has this power, why does he not always act in a controlling state of goodness so that sin never happens? One might argue that because this is not the case, God is a passive author of sin, because he relents his great power to bring about good things in order to permit sinful circumstances. Both Hoeksema and Turretin, like Berkhof, demonstrate the difficulty that hard determinism has in explaining how God is not the author of evil. Berkhof never rejects the title, "author of sin," while Edwards makes it clear that he "dislike[s] and reject[s]" the phrase that God is the author of evil.[53] However, at best Berkhof defaults to it being a mystery: "so that the problem of God's relation to sin remains a mystery."[54] Berkhof uses the term *mystery* to describe God's relation to sin.

46. Berkhof, *Systematic Theology*, 79.
47. Hoeksema, *Reformed Dogmatics*, 1:226.
48. Ibid., 1:329.
49. Ibid., 1:329.
50. Ibid., 1:330.
51. Pink, *The Sovereignty of God*, 115.
52. Turretin, *Institutes of Elenctic Theology*, 1:514.
53. Edwards, *Freedom of the Will*, 399.
54. Berkhof, *Systematic Theology*, 175.

But for a compatibilist, *mystery* is employed with regard to the way in which human freedom is compatible with the sovereignty of God.

In addition to Berkhof's use of the term *mystery* to describe God's relation to sin, he also seems to reject human freedom. Berkhof notes that God through his free will "determines voluntarily what and whom He will create, and the times, places, and circumstances, of their destiny, and uses them for His purpose. And though He endows them with freedom, yet His will controls their actions."[55] Similar to Berkhof, Hodge asserts that God is the cause of power for the human because he governs their actions.[56] This works theologically for Berkhof through divine concurrence: "The Bible clearly teaches that the providence of God pertains not only to the being but also to the actions or operations of the creature. The general truth that men do not work independently, but are controlled by the will of God, appears from several passages of Scripture."[57] He goes on to describe this control over the human being through divine government. This includes (1) that God controls moral agents through various moral influences such as circumstances, persuasion, motives, and (2) that God controls moral agents more directly through the work of the Holy Spirit upon the intellect, will, and heart.[58] For hard determinism and its theory of providence, all things, even sin in the world, are credited to God's work in his creatures' lives. This is to assure the sovereignty of God in that all things are working toward his desired end.

Theological Evidence of Hard Determinism

A thorough review of the theological evidence of hard determinism must include an exposition of the greater-good theory of divine providence and an examination of the argument that there is not a difference between effectual permission and efficient causation in hard determinism. A key aspect of hard determinism is the removal of human freedom. For example, Charles Hodge argues that God's providence extends "over the world of mind, i.e., over rational free agents, as well as over the material universe."[59] Even in declaring such a statement, he assures that the human agent involved

---

55. Ibid., 78.

56. Hodge, *Systematic Theology*, 1:600.

57. Berkhof, *Systematic Theology*, 172. These scriptural passages include: Gen 45:5; Exod 4:11–12; Josh 11:6; Prov 21:1; Ezra 6:22; Deut 8:18; 2 Sam 16:11; Isa 10:5; 1 Kgs 22:20–23.

58. Berkhof, *Systematic Theology*, 176.

59. Hodge, *Systematic Theology*, 1:614.

is responsible as the "author of their own acts."⁶⁰ However, the view that humans are responsible stands in opposition to his own view of God's providence. He writes, "But although free agents have the power to act, and originate their own acts, they are not only upheld in being and efficiency by the power of God, but He controls the use which they make of their ability."⁶¹ With regard to petitionary prayer, Hodge posits that God is able to incline the hearts of men and to "work in us to will as well as to do."⁶² Thus, God produces a human action that will only result in one way and not in another. Hard determinists hold fast to the belief that God is responsible for everything that is taking place in the world and in the affairs of humans. Otherwise, they would say that God would not be sovereign. In order to uphold God's sovereignty, John Frame asserts that there is not a real difference between effectual permission and efficient causation.⁶³ Frame also affirms the greater-good theory, which, along with efficient causation, helps make hard determinism work theologically.

Frame is not clear on why "God should be responsible for what he causes efficiently" only and not responsible for what he permits effectually.⁶⁴ But Berkhof uses similar terminology to explain the differences between God permitting and God doing. He argues that God enables and prompts his creatures "as second causes, to function, and that not merely by endowing them with energy in a general way, but by energizing them to certain specific acts."⁶⁵ Berkhof and Frame believe that God's effectual permission and causation of the act are the same thing. In contrast to Frame, however, in light of God's activity, Berkhof still maintains that man is responsible for his actions. He writes, "The action remains the free act of man, an act for which he is held responsible."⁶⁶ He even employs the illustration that when "wood burns, that God only causes it to burn, but that formally this burning cannot be ascribed to God but only to the wood as subject."⁶⁷ In this instance, the wood had no choice to be something different. Instead, it was always going to be burned. Ironically, in the very same paragraph, Berkhof asserts, "He enables the fire to fall, to burn, and to destroy. So God also works in man in endowing him with power, in the determination of his actions, and in

---

60. Ibid., 1:614.
61. Ibid., 1:614.
62. Ibid., 1:614.
63. Frame, *The Doctrine of God*, 166.
64. Ibid., 166.
65. Berkhof, *Systematic Theology*, 173.
66. Ibid., 173.
67. Ibid.,, 173.

sustaining his activities all along the line."⁶⁸ In essence, Berkhof is saying the complete opposite of what he posed before, that the wood is responsible for burning, yet it had no other choice but to burn. This is similar to Hodges's point above regarding the idea that men are held responsible as the author of their acts in that God "controls the use which they make of their ability."⁶⁹ When human freedom and responsibility are limited, God becomes culpable for both the good and evil that takes place.⁷⁰

According to Berkhof, the theological leap the hard determinist makes that the compatibilist avoids is that God is responsible for the burning of wood and human action. In contrast, the compatibilist would say that God does permit evil and sin in the world; however, humans are free in their actions. Thus, God is responsible as he permits the action but not in the same way as the hard determinists who see no difference between effectual permission and efficient causation.⁷¹ Hard determinism, not compatibilism, prefers the "greater-good defense" with respect to the problem of evil, which claims "that the presence, or at least the possibility, of evil in the world is good, when seen from a broader perspective."⁷² Here, "broader perspective" means God's perspective. By way of an example, Frame points to some ways in which humans inflict evil or harm on other humans for ultimate good:

> . . . surgery to heal, punishment of children to discipline them. So perhaps God has a good purpose in permitting evil, one which outweighs the suffering and pain—one which, in the end, makes this a better world than it would have been without the intrusion of evil.⁷³

Frame even goes so far as to claim that "the possibility of evil is necessary to have an orderly universe."⁷⁴ He writes, "Although evil is to be deplored in and of itself, there are some respects in which it makes the world a better place. Some have argued, therefore, that evils contribute to a greater good."⁷⁵ Like Frame, Charles Hodge attributes both good and evil to the sovereignty of God. He writes,

---

68. Ibid., 174.
69. Hodge, *Systematic Theology*, 1:614.
70. Bloesch, *God the Almighty*, 133.
71. Frame, *The Doctrine of God*, 166.
72. Ibid., 169.
73. Ibid.
74. Ibid.
75. Ibid., 170.

> God is no less sovereign in the distribution of his favours. He does what He wills with his own. He gives to some riches, to others, honour; to others, health; while others are poor, unknown, or the victims of disease. To some, the light of the gospel is sent; others are left in darkness. Some are brought through faith unto salvation; others perish in unbelief. To the question, Why is this? The only answer is given by our Lord. "Even so, Father, for so it seemeth good in thy sight."[76]

In addition to Hodge and Frame, Mark Talbot describes God's work through Christ as working all things, including evil, for good. In order to make this point, he notes,

> Ephesians 1:11 goes even further by declaring that God in Christ "works all things according to the counsel of his will." Here the Greek word for "works" is *energeō*, which indicates that God not merely carries all of the universe's objects and events to their appointed ends but that he actually *brings about* all things in accordance with his will. In other words, it is not just that God manages to turn the evil aspects of our world to good for those who love him; it is rather that he himself brings about these evil aspects for his glory (see Ex 9:13–16; John 9:3) and his people's good (see Heb 12:3–11; James 1:2–4).[77]

The pursuit of an orderly universe (teleological argument) is not a good enough reason to maintain that God has brought about harm and evil in the world so that some greater-good might occur. Sin is not orderly; harm and evil are not orderly. In fact, they are the opposite of order and the reason why believers are anxiously waiting for the return of the Lord when true and holy order will be established once again (1 Cor 15:35–49; Rev 21). The main thrust of Frame's greater-good defense is to provide an explanation of evil. On the other hand, it is also relevant to the divine-human interaction (petitionary prayer) in question throughout this book because this greater-good defense impacts one's view of the providence of God.

Compatibilism vs. Hard Determinism

The writings of Jonathan Edwards and John Piper demonstrate the difference between compatibilism and hard determinism. Both are Calvinistic theologians, academics, and ministers of God's Word, yet they describe

---

76. Hodge, *Systematic Theology*, 1:441.
77. Talbot, "All the Good That Is Ours in Christ," 42.

God's working in the world in two remarkably different ways. This will become most evident with the use of the terms "permitting" and "ordaining" below. In addition to Edwards and Piper, Paul Helm will serve as a modern link continuing the compatibilistic theology from Edwards in contemporary theology. John Frame, coinciding with Piper, will provide further theological context for hard determinism.

In *Freedom of the Will*, Edwards responds to the notion that Calvinistic logic, when pushed to its limits, makes God the author of evil so that "God knew, that if he ordered and brought to pass such and such events, such sins would infallibly follow."[78] From the outset of his argument, Edwards makes it clear that he "dislike[s] and reject[s]" the phrase that God is the author of evil.[79] There are two possible conclusions if God is the author of evil: either he actually enacts evil or he permits it. On one hand, to call God the actor, agent, and doer of a wicked thing would be blasphemy: "In this sense, I utterly deny God to be the author of sin; rejecting such an imputation on the most High, as what is infinitely to be abhorred; and deny any such thing to be the consequence of what I have laid down."[80] Edwards "utterly" denies this depiction of God. On the other hand, if by the "author of sin," one believes God is a "permitter, or not a hinderer of sin; and at the same time, a disposer of the state of events, in such a manner, for wise, holy and most excellent ends and purposes," then Edwards would affirm that God is the author of sin.[81] For Edwards, God being the author of sin does not include being "the *actor* of sin, but on the contrary, of *holiness*."[82] To further illustrate God as an actor of holiness, Edwards writes,

> He may will the disposal of such an event, and its coming to pass for good ends, and his will not be an immoral or sinful will, but a perfectly holy will. And he may actually in his providence so dispose and permit things, that the event may be certainly and infallibly connected with such disposal and permission, and his act therein not be an immoral or unholy, but a perfectly holy act.[83]

78. Edwards, *Freedom of the Will*, 398.

79. Ibid., 399.

80. Ibid.

81. Edwards, *Freedom of the Will*, 399. Oden (an Arminian theologian) also uses the term *actor* when describing both God and the human being. God, for Oden, is the "primary actor," while humans are the "secondary actors" (Thomas, Oden, *Classic Christianity*, 144).

82. Edwards, *Freedom of the Will*, 399.

83. Ibid., 406.

Paul Helm provides a contemporary articulation of compatibilism, which is similar to Edwards: "While God ordains moral evil, he is not the author of it in the sense either that he is himself morally tainted by what he ordains, or that he takes away the responsibility of those creatures who perpetrate the evil."[84] In Edwards's words, "I don't deny that God is the author of sin (though I dislike and reject the phrase, as that which by use and custom is apt to carry another sense), it is no reproach for the most High to be thus the author of sin. This is not to be the actor of sin, but on the contrary, of holiness."[85] Helm elaborates on this idea of God being an actor of holiness. He explains that sin, pain, and unhappiness naturally become the effects of human rebellion. Thus, God permits sin and the effects of sin.[86] Edwards and Helm provide the needed examples to reveal the difference between hard determinism and compatibilism. The lack of human freedom in hard determinism as it relates to God's ordination of all things differentiates hard determinism from compatibilism and middle knowledge.

While Edwards and Helm reject the phrase, "author of sin," hard determinists, such as John Flavel and John Piper, seem to embrace it more easily. Piper describes that when God ordains something, he does so (1) directly or (2) through divine permission. However, for Piper, divine permission is a kind of indirect causing.[87] The language of indirect causing is similar to what Berkhof describes above whereby God controls moral agents more directly through the work of the Holy Spirit upon the intellect, will, and heart.[88] This means that whether God is causing or permitting, he is doing so as the cause or actor of that circumstance so as to assure that the human could not have acted any other way.[89] Hard determinism argues that God is the author or actor of sin in a way that the compatibilist would reject.

---

84. Paul Helm, *The Providence of God*, 196. The terms *compatibilism* and *soft-determinism* could be interchangeable. Feinberg notes, "Soft determinists agree that everything that happens is causally determined, but they also believe that some actions are free. The freedom in view, however, is not libertarian free will, so we must clarify what soft determinists mean by freedom. Soft determinism is also called compatibilism . . ." (Feinberg, *No One Like Him*, 635–6). This book will primarily use the term *compatibilism* in order to maintain consistency.

85. Edwards, *Freedom of the Will*, 399.

86. Helm, *The Providence of God*, 194.

87. Piper, *Spectacular Sins and Their Global Purpose in the Glory of Christ*, 54. See also Cosby, *Suffering and Sovereignty*; Crosby, *A Christian's Pocket Guide to Suffering*.

88. Berkhof, *Systematic Theology*, 176.

89. Piper, *Spectacular Sins*, 56. The biblical passages Piper uses to support this claim are Mark 5:12–13; 1 Cor 16:7; Heb 6:1–3; Gen 45:7; Exod 4:21; Ps 105:25; Ezek 5:17; Amos 8:11.

For hard determinism, no matter how big or small the matter or circumstance, God is in control. Piper uses the language of a "macro-world" and "micro-world" that God manages. God's control over the situation is not difficult to understand. The problem in particular is the idea that human beings are not free in relation to sin because God is in control: "Yes, every horrible thing and every sinful thing is ultimately governed by God."[90] In this 2010 sermon, what "centers" Piper and gives him confidence in proclaiming such a thing is Christ's death on the cross: "When you go to Acts 4:27–28 and you read that Herod and Pontius Pilate and the Gentile and the Jews were all gathered together to do what God's hand and God's plan had predestined to take place in the killing of Jesus, you have God's plan and hand predestining the most horrible sins ever committed."[91] In other words, Piper determines that God is in fact ordaining all matters, including evil, for Christological reasons.

According to Piper's statement above, God's "hand" and "plan" were on the killing of Jesus upon the cross. In fact, he describes it as the "worst wickedness that has ever been performed on the planet or ever will be."[92] Note that Herod, Pontius Pilate, Gentiles, and Jews "were gathered together to do what God's hand and God's plan had predestined."[93] As a result, God is also planning and responsible for the sins people commit in hard determinism.

Similar to Piper, Ronald Goetz argues that the responsibility for our sin lies with God, and he justifies this for Christological reasons.[94] His argument goes that since Jesus was tempted in every way (Heb 4:15) and was without sin, this also includes the temptation to sin while undergoing the evil of the cross by the hand of God. He writes, "I must conclude that Jesus Christ's death entails not just God's atonement for our sins but God own atonement

---

90. Piper, "Has God Predetermined Every Tiny Detail in the Universe, Including Sin?" http://www.desiringgod.org/interviews/has-god-predetermined-every-tiny-detail-in-the-universe-including-sin.

91. Piper, "Has God Predetermined Every Tiny Detail in the Universe, Including Sin?" http://www.desiringgod.org/interviews/has-god-predetermined-every-tiny-detail-in-the-universe-including-sin. See also Piper, *The Pleasures of God: Meditations on God's Delight in Being God*, 157–78.

92. Piper, "Has God Predetermined Every Tiny Detail in the Universe, Including Sin?" http://www.desiringgod.org/interviews/has-god-predetermined-every-tiny-detail-in-the-universe-including-sin. This was later addressed again in the 2012 sermon mentioned above, titled, "The Sovereignty of God: 'My Counsel Shall Stand, and I will Accomplish All My Purpose,'" http://www.desiringgod.org/sermons/the-sovereignty-of-god-my-counsel-shall-stand-and-i-will-accomplish-all-my-purpose.

93. Piper, "Has God Predetermined Every Tiny Detail in the Universe, Including Sin?" http://www.desiringgod.org/interviews/has-god-predetermined-every-tiny-detail-in-the-universe-including-sin.

94. Goetz, "Jesus Loves Everybody," 277.

for being the ultimate agent of evil as well as good."[95] For the Christian, Jesus becomes the ultimate model of how to trust God who is the agent of the evil being experienced. Donald Bloesch observes that Goetz would say that since evil proceeds from God's sovereignty, rather than merely allowed by God, the Christian is able to find comfort that those evil circumstances are preparing him or her for something of greater good.[96] Thus, this imperfect world for Goetz is in the process of being perfected. Brian Cosby, a specialist in John Flavel's theology, displays a similarity between Piper, Goetz, and Flavel as he notes that for Flavel, "God is not only sovereign over all good things that happen, but also over all bad things, even the most severe sufferings that fall upon humanity."[97] For example, Flavel describes that the hand of God "is to be acknowledged in the greatest afflictions that befall us."[98] Cosby argues that Flavel believes affliction comes from the hand of God and believers should "lift up thine eyes to the sovereign, wise, and holy pleasure that ordered this affliction."[99] Not only do these afflictions come from the hand of God, but the Christian is to find pleasure in them because God is pleased "to cast his own people into the fire of affliction."[100] Flavel says that God is pleased with the way he authors such afflictions for his children. Flavel further calls believers to see God as the author of sin when he writes, "In all the sad and afflictive providences that befall you, eye God as the author and orderer of them."[101] Once again, this is acceptable because God ordained the worst sin that was ever committed in the death of Christ. He writes, "To the very torments of hell was Christ delivered, and that by the hand of his own Father."[102] Flavel argues that the hand of his own Father delivered the death of Christ.

The claim was made above that the Christian should take comfort that God is ordaining the suffering and sin people endure because of what Christ endured on the cross.[103] Flavel argues similarly that God's glory and human

---

95. Ibid., 277.

96. Bloesch, *God the Almighty*, 133. For more on the idea of greater-good, see Goetz, "The Suffering God," 385–89.

97. Cosby, *Suffering and Sovereignty*, 47.

98. Flavel, "Exposition on the Assembly's Catechism," in *The Works of John Flavel*, 6:161.

99. Flavel, "Token for Mourners," in *The Works of John Flavel*, 5:627.

100. Flavel, "Touchstone of Sincerity," in *The Works of John Flavel*, 5:583.

101. Flavel, "Divine Conduct," in *The Works of John Flavel*, 4:426.

102. Flavel, "Fountain of Life," in *The Works of John Flavel*, 1:67.

103. For Piper, if Christ can undergo such suffering at the hand of the Father in order to display the glory of the grace of God, then our sufferings are image bearers of the sufferings of Christ and image bearers of the glory of the grace of God. For Piper,

suffering are not meant to be separated; instead, they are held together so that "when the Lord sees these sweet effects of his trial upon them, it greatly pleaseth him."[104] Cosby agrees with and defends Flavel's view, that this is "not to be understood in a sadistic sense, but in a way that brings God glory and His people good."[105] In addition to Flavel's claim not being sadistic, Cosby also asserts that God is glorified as the author of sin. He writes, "God would ordain suffering" due to his desire "to minister to, comfort, and console the sufferer, as well as his desire to encourage the afflicted to respond to suffering in a way that glorifies God."[106]

Sin and suffering for hard determinism is God's handiwork through which to draw his creatures into a relationship with him. Herman Hoeksema argues that God ordains sin in order to demonstrate his hatred towards sin.[107] In other words, God is justified to ordain sin and suffering because it is his megaphone to a dull soul that God exists. Piper uses the imagery of God ordaining sin as a justified megaphone to awaken people.[108] Similarly, Flavel uses the imagery of ordained sin penetrating through to clouded eyes to display God's glory.[109] In both instances, sin is God's handiwork in order

---

not only permitting but also authoring sin in the world is linked to his understanding of the work of Christ (Piper, "Why God Appoints Suffering for His Servants," 106–109). Piper writes, "The ultimate reason that suffering exists in the universe is so that Christ might display the greatness of the glory of the grace of God by suffering in himself to overcome our suffering. The suffering of the utterly innocent and infinitely holy Son of God in the place of utterly underserving sinners to bring us to everlasting joy is the greatest display of the glory of God's grace that ever was, or ever could be" (Piper, *Suffering and the Sovereignty*, 82). Furthermore, Piper believes that the suffering that God brings about marks the whole created order in order to display the glory of the grace of God. He writes, "This coming to suffer and die is the supreme manifestation of the greatness of the glory of the grace of God. Or to say it a little differently, the death of Christ in supreme suffering is the highest, clearest, surest display of the glory of the grace of God. If that is true, then a stunning truth is revealed, namely, suffering is an essential part of the created universe in which the greatness of the glory of the grace of God can be most fully revealed. Suffering is an essential part of the tapestry of the universe so that the weaving of grace can be seen for what it really is" (Piper, *Suffering and the Sovereignty*, 82).

104. Flavel, "Touchstone of Sincerity," in *The Works of John Flavel*, 5:582.

105. Cosby, *Suffering and Sovereignty*, 58–59.

106. Ibid., 59. See also Flavel's description of "sanctified afflictions" in "Divine Conduct," in *The Works of John Flavel*, 4:407–8, and "Navigation Spiritualized," in *The Works of John Flavel*, 5:218, 251–52.

107. Hoeksema, *Reformed Dogmatics*, 1:227.

108. Piper, "Cancer is a Parable about Sin," 1, accessed June 2, 2015, http://www.desiringgod.org/articles/cancer-is-a-parable-about-sin.

109. Flavel, "Touchstone of Sincerity," in *The Works of John Flavel*, 5:582. See also Flavel, "Preparation for Sufferings," in *The Works of John Flavel*, 6:15.

to draw his children into a relationship. Instead, the Christian faith confesses that Adam's sin is imputed upon humans so that men are born sinners naturally (Rom 5:12; Eph 2:1–3). Scripture also confesses that Christ takes upon himself man's sinfulness and becomes sin even though he knew no sin (2 Cor 5:21). Due to this penal substitutionary sacrifice, Christ then bestows righteousness upon the Christian whereby God now looks upon the old creature as a new creation, righteous in his sight (1 John 2:2; Rom 3:21–26). Sin then becomes something inherited, unavoidable, and the result of Adam's willful disobedience and sin. The proclamation that the "centerpiece of worship in heaven for all eternity" will be the "slaughtered Lamb" (Rev 5:9–12) does not justify that suffering must be glorified here and now.[110]

Suffering is better understood as the result of sin and total depravity than as a gift from God's goodness, which has the potential to display the glory of the grace of God. Can good come from sin or evil? Yes, good and redemptive outcomes are possible and likely because God is gracious and merciful. But God does not author such circumstances just so he can display the glory of the grace of God. In other words, a person is not wasting the glory of the grace of God by rejecting God as the author of such evil circumstances. When Piper writes, "Therefore, the ultimate reason that suffering exists in the universe is so that Christ might display the greatness of the glory of the grace of God by suffering," he seems to imply that the cross was not enough and that Christian suffering is needed in order to further display the glory of the grace of God.[111]

Contrary to hard determinism, Edwards argues that the death of Christ was the free and voluntary act of Jesus.[112] Also, Edwards upholds that wicked men, not God, murdered Christ.[113] This dual affirmation of Christ sovereignly offering himself while men freely murdered him is an illustration of compatibilism at work: in the death of Christ, God was sovereign, and humanity was free. The compatibilist view is contrary to Flavel and Piper's view of sin, which is that God ordains sin in order to display that sin is ugly. For example, Piper writes, "God brought down calamities galore, and diseases galore, and death everywhere in order to make plain: Sin is ugly."[114] Thus, in hard determinism, God is the author of sin to demonstrate that (1) sin is ugly and also (2) so that God would obtain glory in light of such

---

110. Piper, *Suffering and the Sovereignty*, 84–85.

111. Piper, *Suffering and the Sovereignty*, 89.

112. Edwards, "The Free and Voluntary Suffering and Death of Christ," 19:496–97.

113. Edwards, "The Free and Voluntary Suffering and Death of Christ," 19:496.

114. Piper, "Cancer is a Parable about Sin," accessed June 2, 2015, http://www.desiringgod.org/articles/cancer-is-a-parable-about-sin. In addition, Piper below describes cancer as something good.

suffering and evil. Hard determinism justifies that God brought down sin by the suffering God authored for the Son of God on the cross. To add to the difficulty of arguing that God makes bad things happen, Piper talks about this while preaching on cancer. God does not have to give someone cancer just to display that sin is ugly. God does not have to give someone cancer so that the human suffering might serve as a megaphone to dull souls around them. As noted earlier, for Piper, God ordains sin for his "wise purposes."[115] This is accomplished through causing sin directly or by means of permitting the sin as a kind of secondary causing. For hard determinism, the ideas of causing and permitting must be located within God's ordination.

It is important to remember that at the beginning of this section, Feinberg described that a key element to hard determinism was its affirmation that God causally determines all acts.[116] He concludes that nothing else could have been done; thus "there is really no room for human free will."[117]

The language of permission is similar to how the compatibilist understands providence; however, the idea that God has caused such things, especially sin, is not. For this reason, hard determinism should be categorized separately from the compatibilist view. God ordaining sin is different from him permitting it. This not being the case would force God into the compromising situation whereby he is the author of sin as Edwards demonstrates above. If *caused* language was similar to that of *permission* language, one could then interpret hard determinism to be articulating a similar view to compatibilism. However, hard determinism seems to bifurcate God's ordaining of evil into two categories: cause and permit.

Similar to Piper and Berkhof above, Mark Talbot writes, "God never *does* evil"; however God does "*create, send, permit,* or even *move others* to do evil, for Scripture is clear that *nothing* arises, exists, or endures independently of God's will."[118] It is understandable that Talbot desires to free God from being the doer of evil; however, his attempt fails to do so. Talbot even describes God as the instigator of evil. He writes, "And so it is not inappropriate to take God to be the creator, the sender, the permitter, and sometimes even the instigator of evil."[119] For example, one cannot be held responsible for an action that they are moved or instigated to do. For Talbot, the discussion is over evil; however, I will argue in chapter 3 that

---

115. Piper, *Spectacular Sins*, 54.

116. Feinberg, *No One Like Him*, 635.

117. Ibid., 649.

118. Talbot, "'All the Good That Is Ours in Christ': Seeing God's Gracious Hand in the Hurts Others Do to Us," in *Suffering and the Sovereignty of God*, 41.

119. Ibid., 44.

petitionary prayer is not a genuine action if one is moved or instigated to offer the prayer. For Talbot, it is not that God merely turns evil aspects of one's life into something good. Instead, God "brings about these evil aspects for his glory."[120] Talbot concludes that the claim that God does evil needs to be repudiated while at the same time "implying that God ordains any evil there is."[121] For hard determinism, both causing and permitting are forms of God's ordination.[122] Once again, the *mystery* involved for the hard determinist is that God has a mysterious relationship to sin. This goes back to Berkhof above and his employment of the term *mystery* as it describes God's relation to sin as well.[123] In compatibilism, *mystery* is understood in terms of God's sovereignty being compatible with human freedom rather than with sin.[124]

In conclusion, words matter, and the difference between producing (actor of sin) and permitting (actor of holiness) is foundational to the discrepancy between compatibilism and hard determinism. In order to fortify the idea that God is not the actor of evil, Edwards writes that men "do will sin as sin, and so are the authors and actors of it."[125] This means that for compatibilism, man, rather than God, is the actor of sin. God does permit sin; however due to his holiness, he is not the actor of sin.[126] On the other hand, instead of man being the author of sin, hard determinism would prefer to say that based upon God's holiness, wisdom, and providential care, people can proclaim with confidence that God ordains sin and thus is the direct and secondary cause of sin. Of particular importance is the notion that God is the secondary cause of sin, which is significant because the human is not responsible since humans do not have freedom within the hard determinist's framework. Moreover, they would say that people can trust God to be in such control whereby good will come out of evil and that glory will be given to God because of that evil. In the end for hard determinism, God must ordain sin for the sake of goodness and glory.

The following demonstrates that in hard determinism, God is responsible for sin, which is for the human's greater-good. If it is theologically acceptable for God to be responsible for sin, then it is also reasonable for God to be responsible for petitionary prayer as it contributes to the

120. Ibid., 42.
121. Ibid., 47.
122. Piper, *Spectacular Sins*, 54.
123. Berkhof, *Systematic Theology*, 175.
124. Lemke, "God's Relation to the World," 213.
125. Edwards, *Freedom of the Will*, 408.
126. Ibid., 408.

human's greater-good. For example, Piper's contribution is built on his own personal experience with cancer. He wrote a small book on the eve of prostate-cancer surgery titled, *Don't Waste Your Cancer* in which he draws upon the good that cancer can bring.[127] Piper claims that cancer is good. He writes, "Christ has taken the curse of our condemnation and the curse of our diseases"; however, "that means the diseases we still bear are not a curse. They have been transformed from a punitive pathway to hell into a purifying pathway to heaven. We are not cursed. As hard as it is to feel this, we believe God is not withholding good. He is doing good."[128] If God permitted and designed evil, and in this case disease, then it becomes imperative to find the good in it.

Flavel provides a similar argument when he asserts, "The reason why [afflictions] become thus sweet and pleasant is, because they run now in another channel; Jesus Christ hath removed them from mount Ebal to Gerizim; they are no more the effects of vindictive wrath, but paternal chastisement."[129] One must not overlook the emotive language of "vindictive" and "chastisement" as being credited to God's actions towards humans.

The argument from Piper and Flavel is flawed: just because God has permitted evil does not necessitate that the evil be good. In reality, good might not ever happen. In the case of disease, healing might never happen. For the Christian, the consequences of total depravity entail that the disease has to run its course, which means there is no promise of good this side of heaven, and certainly God does not have to give us a disease in order to demonstrate his goodness. In contrast to Piper, Oden writes,

> Redemption is the provision God makes to deal with a foreseen, permitted, restrained, condemned, and vanquished evil. Sin has a long career. The divine governance of currently ambiguous moral history must be seen final in the light of God's grace . . . providence is the central bridge between creation and redemption.[130]

In addition, Piper asserts that God has designed and permitted our cancer to drive us away from the "rationalistic, human calculation of odds" that the world offers.[131] Instead, God gives cancer to some Christians so that they learn to rely on the Lord. Piper writes, "The aim of God in our cancer (among a thousand other good things) is to knock props out from

127. Piper, *Don't Waste Your Cancer*.
128. Ibid., 7.
129. Flavel, "Navigation Spiritualized," in *The Works of John Flavel*, 5:252.
130. Oden, *Classic Christianity*, 152.
131. Piper, *Don't Waste Your Cancer*, 8.

under our hearts so that we rely utterly on him."[132] Piper also warns that cancer should not drive us into solitude. Piper writes, "The kind of heart God is aiming to create with cancer" is thus "a deeply affectionate, caring heart for people. Don't waste your cancer by retreating into yourself."[133] Thus, cancer is given by God's design to help the believer form a firm reliance upon the Lord.

For hard determinism, God ordains the evil people experience so that some greater-good might occur, which could not have come about without the attendant suffering. For example, Cosby describes that God ordains suffering so that a sincere faith might be produced. He writes, "God ordains suffering, then, to produce a real, sincere faith that separates the believer from the unbeliever."[134] Cosby also argues that, "When Christians suffer, they suffer so as to bring glory to God through the increase of their own godliness, which is the process of sanctification. In sanctification, believers are refined through suffering to produce godliness."[135] However, it is not as if the only way creatures are going to depend upon God is if he inflicts one of their beloved family members with alcoholism or drug addiction.

As a hard determinist, Frame does not like to call God the *author* of sin or *causer* of sin. God cannot characteristically be associated with authoring or causing evil and sin. God's causing or being the author of evil or sin would nullify aspects of his character. Instead, Frame prefers the term *permission* in reference to God's ordination of sin.[136] Although Frame does not want to say God is the author of sin or causer of sin, he basically says as much with his use of this term.

This "permission" language harkens back to the compatibilism of Edwards's view; however, Edwards and Frame use the term *permission* in very different ways. Edwards as a compatibilist does say that God permits evil and sin in the world, but humans are free in their actions. Edwards asserts as much when he declares, "Men do will sin as sin, and so are the authors and actors of it: they love it as sin, and for evil ends and

132. Ibid., 8.

133. Ibid., 12.

134. Cosby, *Suffering and Sovereignty*, 78.

135. Ibid., 67.

136. Frame, *The Doctrine of God*, 178. Hodge asserts, "This theory [middle knowledge] is inconsistent with the Scriptural doctrine of God's providential government, as it assumes that the free acts of men are not under his control" (Hodge, *Systematic Theology*, 1:400). Later in *Systematic Theology*, he discusses in greater detail God's governmental control over the free acts of men. He writes, "The Bible no less clearly teaches that God exercises a controlling power over the free acts of men, as well as over their external circumstances. This is true of all their acts, good and evil" (Hodge, *Systematic Theology*, 1:588).

purpose."[137] Humans are responsible for their actions, and this freedom is held mysteriously to be compatible with the sovereignty of God. Furthermore, the compatibilist understands that evil does not have to contribute to any good since God only permits it. Edwards goes on to say, "We need not be afraid to affirm, that if a wise and good man knew with absolute certainty, it would be best, all things considered, that there should be such a thing as moral evil in the world, it would not be contrary to his wisdom and goodness, for him to choose that it should be so."[138]

Within the first few sentences of unpacking his understanding of permission, Frame writes, "It is appropriate, therefore, to use *permission* to refer to God's ordination of sin . . . . Permission, then, is a form of ordination, a form of causation."[139] While Frame might think he is saying the same thing as Edwards, it is not the case. This is important as one should link Frame's understanding of permission with that of Piper's understanding above whereby he connects God's ordaining to direct and secondary causation. He writes, "By *ordain* I mean that God either *caused* something directly or *permitted* it for wise purposes. This permitting is a kind of indirect causing."[140] Frame and Piper, in their own ways, are attributing "permission" language not in terms of compatibilism, which argues that human freedom is compatible with divine sovereignty. Instead, for Frame, Piper, Cosby, and Talbot, permission is essentially a form of causation. The way in which these scholars have employed God's permission of an act so as to describe God as causally determining is exactly how the hard determinist would argue according to Feinberg.[141] The human is not responsible, which, in the case of a sinful circumstance, then implies that God is the cause of that circumstance. Frame does not include human freedom in his unpacking of divine permission/causation. However, he does write, "It is not easy to find adequate terms to describe God's ordination of evil. Our language must not compromise either God's full sovereignty or his holiness and goodness."[142] The lack of inclusion of human freedom while discussing God's permission in the ordination of sin is another way in which compatibilism and hard determinism differ because the compatibilist affirms in some measure that human freedom is compatible with divine sovereignty.

---

137. Edwards, *Freedom of the Will*, 408–409.
138. Ibid., 411.
139. Frame, *The Doctrine of God*, 178.
140. Piper, *Spectacular Sins*, 54.
141. Feinberg, *No One Like Him*, 635.
142. Frame, *The Doctrine of God*, 179.

Both compatibilism and hard determinism have been defined as key theories of divine providence. It was necessary to distinguish compatibilism from hard determinism so as to treat them as different theories concerning God's providence, because they employ similar language concerning God's action in the world. The terms *ordain* and *permission* show this as they both employ these terms but with different meaning. Chapter 3 will examine these theories to demonstrate how they employ petitionary prayer. Attention now turns to open theism and middle knowledge as theories of divine providence.

Open Theism

Introduction

Open theism is a theological system that believes that God's knowledge of the future is both settled and open. Gregory Boyd calls determinism, or what is termed *compatibilism* in this book, "future determinism," and he calls *open theism*, "future openness."[143] This is because both compatibilists and open theists adhere to God knowing the past and present in the same way. Open theists debate God's knowledge of the future.[144] Some things that God knows are settled while other things are open or dynamic.[145] This means that the future is not totally known and subject to change. In other words, God does not have an exhaustive knowledge of the future. In *The Openness of God*, the relationship God has with the future is described as give-and-take as he cooperates with his creation in real space and time. This means that "we respond to God's gracious initiatives and God responds to our responses . . . and on it goes. God takes risks in this give-and-take relationship, yet he is endlessly resourceful and competent in working toward his ultimate goals."[146] William Hasker also argues that God takes relational risks and that this is a valuable component in the divine-human relationship.[147] In fact, for open theism, only with this kind of give-and-take relationship can people have a true relationship with God.

---

143. Boyd, "Does God Ever Change His Mind?" 13.
144. Boyd, *God of the Possible*, 13.
145. Ibid., 11.
146. Pinnock, Rice, Sanders, Hasker, and Basinger, *The Openness of God*, 7.
147. Hasker, "A Refutation of Middle Knowledge," 546.

Open Theism Defined

The seminal work concerning open theism is *The Openness of God*. In this work, open theism is defined as God giving humans significant freedom to work with or against God's will.[148] In this dynamic relationship, God takes great risks while remaining endlessly resourceful as he adapts his own plan to fit the changing situations created by human beings. Prior to the publication of *The Openness of God*, David Basinger defines open theism as "present knowledge." He writes, "For a God with [present knowledge], the creative act was a significant gamble."[149] Then again, he argues for "present knowledge," which is the belief that "God knows all that has occurred in the past, is occurring now, and that which will follow deterministically from what has already occurred. But they [open theists] deny that God necessarily knows all that will occur in the future."[150] This definition is not in opposition to *The Openness of God*; rather it displays the early formulations of what would later be termed open theism in that God does not know all that will occur in the future, leaving himself open to a genuine relationship with his creation. Hasker provides another early definition of open theism. He asserts, "God has gifted some of his creatures with libertarian free will, and God's decisions concerning how he will respond to his creatures at each stage of the temporal process are based on what has occurred up until that stage of the process and not on knowledge of free choices which will occur subsequently." The clearest definition comes from Pinnock when he describes the dynamic relationship God shares with his creation. He writes, "God's goal is to make possible relationships of mutual love between God and creatures and therefore set up a dynamic give and take situation in which God can even be said to risk failure to the degree permitted by the overall plan."[151] This dynamic relationship is marked by genuine risk.

Each of the above definitions alludes to a loving dialogue between God and humans. For example, in the case of prayer, the human freely prays, and God freely responds. William Alston provides a view concerning the divine-human dialogue that open theists employ.[152] For example, he describes the divine-human conversation as requiring "two independent participants, neither of which wholly controls the response of the other."[153] Alston then

---

148. Pinnock, et al., *The Openness of God*, 7.
149. Basinger, "Middle Knowledge and Classical Christian Thought," 411.
150. Basinger, "Divine Control and Human Freedom," 58.
151. Pinnock, "Open Theism," 237.
152. Hasker, "Providence and Evil," 94.
153. Alston, "Divine-Human Dialogue and the Nature of God," 148.

illustrates the importance of this dialogue by using the example of a hypnotist and his subject. He writes,

> Consider a "conversation" between hypnotist and subject, in which the latter is doing nothing but carrying out posthypnotic suggestions . . . Here the one party, the hypnotist, really is effectively deciding just what the other says, and the other is as complicated as a human being, in fact *is* a human being. Here we have as close an analogy to divine omnidetermination as we are likely to find, and the verdict, I suppose, would be clear. This is a charade, not a genuine case of communication.[154]

An open theist holds that the interaction between the Creator and creature is paramount. God created man in his image, and, in so doing, the creature has built within its very nature the longing to commune, which takes place between the divine and the human.[155] Furthermore, no member of the Trinity is static in its relationship with the other members of the Trinity, and if humans are created in God's image, then the open theist posits that creatures will participate in communion with one another and love one another.[156]

Biblical Example for Open Theism

Boyd arrived at open theism after a process that started some twenty years prior to writing *God of the Possible*.[157] He tells the story of reading 2 Kgs 20 and Isaiah speaking on behalf of God to Hezekiah that the sickness he was under would eventually take his life. In light of this, Hezekiah should get his house in order (2 Kgs 20:1). He also weeps bitterly and repents of his sin (2 Kgs 20:2–3). The text situates Hezekiah's response to show that his posture towards the Lord provokes God to heal him, and fifteen years are added to Hezekiah's life (2 Kgs 20:6). The question of God's sincerity puzzled Boyd. He writes, "Was God being sincere when he had Isaiah tell Hezekiah he wouldn't recover from his illness? And if so, then must we not believe that God really changed his mind when he decided to add fifteen years to Hezekiah's life?"[158] Furthermore, Boyd began to question

---

154. Alston, "Divine-Human Dialogue and the Nature of God," 9. Hasker provides the link to open theism as he positively refers to Alston in "Providence and Evil," 94.

155. Pinnock, et al., *The Openness of God*, 108–109.

156. Boyd, *God of the Possible*, 97. The Trinitarian implications are addressed in greater detail in chapter 4.

157. Ibid., 7.

158. Ibid.

what he had been taught to believe his entire Christian life. How "could God have truly changed his mind in response to a prayer if the prayer he was responding to was forever in his mind?"[159] Boyd's study of this passage and others where God seemingly changes his mind brought him to the conclusion that God must be open to the future and that he does not know everything that will come to pass.[160]

Theological Characteristics of Open Theism

The following is an examination of the theological characteristics of open theism, including a description of the dynamic relationship between God and humanity, which is expressed in the literature through love, knowledge, and relationship. However, to begin, attention is given to open theism and its understanding of the sovereignty of God.

Sovereignty of God

Even though they define it differently, compatibilism, hard determinism, middle knowledge, and open theism all affirm the sovereignty of God. The freedom that God's creatures enjoy is due to his sovereignty. For the open theist, God sovereignly granted humanity the freedom to work with or against God's will. Pinnock describes this sovereignty as "dynamic, give-and-take relationships with himself. It places the emphasis upon the genuine interactions that take place between God and human beings: how we respond to God's initiatives and how he responds to our responses."[161] With regard to those events, situations, and circumstances that God does not know with certainty, Pinnock reassures the Christian that God is "endlessly resourceful" in adapting circumstances to work towards his ultimate goals.[162] In addition, Pinnock writes, "Divine sovereignty involves a flexible out-working of God's purposes in history. It refers to his ability, as the only wise God, to manage things, despite resistance to his will."[163] The key terms for open theism as outlined by Pinnock are that God is resourceful and flexible in bringing about his desired goals.

---

159. Ibid.

160. Ibid. In chapter 4, a lengthy treatment of the biblical support for open theism and petitionary prayer is given.

161. Pinnock, *Most Moved Mover*, 4.

162. Ibid.

163. Pinnock, et al., *The Openness of God*, 116.

Sanders further unpacks God's sovereignty within the framework of open theism. He puts forward God's specific and general sovereignty. Compatibilism, he asserts, affirms specific sovereignty in that it maintains, "there are absolutely no limitations, hindrances or insurmountable obstacles for God to achieve his will in every specific circumstance of the created order.... Only what God purposes to happen in that particular time and place to that specific creature will happen."[164] For the open theist, general sovereignty more clearly captures the way in which God interacts within his creation. It states that God has sovereignly "established a type of world in which God sets up general structures or an overall framework for meaning and allows the creatures significant input into exactly how things will turn out."[165] This idea allows for God to enter into a genuine give-and-take relationship with his creatures. Sanders writes, "God macromanages the overall project (while remaining free to micromanage some things), God takes risks in governing the world."[166] For open theism, the sovereignty of God is essential because through his sovereignty, human beings are able to exercise their libertarian freedom in a given circumstance. This takes a great amount of risk on the part of God, but for him and the relationship he shares with humanity, it is a risk worth taking.

Dynamic Love, Knowledge, and Reactions

Three words are essential to open theism: love, knowledge, and reactions. Each represents an important characteristic of the relationship God shares with humanity. Both Richard Rice and John Sanders argue that a necessary component to making open theism work theologically is that God's knowledge of the future is dynamic as opposed to static. Rice argues that God is in a dynamic relationship, grounded in love, with his creatures. He writes,

> It [open theism] expresses two basic convictions: love is the most important quality we attribute to God, and love is more than care and commitment; it involves being sensitive and responsive as well. These convictions lead the contributors to this book to think of God's relation to the world in dynamic rather than static terms.[167]

---

164. Sanders, *The God Who Risks*, 224. For more on specific sovereignty see, Feinberg, *No One Like Him*, 677. Feinberg also offers a direct response to Sanders in *No One Like Him*, 706–14.

165. Sanders, *The God Who Risks*, 225.

166. Ibid.

167. Pinnock, et al., *The Openness of God*, 15.

Similar to Rice, Terence Fretheim argues that the divine-human relationship is not static.[168] Instead, when we do not pray, it hurts God "who remains eager for communication" when the human remains silent (Isa 65:2).[169]

In addition to God's dynamic relationship with humanity, open theism also emphasizes the work of God's love. Thomas Jay Oord, an open theist, actually critiques Sanders's view of providence because he believes that Sanders does not emphasize love enough. He writes, "My criticism of Sanders leads to my alternative version of open and relational theology, what I call 'essential kenosis.' At the heart of essential kenosis is the belief that controlling love is logically preeminent in God."[170] This nuance between Sanders and Oord is small, and Oord's term *essential kenosis* has not caught on in the literature; however, this term does demonstrate just how much emphasis an open theist places on love. Continuing on the topic of dynamic love, Sanders focuses on the creature's necessary ability to freely love God.[171] Similar to Sanders, Robin Collins adds that dynamic love involves valuing one's neighbors, which is manifested in the person's ability to love his neighbors for who God created them to be.[172] For open theism, love presents the perfect illustration that humanity must be able to love God freely, which also means that God takes a risk, because some will choose to not love him. In addition to Sanders, Pinnock also refers to the dynamic love shared in relationship between the Divine-human.[173] Like Sanders, Pinnock observes that love is genuine when both God and human are freely expressing their love toward one another. For Pinnock, it is linked closely with the way in which we were created as image bearers of God.

---

168. Fretheim, "Prayer in the Old Testament," 51.

169. Ibid., 54. The question then becomes, does God have to be dynamic in order for real relationship to exist? It seems that the answer is no. In God's free knowledge, which the Christian exists in now, the human being is consumed with "dynamic" experiences. This validates what Rice states in the quote above. However, God does not have to be dynamic for the human experience to be dynamic as well. Rice is in error when he defines the divine human interaction as genuine only when both the divine and human are dynamic. That does not have to be the case. Middle knowledge helps solve this problem as it does not have to wait until the moment the human being acts in the world to become aware and thus enter into a dynamic relationship. For middle knowledge, the relationship began prior to the creation of the world. This difference between open theism and middle knowledge will be discussed in chapters 5 and 6.

170. Oord, *The Uncontrolling Love of God*, 149.

171. Sanders, *The God Who Risks*, 206.

172. Collins, "Prayer and Open Theism," 174.

173. Pinnock, "Open Theism," 238.

God's dynamic knowledge can be displayed as he progressively learns throughout the course of time.[174] The position is called the "open view of God" based on this theological principle, because it "regards God as receptive to new experiences and as flexible in the way he works toward his objectives in the world. . . . Yet we believe that this dependence does not detract from God's greatness, it only enhances it."[175] In other words, God is able to be receptive towards the future because he is endlessly resourceful in bringing the future towards his end.

Another seminal aspect of open theism is God's dynamic responses toward his creation. Said another way, God's actions are by definition also reactions toward his creatures which are created in his image.[176] Furthermore, Rice asserts that God is unchangeable in nature and is changeable (i.e. dynamic) in experience through his give-and-take relationship with humanity.[177] Thus, open theism believes that it is the theory of providence best suited to give an account of the genuine relationship one encounters with God.[178] For this reason, the open theist asserts that God is dynamic in his dealings with humanity. Furthermore, the resourcefulness of God's wisdom gives the open theist hope and reassurance in such a responsive relationship with God. Sanders and other open theists believe that the idea of God being innovative and proficient is paradigmatic. Sanders writes, "God's problem solving ability came out as he overcame various. . . obstacles that stood in the way of accomplishment of the divine project. God has demonstrated in history that he has all the wisdom necessary to work with the sort of world he decided to create, despite the fact that things do not always go as God desires."[179] Open theism does not worry about a world out of control, because due to God's dynamic response to his creation, he is a great problem solver with endless resources at his disposal in order to assure that the world is still orderly. With this confidence, God "voluntarily forfeits control over earthly affairs in those cases" in order to allow humanity to have a genuine give-and-take relationship with him.[180]

---

174. Pinnock, et al., *The Openness of God*, 16.

175. Ibid.

176. Ibid., 38.

177. Rice, "Biblical Support for a New Perspective," 48–49. See also Sanders, *The God Who Risks*, 14–15.

178. See chapter 4, which discusses the interaction humanity has with God through petitionary prayer.

179. Sanders, *The God Who Risks*, 182.

180. Basinger, "Practical Implications," 159; Basinger, *The Case for Freewill Theism*, 108.

The examination of open theism as a theory of providence included defining open theism, discussing its view concerning God's sovereignty, and articulating its theological principles. This focused on the dynamic relationship God shares with humanity as expressed through love, knowledge, and relationship. In chapter 4, open theism will be examined as it relates to petitionary prayer.

Middle Knowledge

At the outset, the agenda was to argue for four theories of providence: compatibilism, hard determinism, open theism, and middle knowledge. In what follows, I will define middle knowledge, which is the final theory in question for this chatper, and discuss its theological principles.

Molina, Hubmaier, and Arminius

The origin of middle knowledge is dated back to the sixteenth century when Luis de Molina wrote *On Divine Foreknowledge*.[181] Middle knowledge first began within Catholicism, setting off a dispute between the Dominican Order and the Society of Jesus.[182] During the Reformation period, Balthasar Hubmaier and James Arminius were developing their views concerning God's omniscience. They both sound very similar to Molina. The difference between Hubmaier and Arminius is that Hubmaier was not aware of Molina's work.[183] However, Arminius uses the very language of Molina (i.e. middle knowledge), and according to Eef Dekker, this is not a coincidence. He writes,

> Now if this train of thought is correct, we may conclude that Arminius was in 1597 (in which year he wrote the *Collatio*) acquainted with the theory of middle knowledge, but did not yet accept it . . . . thus we can say that Arminius somewhere between 1597 and 1603 became convinced of the fruitfulness of the theory of middle knowledge. Arminius most probably

---

181. Kirk MacGregor has written a helpful biography on the life and theology of Molina in *Luis de Molina*.

182. Brown, *From the Ancient World to the Age of Enlightenment*, 161.

183. MacGregor, "Hubmaier's Concord of Predestination with Free Will," 279–99, accessed October 9, 2015, http://www.directionjournal.org/35/2/hubmaiers-concord-of-predestination-with.html.

knew the theory of middle knowledge already in 1597, but endorsed it only later.[184]

Arminius asserts that humans are free in their actions. He writes, "The second cause, both with regard to its power and the use of that power, remains free either to act or not to act, so that, if it be the pleasure of this second cause, it can suspend its own action."[185] In other words, Arminius is arguing that the human is capable of acting freely in a given circumstance. However, Arminius also believes that God is sovereign over these free human actions. He writes, "I place in subjection to divine providence both the free will and even the actions of rational creature, so that nothing can be done apart from the will of God, not even any of those things that are done in opposition to it."[186] One must employ middle knowledge because it is within this framework where a person is able to affirm that God is sovereign over both his will and the actions of humans. This kind of knowledge is not mere foreknowledge, but rather it is knowledge of what humans would do. John Laing notes that this is a common misconception concerning Arminius's views of predestination and election. He writes,

> One of the most common misunderstandings of Arminianism is that its proponents claim that predestination and election are based on God's foreknowledge. This, however, is not quite correct. Rather, the claim is that God's predestining work, his choice of individuals to salvation is based on his knowledge of who would respond to his call in various circumstances, if he were to so act. Thus, according to Arminians, predestination is based on middle knowledge, not foreknowledge.[187]

Furthermore, in Disputation 4.43 Arminius introduces natural, middle, and free knowledge into his own framework concerning God's omniscience.[188] Arminius had an awareness of middle knowledge and the work of Molina, and Arminius's appropriation of the categories demonstrates that at the center of his doctrine concerning the divine nature is the interworking of middle knowledge.

---

184. Dekker, "Was Arminius a Molinist?" 351.

185. Arminius, *The Writings of James Arminius*, 1:296.

186. Ibid., 1:251.

187. Laing, "The Compatibility of Calvinism and Middle Knowledge," 457.

188. Arminius, "Disputation 4: On the Divine Nature of God," in *The Works of James Arminius*, 448–9.

Middle Knowledge Defined

Calvinists and Arminians alike share the theological concerns of those interested in middle knowledge.[189] Thomas Flint defines middle knowledge as: "Molina and his followers have attempted to fashion the strongest notion of divine providence compatible with genuine human freedom, where freedom is understood in the libertarian sense."[190] In other words, middle knowledge attempts to hold a high view of divine sovereignty while at the same time affirming that human freedom is compatible with God's sovereignty. In addition to God's sovereignty being compatible with libertarian freedom, any definition of God's middle knowledge must include a distinction between logical and temporal priority in God's divine knowledge. Also essential to any definition of middle knowledge is an understanding of the logical moments of God's *natural*, *free*, and *middle* knowledge.[191] William Lane Craig provides a concise definition of *middle knowledge* that will be referenced throughout this book.[192] Craig defines *middle knowledge* as "God's knowledge of what every possible free creature would do under any possible set of circumstances," and hence, knowledge of those possible worlds which God can make actual.[193]

Logical Priority

The difference between temporal and logical priority is essential in that middle knowledge depends on three logical rather than temporal moments

---

189. MacGregor, *Luis de Molina*, 13.

190.. Flint, "Hasker's 'God, Time, and Knowledge,'" 104.

191.. Below *natural*, *middle*, and *free* knowledge are defined and discussed at length. At this point only a brief definition of *natural* and *free* knowledge is necessary as providing a definition of middle knowledge is the focus of this section: "*Natural Knowledge*: God's knowledge of all possible worlds. The content of this knowledge is essential to God . . . *Free Knowledge*: God's knowledge of the actual world. The content of this knowledge is not essential to God" (Craig, *The Only Wise God*, 131).

192. David Basinger describes Craig as a leading evangelical proponent of middle knowledge (Basinger, "Divine Control and Human Freedom," 60).

193. Craig, *The Only Wise God*, 130. Terrance Tiessen's definition states, "The term 'middle knowledge' is most often associated with Luis de Molina, who asserted that God has three kinds of knowledge. I use the term in this book to speak more generally of knowledge concerning what would happen if the circumstance were different than they actually are" (Tiessen, *Providence and Prayer*, 366). Tiessen and Craig do not share the exact same definition and are from two different theological systems. However, they are not that far apart regarding their basic definition of middle knowledge. Both affirm and emphasize the three logical moments of God's knowledge: natural, middle, and free.

in God's knowledge: natural, middle, and free. However, God has known these propositions for eternity.[194] To say that a proposition has temporal priority implies that the proposition occurs before the other in time. Logical priority asserts that a proposition provides the grounds for another proposition or that a proposition provides an explanation for another proposition. Kenneth Keathley, a proponent of middle knowledge, describes the logical priority of God's knowledge.

> Since God is omniscient, He innately knows all things—this means He does not go through the mental processes that finite beings do of "figuring things out." God never "learns" or has things "occur" to Him. He already knows all truths. The fact that God is omniscient does not merely mean that God is infinitely more knowledgeable than us, but that His knowledge is of a different type and quality. So the three moments of God's knowledge proposed by Molinism refer to logical order, not a sequence in time.[195]

Furthermore, with logical priority, God's middle knowledge does not have to wait until God's natural knowledge is complete in order for God to have middle knowledge. Instead, logical priority says that God's natural, middle, and free knowledge could in time be working contemporaneously.[196] In light of this, Craig writes, "The premises in an argument are logically prior to the conclusion, since the conclusion is derived from and based on the premises, even though temporally the premises and conclusion are all simultaneously true."[197] This distinction between God's logical and temporal priority is similar to that of the *ordo salutis* in the Reformed tradition. As Wayne Grudem notes, the logical moments of the gospel call, regeneration, conversion, justification, adoption, and part of sanctification all involve "becoming a Christian," and thus work contemporaneously in the life of the believer.[198]

---

194. Craig, "No Other Name," 77.

195. Keathley, *Salvation and Sovereignty*, 16.

196. Calvinistic theologians are familiar with the distinction between logical and temporal priority. This is clearly evidenced within the framework of the *Ordo Salutis*.

197. Craig, *The Only Wise God*, 128.

198. Grudem, *Systematic Theology*, 670.

Logical Moments in God's Knowledge

The very idea that God's knowledge is in moments begs one to consider what specifically these moments are leading up to or moving away from. In this case, the focus is on God's decree to create the world. Using soteriology as his example, Craig asserts that the content of God's middle knowledge prior to the divine decree to create a world is what reconciles predestination and human freedom.[199] The content of God's natural knowledge includes the entire range of logically possible worlds that God could create. The content of God's middle knowledge includes those possible worlds, which are feasible for God to create. Thus middle knowledge also includes his knowledge of how each individual would respond if created and placed in a certain circumstance.[200] Both God's natural and middle knowledge are logically prior to God's decision to create the world. The content of God's free knowledge is posterior to God's decision to create the world.[201] This entails that God has freely chosen one of the possible worlds available to him in his middle knowledge, and he actualizes that world.[202] It is important to note that the content of God's free knowledge could be different if he had chosen to create a different world.[203] In order for middle knowledge to work, the logical order to the content of God's knowledge must be natural knowledge, middle knowledge, God's decree to create, and then the content of God's free knowledge.

Natural Knowledge

The first logical moment in God's knowledge is his natural knowledge. In this moment, God knows all necessary truths. Thomas Flint asserts, "To guide his act of will, such knowledge would have to be prior to that act—that is, it

---

199. Craig, "No Other Name," 179.

200. Ibid., 178.

201. See also MacGregor's discussion of God's middle knowledge as logically prior to the creation of the world (MacGregor, "Hubmaier's Concord of Predestination with Free Will," 283–86). Tiessen makes a similar point (Tiessen, "Why Calvinists Should Believe in Divine Middle Knowledge, Although they Reject Molinism," 353–54).

202. Middle knowledge finds theological strength in the logical moments of God's knowledge. If the content of God's middle knowledge were positioned logically after God's decree to create a world, middle knowledge would still be positioned between God's natural and free knowledge; however, it would break down theologically (Perszyk, "Free Will Defense with and without Molinism," 43). In fact, most problems that arise when dealing with the theological implications of middle knowledge result from an erroneous positioning of God's decree to create a world (see chapter 5).

203. Craig, "No Other Name," 178.

would need to be *prevolitional*. And the kind of knowledge that most readily pops to mind here is knowledge of *necessary truths*."[204] Furthermore, Flint observes that these propositions are independent of God's will. He writes,

> Since such propositions are true independent of any free choice on God's part, and since God is (according to orthodox Christianity) essentially omniscient, it would seem to be part of his very nature to know such truths. It is hardly unnatural, then, for Molina to label God's *prevolitional* knowledge of *necessary* truths as *natural knowledge*.[205]

For example, it is necessarily true that squares have four sides. A contingent truth (discussed below) could either be true or false, but a necessary truth is true in every possible world. In response, a proponent of middle knowledge would argue, in Flint's words, that "God knows all possibilities."[206] Craig notes that God's natural knowledge of all possibilities includes knowledge of all the possible individuals he could create and all the possible circumstances he could place them in.[207] When Craig refers to "natural knowledge," he means that God knows in his natural knowledge "every contingent state of affairs which could possibly obtain and of what the exemplification of the individual essence of any free creature could freely choose to do in any such state of affairs that should be actual."[208] Flint gives a concise description of God's natural knowledge as well:

> Consider, Molinists say, God's knowledge of his world. Some of the truths God knows—e.g. mathematical truths such as *two plus three equals five*—are necessary truths, ones that could not have been other than they are and that are in no sense the result of any free decision on God's part. Knowing such truths can be seen as part of God's very nature; hence, Molina labeled this God's *natural knowledge*.[209]

This is the first moment of God's knowledge. The next section examines God's free knowledge.

---

204. Flint, *Divine Providence*, 37.
205. Flint, *Divine Providence*, 38. See also Molina, *On Divine Foreknowledge*, 168. Berkhof discusses the reality of God's natural knowledge in *Systematic Theology*, 78.
206. Flint, *Divine Providence*, 38.
207. Craig, *The Only Wise God*, 129.
208. Craig, "No Other Name," 177.
209. Flint, "Divine Providence," 274.

Free Knowledge

The third logical moment in God's knowledge includes knowledge of the "actual world" which God has created.[210] For example, the statement, the sky is blue, is true because the world God chose to create contains a blue sky during the day.[211] Important to God's free knowledge is that it has implication both before and after creation. For example, God knew prior to creation which world he would actualize; thus, prior to creation God knew the content of his free knowledge as he made a decision about which world to create. In addition, once the world is created and the content of the "actual world" is set in motion, God's free knowledge is actualized and therefore stands logically posterior to God's decision to create the world.[212] Flint writes,

> God can be thought of as moving from knowledge of which worlds are possible to knowledge of which world is actual, and this movement is mediated by his free creative act of will. Knowing which world is actual adds to God's knowledge by informing him as to which contingent propositions that he might have rendered false are in fact true in the wake of his free activity.[213]

Furthermore, with regard to the posterior nature of God's free knowledge, Tiessen writes, "God's knowledge of how particular creatures would act in particular situations is prior to his decree to create this particular world and it is, therefore, not part of his free knowledge, which is his knowledge of his own decree. If it is not part of God's necessary knowledge, it must therefore be part of a middle knowledge."[214] Tiessen observes that God's knowledge of what a creature could do (natural knowledge), or would do (middle knowledge) is located in God's knowledge prior to the world being created. However, with God's free knowledge, he now has knowledge of the actual world. The content of God's free knowledge is not essential to God as it is dependent upon his will and decision to create a specific world. Craig writes, "For if he had created a different world, the content of his free knowledge would be different."[215] This is the third logical moment in God's

---

210. Craig, *The Only Wise God*, 129.

211. Berkhof discusses the reality of God's free knowledge in *Systematic Theology*, 78.

212. Craig, *The Only Wise God*, 129.

213. Flint, *Divine Providence*, 38. See also de Molina, *On Divine Foreknowledge*, 168.

214. Tiessen, "Why Calvinists Should Believe in Divine Middle Knowledge," 354.

215. Craig, *The Only Wise God*, 130.

knowledge, which is located after the world has been created. Attention will now turn to the logical moment of God's middle knowledge.

Middle Knowledge

The second logical moment in God's knowledge is in-between God's natural and free knowledge: hence, the term, *middle* knowledge.[216] While middle knowledge is logically between God's natural and free knowledge, it also shares with natural knowledge the important position of being logically prior to God's decree to create a world. In middle knowledge, "God knows what every possible creature would do (not just could do) in any possible set of circumstances."[217] For example, God knew that if he were to create the Apostle Peter and put him in certain circumstances, then Peter would deny him three times. Craig writes, "By his natural knowledge God knew in the first moment all the possible things that Peter could do if placed in such circumstances. But now in this second moment he knows what Peter would in fact freely choose to do under such circumstances."[218] The difference between God's natural and middle knowledge is:

> In the second moment, God possesses knowledge of all true counterfactual propositions, including counterfactuals of creaturely freedom [CCF]. That is to say, He knows what contingent states of affairs would obtain if certain antecedent states of affairs were to obtain; whereas by His natural knowledge God knew what any free creature could do in any set of circumstances, now in this second moment God knows what any free creature would do in any set of circumstances.[219]

Molina also explains why middle knowledge should not be thought of as natural or free knowledge. First, middle knowledge is logically prior to his decree to create a world, whereas free knowledge is logically posterior to his decree to create. Also, in God's free knowledge, he does not know

---

216. Ibid. See also Thomas Flint's helpful treatment of middle knowledge in Flint, "Divine Providence," in *The Oxford Handbook of Philosophical Theology*, 274–82.

217. Craig, *The Only Wise God*, 129. Thomas P. Flint provides a helpful definition of middle knowledge. He writes, "My own view, to put it succinctly, is that the Molinist account is the inevitable offspring of two theses to which orthodox Christians are strongly attracted. These two are (1) that God is provident in the strong traditional sense, a sense which entails his foreknowledge of an sovereignty over each and every event that occurs, and (2) that humans are free in the full-blooded libertarian sense" (Flint, "A Death He Freely Accepted," 4).

218. Craig, *The Only Wise God*, 129.

219. Craig, "No Other Name," 177.

anything other than what in fact *is*, because the world has been created, whereas with middle knowledge God knows what the creature would do *if* created.[220] Second, middle knowledge is not natural knowledge because what the human would do is known in his middle knowledge while the possibilities of human free choice are known in his natural knowledge.[221]

God's middle knowledge is made up of various Counterfactuals of Creaturely Freedom (CCF).[222] Flint asserts that CCFs inform God as to how any creature would freely act in a given circumstance in which it is created and left free.[223] Having knowledge of CCFs, God can, "by carefully selecting both the beings He creates and the situations in which He places them, arrange things in such a way that His goals for the world are attained with certainty, but attained largely through the free acts of His creatures rather than through His causally determinative initiatives."[224] Terrance Tiessen agrees with Flint and observes that due to God's middle knowledge, he knows what a creature would do if that set of circumstances were actual.[225] To say it another way, CCFs specify what a creature would do if the creature were in such a situation and free.[226] Perhaps the most iconic passage regarding God's middle knowledge is found in 1 Sam 23:6–10.[227] In this passage, David learns that the Philistines are fighting against Keilah and are about to destroy them. David departs for Keilah after receiving the directive from the Lord to go and fight on behalf of Keilah. The Lord promises David that the Philistines will be handed over to David if he were to go and fight. David departs and fights on behalf of Keilah, and as the Lord promises, the Philistines are handed over to David. Sometime after the battle, Abiathar the priest notifies David that Saul is going to come to Keilah to wage war against David with the intent of capturing David and his men. David then asks the Lord if the men of Keilah will surrender him over to Saul. The Lord replies with the affirmative that Saul will in fact be coming down to capture him

---

220. de Molina, *On Divine Foreknowledge*, 168–69.

221. Ibid.

222. Craig, *The Only Wise God*, 71.

223. Flint, "The Possibilities of Incarnation," 308.

224. Flint, "The Possibilities of Incarnation," 308.

225. Tiessen, *Providence and Prayer*, 365.

226. Craig, *The Only Wise God*, 130.

227. For example, see Gaskin, "Conditionals of Freedom and Middle Knowledge," 414; Bertolet, "Hasker on Middle Knowledge," 7; Campbell, "Middle Knowledge: A Reformed Critique," 7; Adams, "Middle Knowledge and the Problem of Evil," 110; Hasker, "Response to Thomas Flint," 120. Within theology, Charles Hodge illustrates middle knowledge by employing this same passage in *Systematic Theology*, 1:399; see also Hoeksema, *Reformed Dogmatics*, 1:129.

and his men and that the people of Keilah will hand him over to Saul. Upon learning of this coming trouble, David along with 600 of his men depart from Keilah. Once Saul arrives and learns that David had fled, Saul gives up the expedition to capture David.[228]

Molinists interpret the passage as confirming that there can be true CCFs because God knew what David would do were he in the circumstance of Saul coming to Keilah to capture him.[229] David acts freely in his departure from Keilah as well. He could have stayed; however, he would have been captured. God knew not only what could happen but also what would happen.

God's middle knowledge does not imply that God perceives what free creatures would do in a given circumstance so as to look upon already created (i.e., fully instantiated) free creatures and adjudicate what they would do based on God's observation of their free actions. This entails, for example, the idea that a person is instantiated in three possible worlds, and God is merely observing how that person would react. Based upon his actions, God then makes a decision as to which world he is going to create. This is not God's middle knowledge. Rather, God, based on his knowledge of that person, conceives of his choices within God. This kind of knowledge echoes that of the Psalmist, who declares, "Your eyes saw my unformed substance" (Ps 139:16 ESV).[230] Therefore, God's detailed knowledge of the actions of his children is already formed long before their formation. For example, if God were to obtain his knowledge of what a creature would do after his decision to create a world, then the world would already be created, and therefore, God would merely be observing within his created world how the creature is acting. Middle knowledge instead maintains the sovereignty of God as he is not in a responsive posture towards his creatures and their actions.[231]

---

228. See also Ps 5 where David offers a petition of protection, which parallel the events of 1 Sam 23:6–10. See specifically "Lead me, O Lord, in your righteousness because of my enemies; make your way straight before me" (Ps 5:8), and also "But let all who take refuge in you rejoice; let them ever sing for joy, and spread your protection over them, that those who love your name may exult in you. For you bless the righteous, O Lord; you cover him with favor as with a shield" (Ps 5:11–12).

229. William Hasker and Robert Adams reject that CCFs are true. See Hasker, "Response to Thomas Flint," 117–26; Adams, "An Anti-Molinist Argument," 343–53.

230. Kraus, *Psalms 60–150*, 517.

231. To be fair to Keathley, he clearly states at the beginning of his description and definition of middle knowledge, he is "going to simplify things a bit" (Keathley, *Salvation and Sovereignty*, 17). However, placing middle knowledge as a subset to natural knowledge does not achieve the clarity he desires. A better approach would be to highlight the logical moment of God's decree to create a world and how that impacts God's knowledge prior to and after.

Libertarian Freedom

One of the main characteristics of middle knowledge is that human agents are free in a libertarian sense with regard to their actions. For Flint, this kind of freedom, along with how it relates to God's sovereignty, is what makes middle knowledge so attractive.[232] He writes,

> The Molinist account is the inevitable offspring of two theses to which orthodox Christians are quite properly strongly attracted. These two theses are
>
> (1) that God is provident in the strong traditional sense, a sense which entails his foreknowledge of and sovereignty over each and every event that occurs, and
>
> (2) that humans are free in the full-blooded libertarian sense.[233]

Tiessen defines *libertarianism*: "Libertarian freedom is that state of freedom in which there is a real possibility that one could make at least two different choices in exactly the same circumstances, both external and internal."[234] According to Alfred Freddoso, Molina is an unremitting libertarian.[235] Freddoso defines such freedom as having the faculty to choose indeterministically with regard to the circumstance at hand.[236] Furthermore, three options are available to the free agent:

> (i) to elicit an act of willing the object, (ii) to elicit an act of dissenting from or rejecting the object, or (iii) to refrain from either willing or dissenting. So every free action involves a free choice, which then typically issues forth in a "commanded" act—most often, in free human action, a basically bodily movement.[237]

For the proponent of middle knowledge, libertarian freedom is essential because it assures that the human agents are genuinely free and culpable

---

232. Flint argues against what he calls, "Maverick Molinism," a version of Molinism described by Jonathan Kvanvig as maintaining, "though counterfactuals of freedom have their truth-value logically prior to God's acts of will, God could have so acted that these counterfactuals would have had a different truth value from that which they actually have" ("On Behalf of Maverick Molinism," 348). Flint responds to Kvanvig in "The Multiple Muddles of Maverick Molinism," 91–100. Flint first discusses Maverick Molinism in *Divine Providence*, 65–70.
233. Flint, "A Death He Freely Accepted," 4.
234. Tiessen, *Providence and Prayer*, 366.
235. de Molina, *On Divine Foreknowledge*, 24.
236. de Molina, *On Divine Foreknowledge*, 25.
237. de Molina, *On Divine Foreknowledge*, 25.

with respect to their actions while at the same time assuring that God is omniscient. In order to illustrate this, Wes Morriston asserts,

> A great advantage of Molinism is that it allows those who hold it to combine a full-blooded belief in libertarian freedom with the view that all human choices and actions take place in accordance with a detailed divine plan. In the Molinist world, there is no such thing as brute change, and Providence rules all. It rules—not by compelling obedience, but by taking into account what it knows about what every possible person *would* freely do in any possible set of circumstances.[238]

In addition to Morriston above, Thomas Flint summarizes the relationship between libertarianism and middle knowledge well. He writes,

> For if libertarianism is correct, God could not just decide or causally determine which such propositions (which can be referred to as counterfactuals of freedom) would be true; rather, their truth would have to be independent of the divine will. Molina saw such truths as constituting what he called God's middle knowledge, and argued that this middle knowledge would allow God to exercise sovereign control over his world.[239]

Along with Flint and Morriston, Craig offers an appeal to mystery when trying to defend middle knowledge from the charge that God has divine foreknowledge. He asserts, "In other words, all the Christian has to show is that such foreknowledge has not been proved to be impossible, that there is no good reason to reject it. The Christian cannot be expected to explain the actual way that God foreknows future events; all the Christian has to do is suggest some possible way."[240] The Molinist's task is to articulate that there is compatibility between God's knowledge and libertarian human freedom. The work of the Molinist theologian is not to give an account for something unknowable by finite humans, namely the scope of God's knowledge.

Middle knowledge is therefore defined by its adherence to specific sovereignty being compatible with libertarian freedom, a claim that no other theory discussed in this book can make. Also it has been discussed that God's knowledge is that of logical and not temporal priority. Attention was also given to defining the logical moments of God's natural, middle, and free

---

238. Morriston, "Explanatory Priority and the 'Counterfactuals of Freedom,'" 21–22.

239. Flint, "Hasker's God, Time, and Knowledge," 104.

240. Craig, *The Only Wise God*, 119.

knowledge. In chapter 5, I will discuss middle knowledge and its treatment of petitionary prayer.

Conclusion

In conclusion, the theories of compatibilism, hard determinism, open theism, and middle knowledge will serve as a foundation for this book as one's view of providence determines how motivated the person is to offer petitionary prayer. Each of these theories of providence will receive attention in chapters 3, 4, and 5 respectively as each theory treats petitionary prayer differently. In the end, I argue that middle knowledge is the preferred theory of providence due to its ability to affirm the sovereignty of God in petitionary prayer by including both God's omniscience and libertarian human freedom.

2

Petitionary Prayer and Theology

Introduction

THIS CHAPTER WILL ADDRESS petitionary prayer, which will include defining and examining its biblical and theological characteristics. In this book, *petitionary prayer* is a genuine human behavior whereby the creature goes to its sovereign Creator and simply asks. The relationship between petitionary prayer and each theory of providence discussed in chapter 1 will be examined in chapters 3–5. Also, the outline of this chapter will provide the structure for chapters 3–5. For example, each theory of providence will use certain biblical passages and theological topics from this chapter to support their claim. This will provide continuity throughout the remainder of the book and exclude other topics relevant to petitionary prayer.[1]

Eleonore Stump and J. I. Packer offer some general observations regarding the function of petitionary prayer in the life of the believer. First, Stump asserts that "Christian believers of every period have in general taken prayer to be fundamentally a request made of God for something specific believed to be good by the one praying."[2] Those specific things that the creature requests are diverse (1 John 3:22; Luke 11:13). For example, humans ask for forgiveness (1 John 1:8–9; Luke 18:13), healing (Jas 5:14–15; Acts 28:8), blessings (Eph 1:16; Acts 6:6; 13:3), wisdom (Eph 1:17; Phil 1:9), and salvation (John 4:10; Rom 10:1). Humans cry out (Col 4:12) and even plead with God (Rom 15:30; Eph 1:19–23). Sometimes, the petition comes

---

1. For example, one topic excluded is the petitionary prayers of non-believers, see, Berkhof, *Systematic Theology*, 404; Grudem, *Systematic Theology*, 378; Kreider, "Jonathan Edwards's Theology of Prayer," 448; Hodge, *Systematic Theology*, 3:695; Constable, "What Prayer Will and Will Not Change," 100; Kreider, "God Never Begrutches His People Anything They Desire," 84. Another topic excluded is prayer for Jesus to return. See Cosby, *Suffering and Sovereignty*, 77–78; Crump, *Knocking on Heaven's Door*, 300; Redding, *Prayer and the Priesthood of Christ in the Reformed Tradition*, 292; Horton, *The Christian Faith*, 786.

2. Stump, "Petitionary Prayer," 81.

without words but with groaning that the Holy Spirit takes and offers to the Father on their behalf (Rom 8:22–26).

J. I. Packer also demonstrates the significance of petitionary prayer as he reflects on how the "awareness of the divine is natural to human beings through general revelation."[3] For Packer, petitionary prayer is a demonstration of the natural awareness of the divine. He writes, "Everywhere in every era when crises come, children and adults of any faith or no faith find their minds forming the cry, 'Please let this (specified) happen, and not that (specified again).' The dictum that there are no atheists in the trenches bear witness to this. The naturalness of prayer under pressure is a fact of life."[4] The things and circumstances that one petitions God for are diverse and impact the Christian on many levels. Petitionary prayer is defined in the following section.

Petitionary Prayer Defined

Thomas Oden, when defining *petitionary prayer*, notes the link between providence and prayer. He writes, "It is faith in providence that enables Christians to pray that God will carry them through hazards, care for them, and be present to them amid ordinary and extraordinary human struggles. Without God's providing, the act of praying would be absurd."[5] However, in light of divine providence, the issue of the nature of communication between God and humanity emerges. In other words, one's theory of providence determines how necessary petitionary prayer is to them. Also, a person's view of providence determines how motivated he is to offer petitionary prayer. For this book, I define *petitionary prayer* as a genuine human behavior whereby the creature goes to its sovereign Creator and simply asks.[6] Others have defined *petitionary prayer* as well. For example, Joshua Hoffman defines *petitionary prayer* as, "the practice of making a request of God in the hope that one's request will be granted, and in the belief that some such requests, at least, are efficacious."[7] This definition falls short due to its emphasis on receiving from God. Receiving something requested is indeed beneficial; however, it is not the main emphasis of petitionary prayer. Nor does success or failure rest on whether or not a person has received some-

---

3. Packer, "When Prayer Doesn't 'Work,'" 29.

4. Ibid.

5. Oden, *Classic Christianity*, 144.

6. H. P. Owen defines petitionary prayer as signifying, "requests for oneself . . . or on behalf of, other people" (Owen, *The Basis of Christian Prayer*, 43).

7. Hoffman, "On Petitionary Prayer," 21.

thing. Bruce Ware defines petitionary prayer as "requesting or petitioning God, on behalf of oneself or others, to act in some specific manner in order to bring about some specific result, where the action and result are seen as brought about by God's own will and action while they are also, in certain instances, causally tied to the petition that was brought before God and requested of him."[8] This definition falls short due to the particular phrase "in certain instances," because if prayer is only necessary at times, the Christian has difficulty adjudicating those instances when prayer is causally tied to the petition. Also, if prayer is only efficacious in certain circumstances, then the one petitioning is not necessary. There seems to be a lack of confidence built in because the person does not know if that particular moment is a time in which God is going to causally tie prayer to the outcome. Further analysis of Ware's definition will take place in chapter 3. In addition, David Basinger defines *petitionary prayer* as, "Prayer in which God is asked to intervene beneficially in earthly affairs."[9] Basinger's definition is similar to that of Hoffman above; however, instead of hope being the focus, Basinger believes it to be the beneficial intervention of God.

The definition of *petitionary prayer* that I have proposed captures the relational qualities one hopes for in prayer: that the interaction between God and human is genuine in that the human could have also refrained from offering prayer. In addition, nothing is prohibiting the one praying from going before God in prayer. However, once the motivation to go before God in prayer is acted upon, Christ's High Priesthood provides the necessary access one needs to go before God. Also, an affirmative response is most desired; however, due to one's limited knowledge and sinful nature, it is best to have the humility to simply ask instead of assuming that what is asked for is the best or wisest outcome in that particular circumstance. I discuss various biblical examples of petitionary prayer in the following section.

Biblical Examples of Petitionary Prayer

The following are examples in the Bible where individuals offer petitionary prayers to God. These examples illustrate that God graciously and mercifully listens to and answers prayers. Also important to petitionary prayer is that humans freely offer these prayers to God. Scholars of all theological persuasions appeal to these passages for their understanding of providence and prayer.

---

8. Ware, "Prayer and the Sovereignty of God," 129.
9. Basinger, "Petitionary Prayer," 475.

One example is Moses petitioning God so that he would relent from his wrath. Douglas Stuart rightly observes, "Indeed, this is one of many passages in Scripture that demonstrate God's responsiveness to the prayer of a righteous person prayed not for selfish reason but out of a desire to see God's will accomplished."[10] When the people determine that Moses is "delayed" in his return, they ask Aaron to "make us gods who shall go before us" (Exod 32:1). To fulfill their request, Aaron asks that they give him all their gold rings, and from them he fashions a golden calf. The people then declare, "These are your gods, O Israel, who brought you up out of the land of Egypt!" (Exod 32:4). Contemporaneous to these events, the Lord says to Moses on the mountain, "Go down, for your people, whom you brought up out of the land of Egypt, have corrupted themselves. They have turned aside quickly out of the way that I commanded them. They have made for themselves a golden calf and have worshiped it and sacrificed to it and said, 'These are your gods, O Israel, who brought you up out of the land of Egypt!'" (Exod 32:7–8). Because the Israelites are a stiff-necked people, the Lord declares that his wrath would burn "hot against them" and that he would "consume them" (Exod 32:10).[11] Moses then petitions the Lord to relent from his wrath. Observing this conversation, Terence Fretheim writes,

> Remarkably, Moses does not accede to God's request; he does not leave God alone...The boldness of his reply indicates something of the nature of the relationship between God and Moses. God has so entered into this relationship that such dialogue is invited, indeed welcomed: *God is not the only one who has something important to say.*[12]

This petition is twofold: (1) Moses draws upon the possible assumptions that would be made concerning the Lord as people wonder why the Lord would bring his people with a mighty hand out of Egypt into the wilderness just to consume them from the earth (Exod 32:11–12); (2) Moses asks God to remember the promise made to Abraham, Isaac, and Israel, which was a promise of blessing and multiplication (Exod 32:13).[13] The Lord listens to Moses' petition and relents from "the disaster that he had

---

10. Stuart, *Exodus*, 672; Childs, *The Book of Exodus*, 568. See also, Prov 15:29; Jas 5:16; 1 Pet 3:12.

11. Tiessen, *Providence and Prayer*, 340.

12. Fretheim, *Exodus*, 285.

13. Sanders, *The God Who Risks*, 61, 71; Pinnock, *Most Moved Mover*, 173; Grudem, *Systematic Theology*, 377; Carson, *Praying with Paul*, 141; Ellis, *Answering God*, 13–15; Garrett, *A Commentary on Exodus*, 627.

spoken of bringing on his people" (Exod 32:14).[14] Glenn Kreider observes, "God agrees to Moses' request . . . This is an amazing statement of condescension from the Creator of the universe! God will grant Moses' request because he is pleased with him. Moses is not perfect, but Moses brings God pleasure."[15] This chapter from Exodus demonstrates that Moses' interaction with God is genuine. He prays, and God responds to his prayer.

Another example is from Solomon as God promises to hear the Israelites' prayers in the temple. God assures Solomon that "if" the people humble themselves, he will hear their prayer. Some time after Solomon "successfully" finishes the "house of the Lord and the king's house," the Lord visits Solomon in the night (2 Chr 7:11–12). During the appearance, the Lord assures Solomon that he heard the petitions of Solomon, and he has "chosen this place [house of the Lord] for myself as a house of sacrifice" (2 Chr 7:12). Not only does the Lord hear the petitions of Solomon but he also speaks to the way in which his people might have confidence that the Lord will hear their petitions. According to the Lord, "If my people who are called by my name humble themselves, and pray and seek my face and turn from their wicked ways, then I will hear from heaven and will forgive their sin and heal their land" (2 Chr 7:14).[16] Boyd interprets from this passage that "The Lord does not play with words when he teaches and illustrates throughout Scripture that much of what will happen in the future depends on prayer."[17] Boyd sees prayer as essential because depending on whether one prays or refrains from praying will deeply impact the state of events surrounding a given circumstance. Eugene Merrill rightly observes, "The remedy for national sin and its resultant drought, locust infestation, and plague was for God's people to humble themselves, pray, seek Yahweh's face, turn from their sin, God will hear, forgive, and heal both people and the ravaged land."[18] Merrill helpfully asserts the importance of humility, which will become evident in all three theories of providence below (chapters 4–6). The Lord's house is the place that his "eyes will be open" and "ears attentive to the prayer" that take place in this house (2 Chr 7:15). Ralph Klein observes, "These words imply that Yahweh would not refuse the prayer of his anointed

---

14. MacGregor, *A Molinist-Anabaptist Systematic Theology*, 91, 286; Sanders, *The God Who Risks*, 2007), 280; Boyd, *God of the Possible*, 83, 164; Hunter, *The God Who Hears*, 52–53.

15. Kreider, *God With Us*, 81.

16. Tiessen, *Providence and Prayer*, 139; Grudem, *Systematic Theology*, 377; Klein, *2 Chronicles*, 110–11.

17. Boyd, *God of the Possible*, 97.

18. Merrill, *A Commentary on 1 and 2 Chronicles*, 360. See also Japhet, *1 and 2 Chronicles*, 615.

one."[19] Later in the biblical text, Ezra is depicted as humbly petitioning God for a "safe journey for ourselves, our children, and all our goods" (Ezra 8:21). The reason for making such a petition to God is the belief that "the hand of our God is for good on all who seek him, and the power of his wrath is against all who forsake him" (Ezra 8:22). Ezra concludes, "We fasted and implored our God for this, and he listened to our entreaty" (Ezra 8:23). God hears and grants Ezra's request.

In a few instances in the Bible, God commands the people not to offer petitionary prayer on behalf of another. Helm writes, "Petitionary and intercessory prayer are commanded, just as elsewhere such prayers are forbidden (Jer 7:16). So, asking God and being answered by him is also meant to form part of the life story of any disciple of Christ, as well as of the corporate life of the church."[20] In an interesting display of petitionary prayer, God tells Jeremiah not to pray, because he will not respond. As the Word of the Lord comes to Jeremiah, God proclaims that the people are not obeying his voice, that their hearts are evil, and that they reject the words that the Lord commands (Jer 11:6-8).[21] As a result of the people partaking in idolatry, Jeremiah proclaims the Word of the Lord: "Do not pray for this people, or lift up a cry or prayer on their behalf for I will not listen when they call to me in the time of their trouble" (Jer 11:14). Leslie Allen writes, "This time Yahweh would not listen to their lament, as had implicitly happened at the exodus (cf. Exod 2:23–25; 3:9)."[22] In this instance, God prohibits petitionary prayer.[23] This proclamation to not pray on behalf of the people must indicate that petitionary prayer affects the outcome of events, so much so that at this time it is better for Jeremiah to withhold praying.[24] Why would God give such a command if petitionary prayer were not able to affect the circumstances at hand? Or if the circumstance will happen irrespective of the prayer offered, then why give the command not to pray? In other instances, God promises to hear the prayers of his people (1 Kgs 9:3; 2 Chr 7:12; Ps 6:9), and that truth applies here as well, but this biblical text affirms that God will not respond to them.[25]

---

19. Klein, *2 Chronicles*, 112.

20. Helm, *The Providence of God*, 145.

21. Allen, *Jeremiah*, 139–40.

22. Allen, *Jeremiah*, 140.

23. Sanders, *The God Who Risks*, 280; Allen, *Jeremiah*, 140–41; Lundbom, *Jeremiah 1–20*, 629.

24. Thompson, *The Book of Jeremiah*, 347.

25. This theme is taken up again in Jer 14:11, "The Lord said to me: 'Do not pray for the welfare of this people.'"

Zechariah and Elizabeth provide a helpful illustration of petitionary prayer as they pray for a child, and God hears this prayer and responds by giving them John the Baptist. I. Howard Marshall observes, "The answer to prayer is bound up with the birth of a son to Zechariah."[26] The biblical text describes this couple as "righteous before God, walking blamelessly in all the commandments and statutes of the Lord"; however, they are without child (Luke 1:6-7).[27] Zechariah is chosen by lot to enter the temple of the Lord and burn the incense, and while he performs this priestly act, the Angel Gabriel appears before him and frightens Zechariah. The message that Gabriel brings on behalf of the Lord is that his wife Elizabeth is going to give birth to a son, and this son "will turn many of the children of Israel to the Lord their God, and he will go before him in the spirit and power of Elijah, to turn the hearts of the fathers to the children, and the disobedient to the wisdom of the just, to make ready for the Lord a people prepared" (Luke 1:16-17). Gabriel, in order to calm the fear of Zechariah, proclaims to him that the Lord has heard his prayers of petition for a child and that the Lord has answered this petitionary prayer (Luke 1:13-14).[28] God uses the petitionary prayers of Zechariah to advance his kingdom work. In his commentary on Luke, Joel Green notes, "Luke outlines in a compact way John's role in God's redemptive program."[29] Zechariah asks the Lord for a child, and the Lord answers that prayer when Elizabeth conceives John the Baptist. François Bovon gives further support for Zechariah's petitionary prayer: "The old man's barren wife—for this is how the biblical language characterizes the miracle—will give birth. But this answer to personal prayer converges with the 'prayer' of the nation, which, according to Luke, awaits redemption (1:68). For with John the Baptist, the new age dawns for the entire nation (vv. 16-17)."[30] Zechariah does not pray for a child to accomplish the things that John the Baptist does.[31] He merely asks for a child, and God gives him one. God answers Zechariah's prayers in a mighty way and advances his kingdom in the process.

Another example of petitionary prayers comes from Jesus teaching his disciples how they ought to pray and not to lose heart. In fact, it would appear that Jesus is teaching them to be persistent in their petitions. Concerning prayer, Marshall observes, "The fear is that men will give up before

---

26. Marshall, *The Gospel of Luke*, 56.
27. Ibid.
28. Green, *The Gospel of Luke*, 72-74.
29. Ibid., 76; Boyd, *God of the Possible*, 34.
30. Bovon, *Luke 1*, 35.
31. MacGregor, *Luis de Molina*, 124.

they are answered."[32] Jesus accomplishes this through a parable, which is about a widow that kept coming to a judge and begging him saying, "Give me justice against my adversary" (Luke 18:3).[33] At first in the parable the judge refuses, but due to her persistent "bothering," he grants her request (Luke 18:5). Boyd observes, "The parable teaches us about our 'need to pray always and not lose heart' (v. 1). If even an unjust judge will relent and hear a widow's persistent plea, Jesus is saying, how much more will our loving Father be affected by our persistent pleas?"[34] The biblical account notes, "I will give her justice, so that she will not beat me down by her continual coming" (Luke 18:5).[35] In addition, Bovon writes, "In fact, he capitulates and sides with the widow, giving her what she wanted, thus conforming to the wishes of someone other than himself."[36] Jesus upholds this persistence as an example for the disciples to model in their prayers. Helm writes, "Persistent, importunate prayer is answered in a way that intermittent, half-hearted prayer is not (Lk 18:7)."[37]

One final observation concerning biblical examples of petitionary prayer comes from Colossians, as the letter itself forms an inclusio around the idea of petitionary prayer.[38] The letter begins with Paul thanking God, "When we pray for you, since we heard of your faith in Christ Jesus and of the love you have for all the saints, because of the hope laid up for you in heaven" (Col 1:5).[39] This prayer for Paul is described as "without ceasing" (Col 1:9).[40] Paul then describes with greater detail what these prayers entail, which include petitions for wisdom and understanding. F. F. Bruce writes, "Their prayer for the Colossians, then, is that they may gain the full knowledge of God's will through the insight that the Spirit imparts, and thus be able to please him in everything and live in a way that befits his children."[41] Jerry Sumney also observes, "This statement implies that the Colossians

---

32. Marshall, *The Gospel of Luke*, 671.

33. Ibid., 672.

34. Boyd, *God of the Possible*, 96–97; Sanders, *The God Who Risks*, 25; Ellis, *Answering God*, 24; Marshall, *The Gospel of Luke*, 672.

35. Green, *The Gospel of Luke*, 642.

36. Bovon, *Luke 2*, 534.

37. Helm, *The Providence of God*, 146; Grudem, *Systematic Theology*, 387; Hunter, *The God Who Hears*, 79.

38. Carson, *Praying with Paul*, 75-90. For more on the admonition from Paul to pray without ceasing see Rom 1:9; 1 Cor 1:4; Eph 1:15; Phil 1:3-4; 1 Thess 1:2; 3:10; 2 Thess 1:3, 11; Phlm 4.

39. Bruce, *The Epistles to the Colossians, o tPhilemon, and to the Ephesians*, 40.

40. Ellis, *Answering God*, 33; Hunter, *The God Who Hears*, 64.

41. Bruce, *The Epistles to the Colossians, to Philemon, and to the Ephesians*, 45.

do not attain this knowledge for themselves; God grants it to them."[42] This short letter from Paul demonstrates that prayer is mightily important. He begins and ends his letter with the emphasis on praying for himself and one another.

Paul's petitionary prayers also include prayers for strength. He writes, "May you be strengthened with all power, according to his glorious might, for all endurance and patience with joy, giving thanks to the Father, who has qualified you to share in the inheritance of the saints in light" (Col 1:11–12). Concerning this strength, Carson writes, "What is remarkable is that the power for which Paul prays is frequently tied to the power of the resurrection (Eph 1:19–20; Col 2:12), but its demonstration among believers, at least in the first instance, is found not in miracles or in their own resurrection but in great endurance and patience."[43] At the end of the letter, Paul concludes by urging them to "continue steadfastly in prayer" (Col 4:2).[44] Paul also requests that the Colossians would petition God for his benefit as well. He writes, "Pray also for us, that God may open to us a door for the word, to declare the mystery of Christ" while he is in prison (Col 4:2).[45] The letter (Col 1:9–4:2) has the continued theme of ceaseless prayer. James D. G. Dunn writes, "As the letter opening began with assurance of Paul's prayer for the Colossians, so the main section concludes with Paul's encouragement that they should be faithful in prayer . . . this was no mere formality but an expression of the indispensability of prayer for Paul and the early Pauline mission."[46] This emphasis on prayer was not due to formality or Christian ritual. Instead, it was the lifeline for how the church functioned in that day. Also significant is the call to petitionary prayer at both the beginning (Col 1:9–14) and end (Col 4:2–4) of the letter. Richard Melick Jr. observes, "Paul ended his epistle as he opened it, urging his readers to prayer. The structure of these verses resembles the opening prayers of the epistles."[47]

---

42. Sumney, *Colossians*, 45.

43. Carson, *Praying with Paul*, 87-88.

44. Ibid., 53; Kreider, "Jonathan Edwards's Theology of Prayer," 434; Grudem, *Systematic Theology*, 392; Ware, "Prayer and the Sovereignty of God," 140; Sumney, *Colossians*, 256–58.

45. Bruce, *The Epistle to the Colossians*, 172.

46. Dunn, *The Epistles to the Colossians and to Philemon*, 262.

47. Melick Jr., *Philippians, Colossians, Philemon*, 32:321–22. Other passages that discuss petitionary prayer include: Josh 10:6–16; 2 Chr 20:1–23; Ezra 10:1–5; Neh 1:4–11; 9:32–38; 1 Sam 23:6–10 paralleled with Ps 5:8, 11–12; Jer 32:16–35; 33:3.

Petitionary Prayer and Theology

Petitionary prayer presents various problems theologically. Millard Erickson says, "On the one hand, if prayer has any effect on what happens, then it seems that God's plan was not fixed in the first place. Providence in some sense depends on or is altered by whether and how much someone prays."[48] Boyd asks what real difference prayer actually makes if it were not possible to alter God's plan?[49] Similarly, Erickson asks if God's "plan is established and he will do what he is going to do, then does it matter whether we pray?"[50] Furthermore, Paul Helm describes that the relationship between providence and petitionary prayer produces many theological questions. For example, "How can God respond to prayer by answering it, when his purposes are changeless? And why, if God is wise and all-knowing, does he need to be prayed to?"[51] If one believes God to be omnisapient (Matt 6:8), then why does he not foresee "the need to do what he is asked to do without the need for being asked?"[52] In addition, Pinnock questions whether or not prayer even makes sense "in the context of personal relationships" if God cannot respond to the creature?[53] God's omnibenevolence is also related in that it requires God to act in terms of what is morally best (or most good) due to his moral character. If God were always acting out of goodness, then it would seem to preclude prayer making a difference because one is already receiving what is good. These questions provide examples of the complexity in the divine-human relationship.

Petitionary prayer also impacts believers' relationships with God as well as the advancement of the kingdom of God. Wayne Grudem defines prayer as "personal communication with God."[54] In his *Systematic Theology*, he poses the question, "Why does God want us to pray?"[55] His answer is threefold: first when Christians pray, there is a demonstration on the part of those humans that they are dependent upon God, and that they have a faith which declares that they trust God in whatever circumstance is at hand.[56] Also important is the idea that the one praying is humble in

---

48. Erickson, *Introducing Christian Doctrine*, 154.
49. Boyd, *God of the Possible*, 95.
50. Erickson, *Introducing Christian Doctrine*, 154.
51. Helm, *The Providence of God*, 145.
52. Ibid., 146.
53. Pinnock, *Most Moved Mover*, 174.
54. Grudem, *Systematic Theology*, 376.
55. Ibid., 376.
56. Ibid.

her dependence upon God as she is "genuinely convinced of God's wisdom, love, goodness, and power."[57] Second, God wants his people to pray because in their prayers, they are brought into a closer relationship with God, and he greatly delights in their willingness to deepen that relationship.[58] A third reason is that God desires for his creatures "to be involved in activities that are eternally important," which means that humans have a responsibility not only to foster their relationship with God but also to participate within the kingdom activity here on earth.[59]

Grudem's observations are helpful, because each one demonstrates the need for petitionary prayer. In order for personal communication with God to be genuine, the relationship must be genuine too. As believers petition God, their relationship with him deepens, and they come to learn things about him. Thus, a relationship is further forged. Grudem also displays that through the course of this personal communication with God, the kingdom is advanced. He writes, "In this way, prayer gives us opportunity to be involved in a significant way in the work of the kingdom and thus gives expression to our greatness as creatures made in God's image."[60]

Petitionary Prayer, Inspiration of Scripture, and Hypostatic Union

The theological issue at hand when dealing with petitionary prayer is the same for other theological systems. Erickson asserts, "We need to note two facts: (1) Scripture teaches that God's plan is definite and fixed—it is not subject to revisions; and (2) we are commanded to pray and taught that prayer has value (Jas 5:16). But how do these two facts relate to each other?"[61] The affirmation of two truths, which appear to conflict with one another, is common to theology. This is evident, for example, in the inspiration of Scripture and the affirmation that the Bible is a divine-human document in "that supernatural influence of the Holy Spirit on the Scripture writers" produced the Word of God.[62] John Feinberg notes that inspiration necessitates that "both God and the writer be active in the process so as to guarantee that what God wanted was written."[63] For Feinberg, this dual affirmation of the

57. Ibid.
58. Ibid., 377.
59. Ibid.
60. Ibid.
61. Erickson, *Introducing Christian Doctrine*, 154.
62. Ibid., 169.
63. Feinberg, "God Ordains All Things," 35.

divine-human guards the doctrine of inspiration against, for example, a dictation theory of Scripture. Most problematic theories regarding the inspiration of Scripture diminish either the divine or human in their definitions of inspiration. Bruce Ware also asserts that without the dual affirmation of the divine-human work, the doctrine of inspiration "is virtually inexplicable."[64] Another example is the hypostatic union whereby Christians affirm that in one person, Jesus Christ is fully divine and fully God. Again, like inspiration, most Christological heresies fall short due to the diminishing of either Christ's divine or human nature.[65] These examples illustrate that petitionary prayer is no different than the inspiration of Scripture or the Hypostatic Union in terms of appealing to mystery while offering a rational explanation. The affirmation that (1) God's plan is definite and fixed while (2) the Christian is commanded to freely pray is common to Christian theology. Thus, it is quite normal in theology to affirm two principles that appear to be in opposition to one another. Therefore, petitionary prayer should be no different as one tries to affirm that God is sovereign while at the same time, humans are free in their petitions to God.

Petitionary Prayer and Systematic Theology

Petitionary prayer also has implications for various categories within systematic theology: in particular, Jesus' office of High Priest and the impact that has on the believers' ability to offer petitionary prayer. As the theological examination continues, George S. Hendry proposes that the relationship between theology and the doctrine of petitionary prayer is pivotal for the theologian.

For Hendry, prayer is what holds word and faith together. He writes, "If word and faith are the twin poles of theology, prayer is the current that maintains their polarity [separation]."[66] He goes on to note that he employs prayer as the means for forming a judgment about someone else's systematic theology. He concludes, "For some time I have employed a simple device in forming a judgment on the systematic writings of theologians, new and old. I read what they have to say about prayer. It provides a significant clue."[67] Even if he does not agree with the conclusions of that particular author, he writes, "If he takes prayer seriously, I take him seriously, even if I am not able to agree with him in everything. I am disappointed with the theologian

---

64. Ware, "Robots, Royalty and Relationships?" 198.
65. Crump, *Knocking on Heaven's Door*, 282–83.
66. Hendry, "The Life Line of Theology," 25.
67. Ibid.

who disposes of the subject briefly with a few commonplace observations or pious platitudes."[68] All the theories of providence in this book devote time to their understanding of prayer, and in light of Hendry, each viewpoint should be taken seriously.

The office of Jesus' priesthood is what enables the Christian with confidence to go before God and petition him. Ryrie describes this office of Christ: "As a faithful Priest our ascended Lord sympathizes, succors, and gives grace to His people (Heb 2:18; 4:14–16)."[69] As a Priest, he intercedes for his people (Heb 7:25). Norman Nagel observes, "But it all starts with priest Christ, because of whom we may draw near to God."[70] Also, he is a forerunner assuring that his people will enter heaven as Christ has entered already (Heb 6:19–20).[71] Due to Christians' standing in Christ (Rom 6:11; 8:1), they are given grace to share in this priesthood (1 Cor 1:2; 2 Cor 11:21; Eph 2:6). According to Kreider, this work of Christ is quite generous: "In this way, Christ not only represents his people but, in some respect, they are identified with him, they are in Christ. Since God the Father loves his son perfectly and 'we may be sure that [God] begrutches nothing as too good for his Son,' we might also be sure that those who are in the Son are recipients of God's generosity."[72]

While Kreider focuses on the gracious work of Christ, Hodge looks at the redeemed Christian and concludes "that faith in Him secures an interest in all the benefits of his redemption, and that, therefore, a thief on the cross, a prisoner in a dungeon, a solitary believer in his own chamber is near to God, and secure of his acceptance, provided he calls on the name of the Lord."[73] Therefore, the redeeming work of Christ provides for us a priesthood that we are able to share in and petition God with. On a similar note, Millard Erickson asserts that due to redemption, all Christians have access to the Lord. He writes, "And what is true of the initiation of the Christian life is also true of its continuation. Each believer can discern God's will directly."[74] This priesthood of the believer relates to petitionary prayer as the Christian no longer needs a special intermediary, something Kreider

---

68. Ibid., 25–26. I am indebted to Al Glenn for this wisdom.

69. Ryrie, *Basic Theology*, 314.

70. Nagel, "Luther and the Priesthood of All Believers," 298.

71. Ryrie, *Basic Theology*, 315.

72. Kreider, "God Never Begrutches His People Anything They Desire," 76. See also David Crump's similar comments on God's generosity in, *Knocking on Heaven's Door*, 296.

73. Hodge, *Systematic Theology*, 2:468.

74. Erickson, *Christian Theology*, 1004. Concerning Jesus' intercession for his own, see Owen, *The Priesthood of Christ*, 279.

describes as a high privilege.[75] Hodge writes, "He makes intercession for the people. Not merely as one man may pray for another, but as urging the efficacy of his sacrifice and the authority of his office, as grounds on which his prayers should be answered."[76] Thus, the Christian is encouraged from the Lord and his apostles to petition God.[77] Due to sin, however, the communication process between God and humans is fractured, yet Scripture speaks to the mediation of Christ as he goes on believers' behalf in order to bring them into God's presence.[78] First Timothy 2:5 reads, "There is one God, and there is one mediator between God and men, the man Christ Jesus." Grudem writes, "But now, since Christ has died as our meditational High Priest (Heb 7:26–27), he has gained for us boldness and access to the very presence of God."[79] The believers' standing in Christ enables them to share in this priesthood.[80] With a mediator in Christ and our own priesthood brought about by our standing in Christ (1 Cor 1:2), it becomes imperative for the Christian to assume that genuine communication exists between the creature and Creator.[81] Furthermore, the question becomes, which of the various aforementioned theories of providence effectuate the genuine communication between the creature and Creator brought about by the work of Christ as believers share in his priesthood. Put another way, which of the theories of providence take full advantage of the priesthood of the believer offered by Christ?

Pastoral Theology

This section will present a review of petitionary prayer and its implications for pastoral theology. For example, attention will be given to Jesus' claim in Matt 21:22, which states, "And whatever you ask in prayer, you will receive,

75. Kreider, "God Never Begrutches," 76.

76. Hodge, *Systematic Theology*, 2:465.

77. Examples from the Lord to offer petitions: Matt 7:7; Luke 11:9; John 16:24. Examples from the apostles to offer petitions: Jas 4:3; 2 Thess 1:11; Heb 13:18; Jas 5:16.

78. Oden, *Classic Christianity*, 488–89.

79. Grudem, *Systematic Theology*, 378.

80. Ibid. For more on this standing "in Christ," see: Rom 3:24; 8:1–2; 1 Cor 1:2; 15:22; 2 Cor 1:21; 2 Cor 5:17, 19; Gal 2:16–17; 3:14, 26; Eph 1:9, 12, 20; 2:6–7, 10, 13.

81. J. Terry Young argues that God hearing the Christian's prayer is an essential promise based upon the Priesthood of the Believer in "Baptists and the Priesthood of Believers," 28–9. In addition, see Kelly, "Prayer and Union With Christ," 123. Oden also asserts, "We are commanded and permitted to offer our prayers in his name (John 14:13, 14). The essential pattern of Christ's intercessory ministry is already anticipated in the high-priestly prayer of John 17" (*Classic Christianity*, 489).

if you have faith." Petitionary prayer is described as a key form of worship for Christians and is essential for maintaining their relationship with God through repentance and confession. All of these topics address the Christian's spiritual life and need for petitionary prayer.

"Ask and You Will Receive"

A key component of the Christian life is to request from the Lord. Basinger writes, "Most Christians continue to believe that God has granted us the power to decide whether to request his assistance and that at times the decision we make determines whether we receive the help desired."[82] Hodge asserts that one of the requisites for acceptable prayer is faith: "We must believe. (a.) That God is. (b.) That He is able to hear and answer our prayers. (c.) That He is disposed to answer them. (d.) That He certainly will answer them, if consistent with his own wise purpose and with our best good. For this faith we have the most express assurance in the Bible."[83] As an explanation for the phrase, "if you have faith," Hodge observes, "It cannot be supposed that God has subjected Himself in the government of the world, or in the dispensation of his gifts, to the shortsighted wisdom of men, by promising, without condition, to do whatever they ask. No rational man could wish this to be the case."[84] However, this reasoning can be employed in a manipulative way with the intent to persuade the Lord to act the way a person desires (Luke 9:47). For example, the Pharisees would often petition the Lord, but their petitions were with the intent to "test" Jesus.[85] Matthew records, "When the Pharisees heard that he had silenced the Sadducees, they gathered together. And one of them, a lawyer, asked him a question to test him" (Matt 22:34–35). Testing in this instance demonstrates that asking of the Lord has the potential to be an attempt to strong arm him. Chapter 22 states, "But Jesus, *aware of their malice*, said, 'Why put me to the test, you hypocrites?'" (Matt 22:18, emphasis mine). However, graciously, Jesus responds to the petition of the Pharisees and offers them the greatest commandment (Matt 22:37–40).

Another biblical example comes from Pharaoh and his interaction with God in Exodus. During the second plague, the Lord brings upon all the country swarms of frogs (Exod 8:2–3). At this time, Pharaoh calls Moses and asks him to petition the Lord on his behalf that the frogs would be taken

---

82. Basinger, "Practical Implications," in *The Openness of God*, 157–58.
83. Hodge, *Systematic Theology*, 3:703–4.
84. Ibid., 3:704.
85. See Matt 16:1; 19:3 Mark 7:5; Luke 17:20; John 9:15.

away (Exod 8:8). The Lord hears Moses' petitions, and the swarms of frogs depart. The biblical accounts record that once Pharaoh sees that the frogs have left, he hardens his heart once again and would not listen to Moses and Aaron (Exod 8:15).[86] In this case, even the manipulative prayers of Pharaoh are heard and answered, even while God knows the very intent of Pharaoh. Pharaoh hardens his heart "and would not listen to them, as the Lord had said" (Exod 8:15).[87] This demonstrates that God is gracious even to those that attempt to manipulate him with their prayers. God is gracious even to hear and respond to the petitions of those without faith.[88] God hears the petitions of Pharaoh and answers his request with the full knowledge that Pharaoh will not live up to his end.

Petitionary prayer can also function to edify and distinguish believers from the world as adopted sons and daughters of God (Eph 1:5; Gal 4:5; Rom 8:23). One of the characteristics that should define Christians is the normality of their petitions, whether on behalf of others or for themselves. Just like belief produces good works (Eph 2:8–10), belief also produces petitionary prayers (Matt 21:22). Jesus in the Sermon on the Mount speaks to such normality of petitionary prayer. Scripture records, "Ask, and it will be given to you; seek, and you will find; knock and it will be opened to you. For everyone who asks receives, and the one who seeks finds, and to the one who knocks it will be opened" (Matt 7:7–8). Jesus, as High Priest, proclaims that the believer should request from the Lord, and his directive has authority. Hodge writes, "Christ stands before the Father as an authorized intercessor, and as one who can present legal claims. . . The people of God may derive comfort from the fact that they have such a prevailing intercessor with the Father."[89] Furthermore, Jesus describes the relationship between a father and child, saying, "Or which one of you, if his son asks him for bread, will give him a stone? Or if he asks for a fish, will give him a serpent? If you then, who are evil, know how to give good gifts to your children, how much more will your Father who is in heaven give good things to those who ask him!" (Matt 7:9–11). Whether or not the prayers are answered is for another discussion. Regardless, believers are called to petition the Father.[90] This is due to a changed standing that redeemed creatures have before God, which is why God would expect his adopted children to request from him all kinds of things. If God expects

---

86. See also (1) the seventh plague in Exod 9:27–35, specifically verse 27, and (2) the eighth plague in Exod 10:16–20. Both of these passages demonstrate the same pattern from the second plague in chapter 8.

87. See also, Ps 44:21; Acts 15:8; Rom 8:27.

88. Kreider, "Jonathan Edwards's Theology," 448.

89. Berkhof, *Systematic Theology*, 405.

90. See Hodge, *Systematic Theology*, 3:704.

Christians to pray and ask so that they might receive, then the question becomes, which of the various aforementioned theories of providence provide the genuine communication between the creature and Creator brought about by the work of Christ? In other words, which of the theories of providence take full advantage of the privilege and command to petition God?

Petitionary Prayer as Genuine Worship

In his chapter on worship, Grudem makes clear that worshiping God is variegated in its expression. As he concludes his chapter on worship, he warns the readers of the time it takes to acquire necessary spiritual skills. For example, one might relate quickly to forms of worship such as music and singing together as a congregation. However, it may take time to understand or develop the worshipful heart that offers money and trust that the Lord will provide for the believer's needs as he shares his resources with the ecclesia. In this long list of various forms of worship, Grudem identifies petitionary prayer as one of them, because it requires a focus on the needs and concerns of others.[91] In addition, petitionary prayer also reveals the relationship shared between God and the petitioner. Hodge observes, "The God of the Bible, who has revealed Himself as the hearer of prayer, is not mere intelligence and power. He is love. He feels as well as thinks. Like as a father pitieth his children, so the Lord pitieth them that fear Him. He is full of tenderness, compassion, long-suffering, and benevolence."[92] Hodge also notes, "Accordingly, as all Christians are the worshippers of Christ, so He has ever been the object of their adoration, thanksgivings, praises, confessions, and supplications."[93]

The Gospel of Luke displays petitionary prayer as worship, particularly in two parables. The first is in 18:1–8, which discusses the parable of the persistent widow. At the end of the parable, the widow is given her request due to her persistent petitioning of the judge.[94] Jesus affirms, "And will not God give justice to his elect, who cry to him day and night? Will he delay long over them?" (Luke 18:7). The very next parable juxtaposes the prayers of the Pharisee and the tax collector.[95] Both men enter the temple to pray; Fredrick

---

91. Grudem, *Systematic Theology*, 1013.
92. Hodge, *Systematic Theology*, 3:699.
93. Ibid., 3:701.
94. See Goetz, "On Petitionary Prayer: Pleading With the Unjust Judge?" 96–98.
95. A. M. Okorie helpfully demonstrates the difference in their prayers. See "The Characterization of the Tax Collectors in the Gospel of Luke," 27–32. See also Doran, "The Pharisee and the Tax Collector: An Agonistic Story," 259–70.

Holmgren observes the extremes between the characters in this parable: "The first and the last, the humble and the prideful, the poor and the rich, and the insider and the outsider."[96] The biblical text describes the two extremes as the Pharisee prays, "God, I thank you that I am not like other men, extortioners, unjust, adulterers, or even like this tax collector. I fast twice a week; I give tithes of all that I get" (Luke 8:11–12). Jesus denounces this prayer and commends the prayer of the tax collector. The tax collector is described as standing "far off" and would not even "lift up his eyes to heaven" only to "beat his breast" proclaiming "God, be merciful to me, a sinner!" (Luke 18:13).[97] The tax collector petitions God asking for forgiveness. This displays petitionary prayer as genuine worship, because the tax collector understands that God is to be worshiped. Even the very posture of the tax collector communicates his worship of God nonverbally.[98] While the biblical account does not describe the tax collector as falling to the ground, it does portray him as not being able to look up towards heaven, only to look down towards the ground (Luke 18:13). God is perfect and holy, and the tax collector knows his own imperfection and lack of holiness. For Jesus, the tax collector is "exalted" because he has exalted God by humbly asking for forgiveness. These two parables build an inclusio around petitionary prayer. It begins with the positive example of petitionary prayer offered by the widow in vv. 1–8. Then, vv. 9–12 shows a negative example of prayer from the Pharisee followed by vv. 13–14 and the affirmation from Jesus of the petitionary prayer from the tax collector. Notably, the negative example of prayer in this account, the Pharisee, does not petition God. Instead, the prayer is focused on his abilities and accomplishments, which is the opposite of genuine worship directed towards God (Matt 7:7; 15:9).

Robert Letham offers another helpful perspective regarding prayer as it relates to worship within the Trinity. Concerning the Holy Spirit, he writes, "It is the Holy Spirit who creates a desire to pray and worship God. It is he who brings us to faith and sustains us in a life of faithful obedience."[99] Concerning the Son, he observes that one's access to the Father is only through the Son.[100] Moreover, the Christian's standing in Christ now shares

---

96. Holmgren, "The Pharisee and the Tax Collector," 253.

97. Oden, *Classic Christianity*, 579.

98. For example, Joshua, ". . . fell on his face to the earth and worshiped and said to him, 'What does my Lord say to his servant?'" (Josh 5:14). All Judah and the "inhabitants of Jerusalem fell down before the Lord, worshiping the Lord" (2 Chr 20:18). Job also out of sorrow " . . . fell on the ground and worshiped" (Job 1:20). The Psalmist declares, "Help us, O God of our salvation, for the glory of your name; deliver us, and atone for our sins, for your name's sake!" (Ps 79:9).

99. Letham, *The Holy Trinity in Scripture*, 414.

100. Ibid., 414–15.

the same relation Jesus has with the Father, except "He is the Son by nature; we are children by grace."[101] Concerning this relationship, Letham writes, "We now call on God as 'our Father.' Moreover, the Spirit brings us into his own intercession for us (Rom 8:26–27). He thus eliminates the distance between us and God, creating in us the same relation he has with the Father and the Son."[102] For this reason, prayer and worship are understood as the exploration "of the character of the Holy Trinity."[103]

Petitionary prayer is an important form of Christian worship, as humans declare with their words, rather than with songs that are sung along with a melody, the greatness of God in the midst of their depravity and need for help. If petitionary prayer is a form of worship, then does one of the aforementioned theories of providence provide a more genuine worship experience? For example, if human freedom is limited so that the human is not able to do anything other than petition God, one might conclude that worship in this instance is mundane. In addition, one might question the desire to pray to a God with limited sovereignty. Even if God willingly gave up some of his sovereignty so that the Christian might freely worship him through prayer. In the following chapters, each of the theories of providence will address this question.

Repentance and Confession

When a human petitions God, that human displays an awareness of his relationship with God. That relationship reveals, for example, that God is perfect, and the human is not. God is holy, and the human is not. God is incorruptible, and the human is not. Believers can display repentance in two ways. On the one hand, they display this as they "turn to the Lord" (2 Cor 3:16), and their salvation is secured.[104] This petition comes to life in the biblical narrative when Paul and Silas are imprisoned, and in the witness of miraculous events, the jailer falls down before them. He petitions them, "Sirs, what must I do to be saved?" Paul and Silas respond, "Believe in the Lord Jesus, and you will be saved, you and your household" (Acts 16:30–31).[105] Another example comes from the cross of Christ when one of the criminals beside Jesus petitions him to remember him when he enters into his kingdom (Luke 23:42). Both of these examples illustrate that non-

101. Ibid., 415.
102. Ibid.
103. Ibid.
104. Oden, *Classic Christianity*, 569–70.
105. Ibid., 581.

believers petition God for salvation. Ultimately, their salvation is based on their belief in the Lord; however, it cannot go unnoticed that in the case of the jailer, he petitions Paul and Silas. Similarly, the criminal petitions the Lord regarding his salvation. In other words, through Christ, petitionary prayer is an example of humanity seeking a relationship with God.

On the other hand, petitionary prayer is a means whereby Christians are able to turn back to God and restore their relationship in light of sin committed. John Calvin asserts that the Christian should be fully committed to confession of sin as a form of reconciliation between God and the sinning party. He writes, "There is a reconciliation with God ready and prepared for us; otherwise we shall always be carrying hell within us."[106] Augustine also affirms the necessity of confession as it serves as the beginning of our righteousness.[107] This form of prayer is also termed, "prayers of confession"; however, even prayers of confession are based on a person petitioning the Lord and pleading for forgiveness.[108] Due to the atonement of Christ, believers have the assurance that when this petition is made, "he is faithful and just to forgive us our sins and to cleanse us from all unrighteousness" (1 John 1:9). Calvin affirms this by proclaiming that there is a double fruit that comes from confession, "that God, being reconciled by Christ's sacrifice, forgives us and that he renews and reforms us."[109] Calvin believes that the confidence for the Christian is linked with the atoning sacrifice of Christ.

Also, due to the priesthood of all believers, Christ becomes the intermediary between the Father and the believer, so that those petitionary prayers of confession are made directly to God. A helpful example of this form of petitionary prayer comes from the brother of Jesus. James admonishes the faithful to "confess your sins to one another and pray for one another that you may be healed. The prayer of a righteous person has great power as it is working" (Jas 5:16).[110] In this case, the righteous person is not living such a righteous life that they do not sin. Instead, for James, the righteous person that

---

106. Calvin, *1, 2, and 3 John*, 23. See also Oden, *Classic Christianity*, 582.

107. Augustine, *Homilies on the First Epistle of John*, 66.

108. "The first movement of the prayer of petition is *asking forgiveness*, like the tax collector in the parable: 'God, be merciful to me a sinner!' It is a prerequisite for righteous and pure prayer. A trusting humility brings us back into the light of communion between the Father and his Son Jesus Christ and with one another, so that 'we receive from him whatever we ask.' Asking forgiveness is the prerequisite for both the Eucharistic liturgy and personal prayer" (Ratzinger, *Catechism of the Catholic Church*, 694).

109. Calvin, *1, 2, and 3 John*, 24. See also Oden, *Classic Christianity*, 579.

110. Sinclair Ferguson notes that the prayer of faith is, " . . . to ask God to accomplish what He has promised in His Word. That promise is the only ground for our confidence in asking" (*In Christ Alone: Living the Gospel Centered Life*, 146). See also Warrington, "James 5:14–18: Healing Then and Now," 357–58.

possesses powerful prayers is petitioning the Lord in the form of confession (Jas 5:17, "Elijah was a man with a nature like ours"). This confession heals the confessor and then enables the confessor to petition the Lord for the suffering and sick.[111] The restored relationship between the believer and God, brought about by the believer's confession of their sin to God, brings about petitionary prayer that works. James uses Elijah as an example as he "fervently" petitions God that it might not rain, "and for three years and six months it did not rain on the earth" (Jas 5:17). Then, Elijah petitions God again but this time for rain, "and heaven gave rain, and the earth bore its fruit" (Jas 5:18). Elijah was not perfect, but his righteousness enabled his petitionary prayers to become efficacious.[112] James asserts that Christians should confess their sins because in so doing they maintain their righteousness, which makes sense in light of 1 John 1:9, "If we confess our sins, he is faithful and just to forgive us our sins and to cleanse us from all unrighteousness." Augustine writes, "Flee *to* him by confessing, not *from* him by hiding, for you cannot hide, but you can confess."[113] Also important is the tax collectors' prayer in Luke 18. The previous section above explains this specific chapter. The tax collector humbly petitions God to be "merciful to me, a sinner!" (Luke 18:13), which is a wonderful example of the powerful restoration that takes place as people confess their sin. After this confession, Jesus declares that this man and his house are "justified," unlike the Pharisee (Luke 18:14). Later chapters will address issues of confession as they relate to the specific theories of providence. For example, if God's sovereignty does not include knowledge of the sin committed until the act is performed, then why would one seek forgiveness from a God with diminished sovereignty? In addition, if the human is not libertarianly free in the confession of sin, then the prayer offered is not genuine because the option to forgo praying was not given.

Conclusion

Petitionary prayer is a genuine human behavior whereby the creature goes to its sovereign Creator and simply asks. This form of prayer has biblical and theological (systematic and pastoral) significance. Chapter 1 provided an explanation of compatibilism, hard determinism, open theism, and middle knowledge, and now these theories of providence and their explanation of petitionary prayer will be examined.

---

111. Warrington, "James 5:14–18," 352.
112. Manton, *James*, 348–49.
113. Augustine, *Homilies on the First Epistle of John*, 90.

3

Compatibilism, Hard Determinism, and Petitionary Prayer

Introduction

IN THIS CHAPTER, I will examine a compatibilist's understanding of petitionary prayer. John Calvin and Jonathan Edwards will primarily demonstrate the role of God's sovereignty in petitionary prayer. Also, various theological implications for petitionary prayer will be examined, which will include systematic and pastoral theology. In addition, I will examine hard determinism and its understanding of petitionary prayer. As noted in chapter 1, hard determinism holds a position similar to compatibilism; however, these two views have a fundamental difference as hard determinism greatly diminishes human freedom. This will present problems with respect to petitionary prayer. In the end, it will be argued that while compatibilism and middle knowledge are similar in the pursuit of demonstrating that God's sovereignty is compatible with human freedom, middle knowledge is preferred over compatibilism due to its ability to define human freedom in a libertarian sense while also maintaining the sovereignty of God. Also, middle knowledge is much more suitable to handle the question as to how God can remain sovereign while humans offer genuine prayers of petition to God than hard determinism. This is due to the lack of human freedom in hard determinism.

Before the work of this chapter begins, it is important to note that there is a paucity of literature on petitionary prayer from the compatibilist and hard determinist positions. For example, Wayne Grudem references Calvin in an attempt to establish the seminal work(s) on petitionary prayer: "Calvin has some good material on prayer in his *Institutes*. I think my chapter on Prayer in my *Systematic Theology* is representative of a Reformed position. At least John Frame from RTS—Orlando speaks highly of the chapter in his systematic theology."[1] In addition to having limited primary sources,

---

1. Wayne Grudem, e-mail message to author, 4 May 2015. W. Bingham Hunter

there is a great deficiency of secondary literature that addresses petitionary prayer within compatibilism and more so hard determinism. This results in a dependency on a limited amount of sources for my argument. Jeremy Koons notes the shortage of hard determinism in the secondary literature.[2] In addition, Saul Smilansky asserts that hard determinism does not translate well into the moral sphere as it rejects human responsibility.[3] Moreover, hard determinism often leads to God being responsible. The purpose of this book is not to answer the question as to why there is such silence; however, Koons and Smilansky demonstrate that silence exists. The next section will explain how a compatibilist understands petitionary prayer in relation to the sovereignty of God.

Sovereignty, Compatibilism, and Petitionary Prayer

One of the main features of compatibilism is the desire to uphold the sovereignty of God; it is the lens by which this theology is accomplished. Also significant for the compatibilist is the affirmation that humans are able to freely offer prayers to God, that God hears their prayers, and that he answers their prayers. However, for the compatibilist, this must be understood within the framework of God's sovereignty as will become evident below. Thus, compatibilism affirms that God is sovereign while humans are also capable of petitioning God with some measure of freedom in accord with the desires they have, which he ordained through secondary causes. John Calvin and Jonathan Edwards will provide the necessary commentary to explain the relationship of God's sovereignty and petitionary prayer.

John Calvin

Calvin holds that prayer is necessary in the life of the Christian as it is an expression of one's faith in a sovereign God.[4] Prayer, whereby the human

---

demonstrates four reasons why there is not a lot of literature devoted to petitionary prayer. See *The God Who Hears* (Downers Grove, IL: InterVarsity Press, 1986), 9–13. Henry W. Holloman, Professor Emeritus at Talbot School of Theology teaches a course on the Theology of Prayer. He makes the point that "few theologies give proper place to a doctrine of prayer." The one exception is Calvin's *Institutes* (Holloman, "Lecture Notes on Theology of Prayer.")

2. Koons, "Is Hard Determinism a Form of Compatibilism?" 81.
3. Smilansky, "Free Will and Moral Responsibility," 226.
4. Calvin *Institutes* 2.20.11.

calls upon the stronghold and safety found in the name of God, invokes God's providence, strength, and goodness.[5]

Necessity of Petitionary Prayer

Calvin teaches that the necessity of petitionary prayer is manifold as it is understood as refuge, accountability, supplier, and worship. For example, one might turn to God in order to seek refuge.[6] The one that loves God will develop a sacred habit of fleeing to God. Petitionary prayer also forms a kind of accountability between the human and God whereby the human is more mindful of not only what he says but to whom he is speaking.[7] In prayer, Christians are held accountable as their eyes and hearts are fixed upon God. Another example is that the person offering petitionary prayer is recognizing God to be the supplier of his needs by the very fact that he is praying.[8] Thus, for compatibilism, prayer is a humbling experience, because the human recognizes his dependency on God to meet his needs. In the end, due to God's answer to their prayers, Christians should be led to worship and meditate upon God's kindness.[9] As Christians are mindful about to whom they are accountable, taking refuge in, and who is supplying their needs, it is understandable that one would then be led to worship. These examples demonstrate that for Calvin, the human and God play essential roles in prayer; however, even in the midst of petitionary prayer, God's sovereignty remains the focal point in the divine-human interaction.

Humility and Prayer

According to compatibilism, Christian prayer is most favorable when it is accompanied by humility.[10] For people to stand before God, they must abandon their glory and worthiness. David Crump agrees with Calvin and also understands the value of humility; in fact, the one who is humble is best suited to engage in the mysterious interface between finite humanity and

---

5. Ibid., 3.20.2.
6. Ibid., 3.20.3.
7. Ibid.
8. Ibid.
9. Ibid.
10. Ibid., 3.20.8. This idea of humility is also evident in the work of Edwards, another compatibilist.

the infinite God.[11] In addition, Arthur Pink notes that as a person enters into the presence of God through prayer, this should rightly humble the person praying. For Pink, God designs prayer to bring about a humbling experience.[12] Thus, for Calvin, Pink, and Crump, the proper understanding of prayer is measured by the humility of the person praying as she understands that she is inferior to God.

In addition, for Edwards, the bond between humility and God's sovereignty in prayer is strong. In fact, the believer's humble prayers offered in faith are the visible manifestations of a heart that resembles a beggar in need and dependent upon God. The heart of a creditor demanding his dues does not fool God.[13] In other words, if humility communicates non-verbally a belief in a sovereign God, then prayer communicates verbally one's belief in the sovereignty of God. Humility also communicates the extent of human freedom in petitionary prayer as a prayer without humility is akin to "creditors that demand their dues," which for Edwards are "no real prayers."[14]

For Calvin, as one humbly petitions God, two things occur. First, forgiveness is one of the primary reasons that the Christian is to petition God.[15] Similar to Calvin, Joel Beeke adds that confession is not something that merely begins the Christian life but that *is* the Christian life.[16] Hodge adds that humility is a requisite to prayer as it displays people's ability to recognize sin in their life. For Hodge, this should lead to repentance.[17] This particular work of petitionary prayer is a preparation and washing from sin so that the Christian is cleansed from unrighteousness (1 John 1:8–10).[18] Once sin is confessed and forgiven, the Christian is prepared to offer any remaining petitions.[19] This plea for forgiveness is rooted within one's humility; as such, the Christian is aware of his sinfulness in light of God's goodness and that any prayer offered is in light of extreme need due to the lack of ability on the part of the Christian to achieve anything. The second thing that occurs when Christians petition God is that they

---

11. Crump, *Knocking on Heaven's Door*, 15.
12. Pink, *The Sovereignty of God*, 136.
13. Edwards, "The Terms of Prayer," 19:787.
14. Edwards, "The Terms of Prayer," in *Sermons and Discourses*, 19:787.
15. Calvin *Institutes* 3.20.9.
16. Beeke, *Living for God's Glory*, 182.
17. Hodge, *Systematic Theology*, 3:703.
18. Calvin writes, "It is important to be fully persuaded that when we have sinned, there is a reconciliation with God ready and prepared for us . . . " (Calvin *1, 2, and 3 John*, 23).
19. Calvin *Institutes* 3.20.9.

become keenly aware of their insufficiency.[20] In this framework, humility is not shame; instead, humility provides confidence for Christians that God will answer their prayers.[21] Thus, prayer is not shameful, but humans are fully aware that they are in a position of weakness in this conversation. For both Calvin and Edwards, humility is the non-verbal communication that God is sovereign while petitionary prayer is the verbal communication that he is sovereign.

Jonathan Edwards

Jonathan Edwards provides another compatibilistic account of petitionary prayer. In order to demonstrate this, attention will be given to Edwards's sermon, "The Most High a Prayer-Hearing God," which is a seminal piece of Edwardian literature expounding on his views regarding prayer.[22] Attention is also given to Peter Beck and Glenn Kreider's work on Edward's theology of prayer.[23]

For Edwards, compatibilism will present itself as he affirms the human necessity and privilege of praying to God. In addition, God is sovereign with complete knowledge of the needs of the one praying. Along with the affirmation of these two theological truths, Edwards begins and ends with God's sovereignty. Even where he affirms the human ability to have free access to God, those instances are only understood within the framework of the sovereignty of God. Holding these two truths in tension warrants the label, *compatibilism*.

Knowing God Correctly Is Paramount to Prayer

The beginning to any knowledge about prayer or the functionality of prayer in the life of the Christian must first be measured by the Christians' understanding of who God is.[24] In addition to Edwards, David Crump also as-

---

20. Ibid., 3.20.6. See also chapter 4, which discusses the similar idea of human insufficiency from the openness position.

21. Ibid., 3.20.11. Open theism and middle knowledge would not reject humility in petitionary prayer. Yet, humility is discussed in this chapter as it is a clear emphasis in the literature on prayer within this theory of providence.

22. Edwards, "The Most High a Prayer-Hearing God," 2:113–18. This work is not available in The Works of Jonathan Edwards series.

23. Beck, *The Voice of Faith*; Kreider, "Jonathan Edwards's Theology of Prayer," 434–56.

24. In chapter 4, I demonstrate that open theism similarly argues that one must

serts that the ability that one has to pray is largely determined by what the one praying believes about God.[25] In other words, knowing God correctly, coupled with humility, grounds the Christian so that pride and dogmatism can be avoided.[26] Robert Young notes that how one conceives of the whole activity of prayer will necessarily reflect one's conception of God.[27] Michael Horton also asserts that identifying the correct God is paramount if invoking the Triune God is of any importance to the theologian.[28] Even hard determinists, who are discussed later in this chapter, make the same argument. Arthur Pink observes that the problem of the modern concept of prayer is its emphasis on man rather than God.[29] Thus, if Christians get God wrong, then they do not know where, or to whom, petitionary prayers are going. Also, how can believers be confident that God hears their prayers if they do not properly understand who they are praying to? Beck affirms Edwards's claim, "Faith must be placed in the right God, the one and true God, recognizable by his attributes and character."[30] This means that a compatibilist's account of prayer begins with and focuses on God's sovereignty and character and from there is finalized in the actual human prayer.

Beck also notes that once God is known correctly, the Christian can with confidence understand that God hears the prayers of his children and desires to grant them their requests.[31] This means that prayer is more than "mere duty and responsibility"; instead, prayer is "Christian privilege and joy."[32] Similar to Beck, Kreider notes that the Christian should confidently believe that God hears and answers prayer. Furthermore, prayer is one of the means whereby God accomplishes his sovereign will in the world.[33] For the compatibilist, God must be rightly conceived prior to undergoing the work of prayer.

---

know God correctly prior to engaging in prayer.
25. Crump, *Knocking on Heaven's Door*, 280.
26. Ibid., 14–15.
27. Young, "Petitioning God," 193.
28. Horton, *The Christian Faith*, 111.
29. Pink, *The Sovereignty of God*, 134.
30. Beck, *The Voice of Faith*, 2.
31. Edwards, "The Terms of Prayer," in *Sermons and Discourses*, 19:787.
32. Beck, *The Voice of Faith*, xiv.
33. Kreider, "Jonathan Edwards's Theology of Prayer," 434.

Petitionary Prayer and Worship

Once God is known correctly, prayer is properly understood as an outworking of one's faith, which leads the Christian to worship God.[34] Similar to Edwards, Thomas Goodwin asserts that speaking to God through prayer is one of the great acts of worship in a Christian's walk with God.[35] Prayer in faith becomes a form of worship for the Christian.[36] Beck agrees with Edwards, "Prayer, offered in humble dependence upon God, becomes the means by which the believer can worship his Creator and Sustainer."[37] In other words, prayer becomes an audible declaration that man is humble before God.[38] Similar to Edwards and Beck, Pink argues that prayer is an act of worship as one calls upon God's goodness, power, and grace.[39] In the end, the one praying is recognizing and submitting to God through prayer. Such an act is worshipful.

Edwards, Prayer, and the Omniscience of God

Regarding the relationship between God's sovereignty and prayer, Edwards writes that God "perfectly knows the circumstances of every one that prays to him throughout the world" and that "God is so perfect in knowledge, that he doth not need to be informed by us, in order to have a knowledge of our wants for he knows what things we need before we ask him."[40] Kreider rightly observes that Edwards bases God's ability to hear and answer prayer upon his knowledge.[41] Edwards also explains that prayer offered to God does not direct him toward human wisdom; rather, God knows 10,000-times better what is best for the one petitioning.[42] For Edwards, God would sometimes answer prayer before the petition was offered based upon

---

34. Edwards, "The Terms of Prayer," in *Sermons and Discourses*, 19:787. Kreider has written a helpful article that focuses on this particular sermon of Edwards: Kreider, "God Never Begrutches," 71–91.

35. Goodwin, *The Works of Thomas Goodwin*, 3:362.

36. Beck, *The Voice of Faith*, xiv.

37. Ibid., xv.

38. Ibid.

39. Pink, *The Sovereignty of God*, 135-6.

40. Edwards, "The Most High a Prayer-Hearing God," in *The Complete Works of Jonathan Edwards*, 2:115.

41. Kreider, "Jonathan Edwards's Theology of Prayer," 442.

42. Edwards, "The Most High a Prayer-Hearing God," in *The Complete Works of Jonathan Edwards*, 2:117.

his readiness and knowledge of the one praying.[43] Edwards's description of God as prayer-hearing is built on the foundation that God is sovereign, omniscient, and merciful as he accepts the supplications of his children.[44] Furthermore, with respect to God's sovereignty, Edwards proclaims that God "gives them sweet views of his glorious grace, purity, sufficiency, and sovereignty; and enables them, with great quietness, to rest in him, to leave themselves and their prayers with him, submitting to his will, and trusting in his grace and faithfulness."[45] Similar to Calvin above, Edwards believes petitionary prayer becomes an indispensable verbal expression that God is sovereign. Beck agrees with Calvin and Edwards, "Prayer, especially those of petition and supplication to which Edwards encouraged his flock, is a 'Great duty,' even a necessity, because such prayer acknowledges the goodness and greatness of God."[46] Thus, God is sovereign in the divine-human relationship, and for compatibilism, this is demonstrated by Calvin, Edwards, Kreider, and Beck's understanding of prayer.

Edwards's Compatibilism

In addition to the relationship between prayer and the sovereignty of God discussed above, it is also foundational that God's children have "free access" to pray to him.[47] The free access the human possesses is gracious and merciful as we are unworthy to do so. In support of the claim that humans are unworthy, Kreider writes, "There is nothing in anyone to merit an audience with God. There is nothing in anyone that deserves anything good from God. There is nothing in anyone that God needs. Yet. . .God inclines His heart toward His people."[48] In order to demonstrate this, Edwards asserts that God has given his children the privilege to access God with boldness as often as one desires.[49] This prayerful boldness that the Christian can bring to God is remarkable for Edwards in light of sin nature.[50] This free

---

43. Kreider, "Jonathan Edwards's Theology of Prayer," 440.

44. Edwards, "The Most High a Prayer-Hearing God," in *The Complete Works of Jonathan Edwards*, 2:114.

45. Ibid., 2:114.

46. Beck, *The Voice of Faith*, xvi.

47. Edwards, "The Most High a Prayer-Hearing God," in *The Complete Works of Jonathan Edwards*, 2:114.

48. Kreider, "Jonathan Edwards's Theology of Prayer," 444.

49. Edwards, "The Most High a Prayer-Hearing God," in *The Complete Works of Jonathan Edwards*, 2:114. Here Edwards draws upon: Heb 4:14, 16; 1 Cor 1:2–3; Prov 15:8; Isa 62:6–7; Luke 11:5; Luke 18:38–39; Phil 4:6.

50. Ibid., 2:116.

access is worthy of praise. He writes, "We consider the distance between God and us, and how we have provoked him by our sins, and how unworthy we are of the least gracious notice."[51] Yet God richly "delights in mercy and condescension."[52] Thus, for Edwards, even the free access one obtains as a child of God is inherently linked to the sovereignty of God.

The dual affirmation of both human necessity and God's sovereignty in petitionary prayer are both seen in Edwards's thought as (1) the charge to offer petitions and supplications to God, and yet (2) God already knows our needs long before the prayer is offered. The affirmation of these two truths regarding the divine-human interaction is imperative and provides a helpful example of the compatibilist nature of Edwards's theology of prayer. For Beck, Edwards did not have to resolve the question as to why God requires that one request even though he already knows the need. Instead, for Edwards, "the resolution of the apparent theological conundrum required no resolution at all."[53] Rather, Edwards accepts both as he argues for God's absolute sovereignty concerning the content of one's prayer while also urging the Christian to petition God.[54] In addition to Edwards and Beck, Kreider adds, "Perhaps the ambiguity is intentional and appropriate. Perhaps the most that humans can affirm is that God hears and responds to prayer and He also remains the Sovereign of His universe. Perhaps a solution to this difficulty will remain forever outside the grasp of humans."[55] Although, the free access granted to the human in prayer is not libertarian freedom, Kreider, Beck, and Edwards accept and understand that God remains sovereign while also granting humans free access to pray to him in terms of mystery.[56]

Edwards's sermon, "The Most High a Prayer-Hearing God," is helpful as it details his understanding of prayer and brings to light his compatibilism. Edwards maintains that due to God's omniscience he does not require prayer so that he might learn something about his creation.[57] Instead, God has sovereignly planned that prayer would act as an antecedent to the bestowment of mercy.[58] Consequently, when "the people of God are stirred up to prayer, it is the effect of his intention to show mercy; therefore he

---

51. Ibid.
52. Ibid., 2:116.
53. Beck, *The Voice of Faith*, xix.
54. Ibid.
55. Kreider, "Jonathan Edwards's Theology of Prayer," 455.
56. Lemke, "God's Relation to the World," 213.
57. Edwards, "The Most High a Prayer-Hearing God," in *The Complete Works of Jonathan Edwards*, 2:115.
58. Ibid., 2:116.

pours out the spirit of grace and supplication."[59] Furthermore, prayer acts in the divine plan as the antecedent to the bestowment of mercy for two reasons. First, it displays the Christians' dependence on God.[60] In light of the discussion above, dependence on God brings to light even more the necessity of humility on the part of the one praying. A person must be humble in order to be dependent on another. Prayer is also the antecedent to the bestowment of mercy "because it tends to prepare us for its reception. Fervent prayer many ways tends to prepare the heart. Hereby is excited a sense of our need, and of the value of the mercy which we seek, and at the same time earnest desires for it."[61] These are the two primary reasons why God requires prayer in order to grant mercy to the petitioner for Edwards. Similarly, Kreider observes, "Clearly for Edwards to say that God hears prayer is not simply a claim that God is aware of the prayers of His people. Edwards believed that God acts in response to those prayers. In some sense prayer is effectual in the outworking of God's providence."[62] The compatibilist's reasoning cannot be missed as there is human priority given to prayer as the antecedent to divine action, yet at the same time God knows fully the needs of the one praying and the specifics of what they are praying for.

Calvin and Edwards both demonstrate the necessity of petitionary prayer in the life of the Christian. Both uphold human ability to offer petitionary prayers while contemporaneously affirming that God is sovereign. For Calvin and Edwards, the entire structure of petitionary prayer is built from within the framework of God's sovereignty so that as one humbly petitions God, they do so (1) freely and (2) as an expression of the sovereignty of God.

Compatibilism, Petitionary Prayer, and Theology

Calvin and Edwards argue that petitionary prayer must be understood in light of God's sovereignty. Attention now turns to the theological employment of compatibilism and petitionary prayer. This includes a discussion on the emphasis of aligning oneself with God's purposes. Attention is also given to the compatibilist argument that God's sovereignty and human freedom are not mutually exclusive concepts. Calvin, Edwards, and the contemporary discussion below form a bridge linking compatibilism throughout the history of Christianity. This uniformity is especially important, because

59. Ibid.
60. Ibid.
61. Ibid.
62. Kreider, "Jonathan Edwards's Theology of Prayer," 439.

it exposes the departure of hard determinism from compatibilism, which is discussed later in this chapter.

God's Sovereignty and Human Freedom Are Not Mutually Exclusive

Millard Erickson contributes to the contemporary discussion of compatibilism in that he affirms that human activity and God's activity are not mutually exclusive.[63] In the face of God's providence and the work in accomplishing his goals, humanity has no "basis for laxity, indifference, or resignation."[64] Similarly, Calvin asserts that God does not ordain idleness in prayer; rather, prayer is a trained discipline that Christians undergo whereby their behavior changes from idleness to action.[65] The grounds for such a statement is due to God's providence, which "includes human actions."[66] Crump also describes that God does not control every human decision; instead, he "possesses an all-powerful ability to seamlessly weave" human decisions into his plan.[67] Like Calvin and Crump, Erickson asserts that humans are free in their actions, and the extent of that freedom is clear.[68] Crump also argues that petitionary prayer is evidence of a personal relationship God shares with his children.[69] God carries out his purposes by enlisting the free actions and responses of those who love him.[70] How God carries out his purposes is discussed in greater detail later in this chapter while covering free will and the priesthood of the believer.

The difficulty for the compatibilist is the lack of clarity regarding the freedom of the one praying. Feinberg rejects the claim that for compatibilism, humans do not have the freedom to refrain from doing something in a particular instance.[71] In other words, he takes exception to the idea that

---

63. Erickson, *Christian Theology*, 376.
64. Ibid.
65. Calvin *Institutes* 3.20.3.
66. Erickson, *Christian Theology*, 376.
67. Crump, *Knocking on Heaven's Door*, 292.
68. Erickson, *Christian Theology*, 368.
69. Crump, *Knocking on Heaven's Door*, 284.
70. Ibid.
71. His argument is adapted from, Canfield, "The Compatibility of Free Will and Determinism," 352–68; Nesbitt and Candlish, "On Not Being Able to do Otherwise," 321–30; Nesbitt and Candlish, "Determinism and the Ability to do Otherwise," 415–520.

the agent could not have done otherwise.[72] Instead, his understanding is that the agent could have acted differently, but it was unreasonable for him to do so. For example, one refusing to pray on Monday due to a busy schedule does not negate the ability to cancel meetings, reschedule meetings, or skip lunch in order to pray. In a real way, the individual could have prayed but chose to refrain.[73] Therefore, compatibilism "counts as freedom just as much as does libertarian freedom."[74] According to Feinberg, what differentiates compatibilist freedom from libertarian freedom is the "causal factors playing on one's will at the time of decision making." For libertarian freedom, someone could have done otherwise irrespective of the causal factors at hand, and because compatibilism allows for God to incline the person's will one way or another, the proponent of libertarian freedom questions how genuine the motivation to act is for the compatibilist. However, compatibilism still argues that the divine-human activity in prayer is not mutually exclusive.[75] Erickson supports this claim: "We need to note two facts: (1) Scripture teaches that God's plan is definite and fixed—it is not subject to revision; and (2) we are commanded to pray and taught that prayer has value (James 5:16)."[76] For Erickson, these two facts work themselves out as "God works in a sort of partnership with humans," and God does not act unless humans play their part.[77] Similar to Erickson, Crump highlights the relationship God shares with Christians in that God honestly listens to and allows himself to be affected by our prayers.[78] In the end, "prayer does not change what [God] has purposed to do. It is the means by which he accomplishes his end. It is vital, then, that a prayer be uttered, for without it the desired result will not come to pass."[79] However, even though prayer is an essential part of the accomplishment of God's will, the reality is still that the prayer would not happen unless God willed it. Thus, what is God's motivation to will that a prayer be uttered if he already intended to act? Nevertheless, in compatibilism, these truths must be agreed upon without having to describe the extent of human freedom.

72. Feinberg, *No One Like Him*, 723.

73. For Feinberg there are reasons why one does not have the ability to carry out a choice. For example, one might desire to walk two miles, but is paralyzes from the waist down. Or one might have all the physical means necessary to swing a club and play golf but is in prison and thus not able to golf (Ibid., 722).

74. Ibid., 724.

75. Kreider, "Jonathan Edwards's Theology of Prayer," 455.

76. Erickson, *Christian Theology*, 378.

77. Ibid.

78. Crump, *Knocking on Heaven's Door*, 285.

79. Erickson, *Christian Theology*, 379.

John Feinberg provides some clarification as to what the compatibilist *does not* mean by the employment of the term, *free will*. He explains, " . . . libertarian free will creates tremendous problems" for petitionary prayer, specifically those petitions about ourselves.[80] Similar to Feinberg, Terrance Tiessen, once a proponent of middle knowledge, argues for a version of middle knowledge that does not include libertarian freedom.[81] Steve Lemke observes that for Tiessen, only two options of human freedom exist: hard determinism and hard indeterminism.[82] Lemke concludes that Tiessen's view is too extreme and would benefit from a more modest view, which does not insist that the only two options are hard determinism or hard indeterminism.[83] More on the viability of Tiessen's argument is discussed in chapter 5. In addition to Tiessen, Feinberg notes that praying for oneself independent of our free will does not run aground on libertarian free will—for example, praying for healing from a disease.[84]

However, the petitions made concerning ourselves pose the greatest problem for libertarian freedom. In order to illustrate this, Feinberg uses the example of one praying on their own behalf to be more faithful in Bible reading, prayer, witnessing, and loving one's neighbor.[85] These prayers make no sense in a libertarian framework, because it would be impossible for God to accomplish what we are asking. In order for God to answer such a request, he would have to override libertarian freedom. However, Feinberg's line of reasoning is flawed; just because a person asks God to make her a more faithful Bible reader or evangelist does not mean that what she asks for is appropriate, even if it might appear to be something good. Feinberg is correct in this instance to assume that God cannot override libertarian human freedom and force people to be more faithful in various spiritual practices. Those are areas of people's spiritual life whereby as they mature, they become more adept. However, Christians can pray for example that the Holy Spirit would assist them as they undertake the difficult task of developing a more consistent habit of reading the Bible. In that instance, God is not overriding human freedom but instead is invited to help in the change the human is

---

80. Feinberg, *No One Like Him*, 704. As a compatibilist, Feinberg does not want to define freedom as libertarian. Bruce Ware, described in this book as a hard determinist, also does not want to define freedom as libertarian. See below for Ware's discussion of what human freedom is not. Both Feinberg and Ware do not define in a positive sense what freedom is, but they each define what freedom is not.

81. Tiessen, "Is God's Knowledge of Counterfactuals Necessary, Middle or Free?".

82. Lemke, "God's Relation to the World," 208.

83. Ibid.

84. Feinberg, *No One Like Him*, 704.

85. Ibid., 705.

seeking. Feinberg is wrong in assuming that because God cannot override human freedom in this instance, libertarian freedom must not be plausible. Instead, the person praying is petitioning for the wrong outcome, thus demonstrating that within libertarian freedom, one can ask God for the wrong thing. In other words, the person praying to be more faithful in Bible reading in Feinberg's example is using his libertarian freedom to pray incorrectly for God to override his libertarian freedom. For example, this would be similar to someone praying that God would make her stronger without ever going to the gym to exercise. God does not force people to go to the gym, but they might pray for a companion to workout with for encouragement and accountability, or they might pray that the Holy Spirit would convict them as they do not take appropriate care of their body.

This is why Paul speaks of maturing in the believers' faith so as to stop drinking breast milk and begin eating solid food. God does not force people do such a thing (1 Cor 3:2, Heb 5:12). For example, if a college professor asks for prayer requests prior to class and a student asks for prayer that he can finish his term paper, the professor could be thinking that the student is responsible for finishing the term paper, not God. The student needs to make better use of his time, not God. Feinberg's argument is that libertarian freedom is not possible as evidenced by praying for oneself. However, the illustration provided by Feinberg demonstrates that the petition is flawed, not libertarian freedom, and thus the premise of his argument is wrong.[86] In fact, one might argue that Feinberg has made the case *for* libertarian freedom, as the one petitioning has the freedom and ability to petition incorrectly. Attention now turns to the compatibilist's emphasis of aligning prayer with God's will.

Petitions Should Align with God's Purposes

The compatibilist position holds that it is essential to align prayer with God's will, which does not mean that prayer changes something in God's plan or God's action. For example, D.A. Carson measures the success of petitionary prayer by the petitioners' ability to align their prayers with God's purposes.[87] In addition to Carson, W. Bingham Hunter also asserts that only those prayers that are according to God's will are granted.[88] He also warns that any other technique, in addition to aligning oneself with

---

86. The subject matter in this section is also discussed in greater detail in chapter 5.
87. Carson, *Praying with Paul*, 177.
88. Hunter, *The God Who Hears*, 60.

God's will, is employed by the spiritually immature.[89] In this instance, hard determinists also assert something similar to Carson and Hunter; for example, Flavel warns of certain destruction if a person trusts in his own will.[90] Pink agrees with Flavel in that prayer is designed not to change God's will but to fulfill it.[91] For Carson, in this particular instance, Paul is in view as his "prayers are entirely in line with God's purposes."[92] Once those prayers fall in line with God's purposes, then Paul, with confidence, has "a reason for advancing these particular petitions to his heavenly Father."[93] Similar to Carson, Hunter, Flavel and Pink, Robert Young asserts that when prayer is not aligned with God's will, this results in a negative response.[94] In addition to compatibilism and hard determinism, open theism also emphasizes that prayer should align with God's purposes. For example, Paul Sponheim warns against wrong-hearted prayer that seeks to change the will of God.[95] Similar to Sponheim, Robin Collins argues that true co-creators with God are those abiding in Christ, which means that one's intention and will in prayer are aligned with God.[96] Thus, open theism agrees with compatibilism and hard determinism on this point. This demonstrates a consensus that in order for prayer to be efficacious, a person must align her petitions with God's will.[97]

A compatibilist also understands that God created people with the knowledge that he will use Christians to bring about his will through petitionary prayers. Feinberg argues that Christians are foolish not to communicate with God because he has at times ordained to use prayer to bring about his desired end.[98] However, in those cases when God has not ordained that he would use the prayers of people to bring about his purposes, it would

---

89. Ibid.
90. Flavel, "The Seaman's Farewell," 5:349.
91. Pink, *The Sovereignty of God*, 138.
92. Carson, *Praying with Paul*, 177.
93. Ibid.
94. Young, "Petitioning God," 193.
95. Sponheim, "The God of Prayer," 74.
96. Collins, "Prayer and Open Theism," 176.
97. Addressing petitionary prayer to the Father is another instance whereby a consensus is reached between the theories of providence. For example, in compatibilism see Carson, *Praying with Paul*, 178; Crump, *Knocking on Heaven's Door*, 205. For hard determinism see, Berkhof, *Systematic Theology*, 403; Hodge, *Systematic Theology*, 3:699. For open theism, see Basinger, "Why Petition an Omnipotent, Omniscient, Wholly Good God?" 25–26. For middle knowledge see MacGregor, *A Molinist-Anabaptist Systematic Theology*, 152.
98. Feinberg, *No One Like Him*, 703.

seem as though prayer is shallow and certainly not efficacious in the sense that a human has offered prayer despite the ability to refrain from said prayer. For compatibilists, only prayers that align with what God purposed are efficacious. Furthermore, only the times when God ordained that he would allow prayer to bring about his purpose become efficacious. Thus, one might ask whether (or not) the desired outcome would have happened if the person never prayed. In addition, it seems like he could simply perform the action and skip the prayer. In other words, one could ask why God ordains that he will only act if a prayer is uttered, when he must ordain that the prayer be uttered in order for the person to pray. For example, in praying to become a more faithful Bible reader, one must ask why God could not have achieved that end without the prayer. Also, one must ask if the prayer was really efficacious. Helm asserts that a possible solution is that "there may be situations where only prayer is efficacious, where God indicates that certain events will take place only if people pray."[99] Thus, it is prudent not to question God's motives in bringing about prayer: "God, who ordained certain ends, also ordained the means to accomplish those ends. Now in some cases, in God's wisdom, the means include people warrantably asking him to do certain things."[100] I prefer middle knowledge over compatibilism, because when free will is mitigated to something other than libertarian free will, God is receiving what he has influenced in terms of causation, which is the Christians' compatibilist free will to bring about prayer.

Grudem uses stronger language than Carson to express the same outcome: that the petitionary prayers of people bring about God's will. He asserts that prayer changes the way God acts. Similar to Grudem, Thomas Constable argues that prayer changes the person, the situation, and occasionally God himself.[101] This idea is based on James 4:2, "You do not have, because you do not ask."[102] Grudem writes, "He [James] implies that failure to ask deprives us of what God would otherwise have given us. We pray, and God responds."[103] Furthermore, in Luke 11:9–10, Jesus is recorded as saying, "Ask, and it will be given to you; seek, and you fill find; knock, and it will be opened to you. For everyone who asks receives, and the one who

---

99. Helm, *The Providence of God*, 156.

100. Ibid., 157.

101. Constable, "What Prayer Will and Will Not Change," 105.

102. Grudem admonishes that if the Christian truly believes that prayer changes the way God acts, "and that God does bring about remarkable changes in the world in response to prayer. . . then we would pray much more than we do. If we pray little, it is probably because we do not really believe that prayer accomplishes much at all" (Grudem, *Systematic Theology*, 377).

103. Grudem, *Systematic Theology*, 377.

seeks finds, and to the one who knocks it will be opened." At its most basic level, Grudem desires that one see the connection between "seeking things from God and receiving them. When we ask, God responds."[104] Crump notes that while God is never coerced through one's prayer, he may be influenced by them.[105] For the compatibilist, it is essential to uphold God's sovereignty while additionally asserting that humans are free in their prayer, which makes prayer quite mysterious.

In addition to aligning prayer to God's will, Erickson warns that the efficacy of prayer might result in a different outcome than the one praying expected.[106] Crump agrees with Erickson and links prayer to divine revelation. He notes that answered prayer might be revealed to the Christian in an unexpected way.[107] Furthermore, for Feinberg, petitionary prayer displays that while prayer may have been for one intended goal, God could have meant it for many intended goals. In other words, because God has ordained ". . . . that he would be moved to act as a result of our prayer," this could have happened with the intended purpose of bringing about many other outcomes that the Christian was unaware of.[108] It is wonderful to think that God brings about a multiplicity of outcomes that were unintended based on one petitionary prayer; however, the lack of libertarian free will in the compatibilist model of petitionary prayer brings into question the genuineness of that prayer. Particularly in this instance, why would God ordain that a prayer be offered when his intention was always to answer it in a different way? The idea that God answers prayer in a different manner from the original request provides a potential argument for libertarian freedom as the human freely offered a prayer, yet God sovereignly chose to answer the prayer with a different outcome. This does not nullify the importance of prayer or the sovereignty of God. However, if the one praying lacks libertarian freedom, then only one petition was available to offer God, which was not God's will. Both Molinists and compatibilists agree that God is providential over prayer. However, the Molinist has a way of dealing with improper prayer as God knew that there was not a situation where the Christian would offer appropriate prayer. The compatibilist cannot make that claim. Thus, God ordained that prayer, not aligned with his will, would be offered just so that he could demonstrate that non-efficacious prayer was offered.

---

104. Ibid. He also provides other examples of God answering prayers: Gen 18:22–33; 32:26; Dan 10:12; Amos 7:1–6; Acts 4:29–31; 10:31; 12:5–11.

105. Crump, *Knocking on Heaven's Door*, 289.

106. Erickson, *Christian Theology*, 379.

107. Crump, *Knocking on Heaven's Door*, 280.

108. Feinberg, *No One Like Him*, 703.

For the compatibilist, petitionary prayer must be aligned with God's will. In addition, God uses prayer, which is freely offered, to bring about his will. Thus, petitionary prayer is compatible with God's will. Since the focus is upon God's will and not merely the outcome prayed for, Christians should also be aware that God may answer their prayer differently than expected. The focus of this chapter will turn now to the implications the priesthood of the believer has upon petitionary prayer in compatibilism.

Compatibilism, Petitionary Prayer, and Systematic Theology

Systematic theology, and specifically the doctrine of the priesthood of the believer, will provide a helpful example as to how compatibilism employs petitionary prayer. In compatibilism, due to the priesthood of the believer, one is able to go before God and offer prayer without an intermediary. In addition, the human petitioning God does not possess libertarian freedom thus restricting her ability to refrain from praying. Reconciling the priesthood of the believer with the non-libertarian freedom of compatibilism demonstrates how this theory of providence utilizes petitionary prayer.

As discussed in chapter 2, the Christian should rightly assume that communication exists between the creature and Creator. Theologically, one of the primary ways in which this communication is made possible is through Jesus' priesthood. Norman Nagel asserts that the Christian's ability to draw near to God starts with Christ.[109] As a Priest, he intercedes for his people (Heb 7:25). Graham Redding notes that Christ is the forerunner assuring that his people will enter heaven as he has entered it already (Heb 6:19–20).[110] In addition to being a forerunner, Douglas Kelly speaks to Christians being present with Christ in his life, death, resurrection, and continuing intercessions, so that their prayers "find glad entrance to the Father."[111] Due to Christians' standing in Christ (Rom 6:11; 8:1), they are given grace to share in this priesthood (1 Cor 1:2; 2 Cor 11:21; Eph 2:6). David Crump argues that the priesthood of the believer relates to petitionary prayer as the Christian no longer needs a special intermediary.[112] John Flavel asserts that only through Christ and his mediation are prayers directed toward God.[113] Therefore, the Christian is encouraged from the Lord

109. Nagel, "Luther and the Priesthood of All Believers," 298.
110. Redding, *Prayer and the Priesthood of Christ in the Reformed Tradition*, 286.
111. Kelly, "Prayer and Union With Christ," 109.
112. Crump, *Knocking on Heaven's Door*, 94.
113. Flavel, "An Exposition of the Assembly's Catechism," in *The Works of John*

and his apostles to petition God. Redding insists that petitioning God is not something the Christian merely does but something that he participates in.[114] The question becomes: how does compatibilism reconcile the priesthood of all believers with petitionary prayer? The compatibilist affirms the priesthood of all believers and as such takes advantage of the ability to offer petitionary prayers to God without an intermediary. The compatibilist also rightly affirms that she can offer anything to God. David Crump asserts that Christians are invited to pray concerning all things, that "no request is ever too great. No need is beyond the reach of God's ability."[115] For example, in 1 Tim 2:1–7, Paul charges that "supplications, prayers, intercessions, and thanksgiving be made for all people," implying that there is not a limit to the scope of prayer offered for people. Also concerning unbounded prayer, Matt 7:7 states, "Ask, and it will be given to you; seek, and you will find; knock, and it will be opened to you," and similarly, Matt 21:22 states, "And whatever you ask in prayer, you will receive, if you have faith." The purpose of these verses is not to determine why one might not receive from the Lord, but rather, these verses put forward that Christians are called to pray without any restrictions. Prayers offered to God without any restrictions are only made possible through Jesus' priesthood, which Christians share in. The difficult question for the compatibilist is how free the Christian is when petitioning God.[116] Feinberg makes it clear that freedom does not entail libertarian freedom.[117] Tiessen and Crump reject libertarian freedom as well.[118] Thus, as it relates to petitionary prayer, God has (1) given Christians limited freedom while (2) granting them unlimited access to pray to him through the priesthood of the believer. If God has ordained the prayers that would be offered, then why is it necessary to access the unlimited nature of the priesthood of the believer? In other words, only those prayers, which God has ordained, will be offered regardless of whether or not the person is part of the priesthood of the believer. Would God ordain a prayer that could not access the Father? Thus, it is possible to assume that the priesthood of the believer is restricted for compatibilism—not restricted in the amount available to the believer but instead with how much of their priesthood they are taking advantage of as a theory of providence. J. Terry Young argues that by reducing the significance of the priesthood of believers is to "reduce the

---

Flavel, 6:291.

114. Redding, *Prayer and the Priesthood*, 288.
115. Crump, *Knocking on Heaven's Door*, 33.
116. As noted above, Feinberg rejects libertarian freedom.
117. Feinberg, *No One Like Him*, 704–06.
118. Tiessen, *Providence and Prayer*, 290; Crump, *Knocking on Heaven's Door*, 290.

significance of both the sovereignty of God and the meaning of persons created in the image of God."[119] Young's point is interesting in light of compatibilism's strong adherence to the sovereignty of God. In this instance, middle knowledge is preferred because the believer is free, in a libertarian sense, meaning that they are able to either (1) offer a petitionary prayer without the need of an intermediator or (2) not offer a petitionary prayer and thus not take advantage of their access to the Father provided by Christ.[120] Thus, for the human, when left with the proposition of whether (or not) to pray, the conclusion is always to pray. That does not mean that they will receive everything they pray for or about, but it does affirm libertarian freedom to pray for all people concerning all things.

I am not advocating that the compatibilist rejects the idea of the priesthood of all believers. Instead, without libertarian freedom, Christians are not maximizing their priesthood, which affords them the ability to, without restriction, go before God and offer their petitionary prayers. In other words, since freedom is limited for the compatibilist, the priesthood must also be limited because it would then imply that their ability to petition God has limits. Next, the various implications compatibilism presents for petitionary prayer within pastoral theology will be discussed.

Compatibilism, Petitionary Prayer, and Pastoral Theology

With regard to a compatibilistic understating of petitionary prayer, one implication for pastoral theology includes the admonition to persevere in prayer. For Christ, the motivation in one's heart to persistently pursue God and not lose faith is a model of a mature believer. Thus, it is necessary to examine how free, in terms of motivation, the one persistently praying is within compatibilism.

Calvin, in the unfolding of petitionary prayer, asserts that Christians should not lose heart when they make a request to God and it seems as though God has neglected the prayer. Calvin instead insists that Christians not "fall into despair," because they "so call upon God that unless he attends upon their first act of prayer and brings them help at once, they immediately fancy him angry and hostile toward them and, abandoning all hope of

---

119. Young, "Baptists and the Priesthood of Believers," 27.

120. This is based on Terrance Tiessen's definition of libertarian freedom, which states, "Libertarian freedom is the state of freedom in which there is a real possibility that one could make at least two different choices in exactly the same circumstances, both external and internal" (Tiessen, *Providence and Prayer*, 365).

being heard, cease to call upon him."[121] Rather, Calvin calls for perseverance whereby the Christian, worn out from praying seemingly to a deaf God, still continues to pray.[122] In addition to Calvin, Berkhof grounds the admonishment to persevere in prayer upon Christ. He notes that every moment Christ is engaging with the Father on our behalf and is always on the alert so that no prayer escapes him.[123] Also, Hunter adds to Calvin and Berkhof, asserting that when a Christian is persistent in prayer, it is a form of humility as well as an expression of faith.[124] In other words, the one persistent in prayer is readily dependent upon God. In addition to Calvin and Hunter, Erickson adds that persistent prayer reveals just how important the petition is, which then forges a greater bond between God and the one praying.[125] Thomas Manton observes that God is not waiting for eloquent language; in fact, there is a spiritual kind of language in groans and sighs that are quite articulate to God (Rom 8:26).[126] For Manton, persistency in prayer should not be linked to one's ability to fashion the right words because God is capable of discerning a variety of languages.

In addition, Crump offers a warning against the confidence that merely persevering or repeating will produce the desired end of the one praying.[127] The manner in which God answers prayer was discussed above. However, the warning is applicable here as well. At the same time, Crump does affirm that somehow the sovereign Lord does things because they are persistently prayed for.[128] Similar to Crump, John Rice notes a kind of spiritual honesty as one persistently prays. He describes this form of petitionary prayer as one kneeling before the "gate of pleading."[129] Thus, Christians should remain steadfast in their prayer and persevere like King David. However, what about a mother praying repeatedly for her son that struggles with an alcohol addiction? She persistently prays that he will stop and overcome this addiction. A compatibilist might ask whether (or not) the desired outcome would have happened if the mother never persistently prayed, especially if only those times when God has ordained that prayer to bring about his purposes do those prayers become efficacious. In that case, God could have

---

121. Calvin *Institutes* 3.20.51.
122. Ibid.
123. Berkhof, *Systematic Theology*, 405.
124. Hunter, *The God Who Hears*, 171.
125. Erickson, *Christian Theology*, 379. See also Ellis, *Answering God*, 23–24.
126. Manton, *James*, 347.
127. Crump, *Knocking on Heaven's Door*, 289–90.
128. Ibid., 290.
129. Rice, *Whosoever and Whatsoever*, 77.

performed the action and skipped the repeated prayer. In addition, one could ask why God ordains that he will only act if a prayer is repeatedly uttered, when he must ordain that the prayer be uttered in order for the person to pray. Thus, the mother's persistent prayer was merely an action that God had persistently ordained.

Middle knowledge offers an additional option for understanding the value of being persistent in prayer. If the mother is free in a libertarian sense, she has the ability to refrain from being persistent in prayer. She also has the ability to pray once and never again. The Bible places great value upon persistently praying, and middle knowledge captures this in the divine-human relationship best due to the risk that the Christian might not persevere in prayer. In addition, this emphasizes the pleasure God must have in receiving a repeated prayer from his children when he knows they could have chosen to refrain from prayer. Nevertheless, for the compatibilist, perseverance demonstrates a certain measure of spiritual discipline to withstand even when it seems as though the words are falling upon a deaf God.[130]

In compatibilism, the divine-human interaction of prayer is illustrated in pastoral theology through the act of patient perseverance in prayer. This form of petitionary prayer is a learned discipline exhibited by the spiritually mature. Attention now turns to hard determinism and its treatment of petitionary prayer.

Hard Determinism

Introduction

The works of John Flavel, Charles Hodge, Arthur Pink, John Piper, Brian Cosby, and Bruce Ware will provide helpful examples of how hard determinism theologically employs petitionary prayer.[131] This will include Piper's reflection on praying through his battle with cancer. Also, Ware will provide a definition of petitionary prayer along with his understanding

---

130. Calvin *Institutes* 3.20.51.

131. As noted in chapter 3, the literature on petitionary prayer within hard determinism is limited. For example, Piper does not author a specific chapter or section to petitionary prayer in any of his books or sermons (he is a prolific speaker and writer). However, he does write a great deal on the topic of prayer, which makes the exclusion of the specific area of petitionary prayer all the more glaring, and it seems like he is making an argument from silence. This silence does not weaken a hard determinist's exposition on petitionary prayer. In fact, it bolsters it, because it reveals the theological consistency between hard determinism and how it would affect one's view regarding petitionary prayer.

of God's ultimate purpose for petitionary prayer. Finally, discussion will turn to the Christian's participation in the kingdom of God as understood through petitionary prayer.

Petitionary Prayer and Cancer

On the eve of prostate cancer surgery, Piper authored what would later be published in a small book titled, *Don't Waste Your Cancer*. Concerning the source of cancer, Piper writes, "It will not do to say that God only *uses* our cancer but does not design it. What God permits, he permits for a reason. And that reason is his design. If God foresees molecular developments becoming cancer, he can stop it, or not. If he does not, he has a purpose. Since he is infinitely wise, it is right to call this purpose a design."[132] Furthermore, he emphasizes that "we are not cursed [with cancer]. As hard as it is to feel this, we believe God is not withholding good. He is doing good."[133] Similarly, John Flavel asserts that God designs afflictions in order to awaken the believer to "pray more frequently, spiritually, and fervently."[134] For example, Piper uses Job's acknowledgement that "They . . . comforted him for all the evil that *the* Lord *had brought upon him*" (Job 42:11, emphasis mine). This verse implies that all those evil things that happened to Job were brought about by design from God. Piper thus concludes, "If we don't believe our cancer is designed for us by God, we will waste it."[135] This means that for Piper, God and not Satan is responsible for the evils Job encounters. A compatibilist contends that God sovereignly works with Satan's freedom to permit the evil that Job experiences.[136] For the compatibilist, this releases God from being responsible for sin while still remaining sovereign.

Next, Piper transitions into a discussion regarding the Christian's response to cancer through petitionary prayer. He writes,

> I believed then, and I believe now, in God's power to heal—by miracle and by medicine. I believe it is right and good to pray for both kinds of healing. Cancer is not wasted when it is healed

---

132. Piper, *Don't Waste Your Cancer*, 6.
133. Ibid., 7.
134. Flavel, "Divine Conduct," in *The Works of John Flavel*, 4:482. The difference between the compatibilist and the hard determinist understanding of God designing is discussed in greater detail in chapter 2.
135. Piper, *Don't Waste Your Cancer*, 6.
136. Feinberg, *No One Like Him*, 518.

by God. He gets the glory, and that is why cancer exists. So not to pray for healing may waste our cancer."[137]

I disagree. Cancer does not exist to bring God glory. Cancer exists because total depravity unfortunately has to run its course. Cancer is a physical manifestation of the fact that bodies are broken due to man's sinful nature.[138] In the Bible, when Jesus enters a town and heals the sick, he does not heal all the sick. Even when Jesus works his ministry, he does not completely eradicate sickness in each village. Many are healed but not all. Even after he raises Lazarus from the dead, the biblical narrative does not declare that he goes on to live forevermore and ascend to heaven like Elijah. Instead, the assumption is that Lazarus dies again. Until glorification and the return of Christ, death has to run its course. Cancer exists to destroy. For this reason, Graham Redding points to a certain "restlessness and dissatisfaction with the way things are here on earth."[139] Redding explains that death drives the Christian to pray for the return of Jesus, which brings to light the eschatological consequences to our prayer. Piper, on the other hand, goes on to assert that "healing is not God's plan for everyone in this life."[140] For proponents of compatibilism and middle knowledge, this does not mean that God withholds healing from some while granting it for others. Instead, it means that until Jesus returns and our bodies are glorified, cancer has to run its course. Some prayers for healing are answered while other prayers for healing are not.[141] This truly is a mystery.[142]

Hard Determinism and Petitionary Prayer

In a sermon he gave in December 2003, Piper proclaims, "Bethlehem exists mainly to do the humanly impossible."[143] This means that the people who attend Bethlehem must align themselves with God's will in such a way that they are able to adjudicate the will of God and then pray for the will of God to take place in their church. In hard determinism, God already has

137. Piper, *Don't Waste Your Cancer*, 3.
138. Fretheim, *Exodus*, 303.
139. Redding, *Prayer and the Priesthood*, 292.
140. Piper, *Don't Waste Your Cancer*, 3.
141. Crump, *Knocking on Heaven's Door*, 302.
142. Lemke, "God's Relation to the World," 213.
143. Piper, "Let Your Requests Be Made Known to God," 1, accessed May 5, 2015, http://www.desiringgod.org/sermons/let-your-requests-be-made-known-to-god. Bethlehem here is in reference to the church in Minneapolis, Minnesota where Piper served as a pastor for 33 years.

ordained the humanly impossible, and once the church aligns itself with God's will, it will come to realize what God has planned. Though minor in difference, the theological gap is wide. On the other hand, compatibilists maintain that prayer is not merely driven by adjudicating God's will and then praying specifically for God's will to happen. Instead, compatibilism notes that prayer changes the way God acts, and as such, God does the humanly impossible due to the Christians' prayers. For example, Richard Phillips argues that prayer "changes things," because God is sovereign and uses human prayer to bring about his will and plan.[144] In addition, Grudem writes, "God does bring about remarkable changes in the world in response to prayer, as Scripture repeatedly teaches that he does."[145] He concludes that if the church adopted such a view of God's working in the world, "then we would pray much more than we do."[146]

Understanding the difference, then, provides the avenue to push hard determinism to its limit and thereby observe what prayer becomes. Based on those theological principles from chapter 1 on hard determinism, it would appear that God will make prayer happen so that he will accomplish his goal through prayer. Arthur Pink also argues that prayer is one of the means that God has decreed, so that God will use prayer to bring about his ends.[147] He will see to it that churches are praying. This is intended so that the Word might "speed on and be honored."[148] However, this interpretation is not convincing when Paul writes, "Pray for us, that the word of the Lord may speed ahead and be honored" (2 Thess 3:1). This sounds like an admonition for the church to pray. If the church were going to pray regardless, then why would Paul give his time to asking for prayer?[149] Piper interprets this verse as Paul warning them that whether they want to or not, God will cause them to pray. Hodge also looks to God's governmental control over humans, which extends to the minds, thoughts, feelings, and volitions. For Hodge, it is perfectly acceptable to admit that God controls the operations of nature as well as the character and conduct of men, which includes prayer.[150] Pink also argues that prayer is just another appointed decree from God, which

---

144. Phillips, "Prayer and the Sovereignty of God," 95.

145. Grudem, *Systematic Theology*, 378.

146. Ibid.

147. Pink, *The Sovereignty of God*, 134.

148. Piper, "Let Your Requests Be Made Known to God," http://www.desiringgod.org/sermons/let-your-requests-be-made-known-to-god.

149. Piper, "Let Your Requests Be Made Known to God," http://www.desiringgod.org/sermons/let-your-requests-be-made-known-to-god.

150. Hodge, *Systematic Theology*, 3:695.

brings about his desired end.[151] The connotation is such that God planned the prayers and the requests that the people would make, which removes the genuine relational aspects between the Creator and his creature. It also removes the necessity of human freedom in prayer. Thus, for hard determinism prayer becomes something unavoidable for humans, because God has ordained that their prayers serve as a means to his end.

Sovereignty and Petitionary Prayer Defined

Bruce Ware contributed a chapter titled, "Prayer and the Sovereignty of God," in a festschrift for John Piper.[152] His chapter on petitionary prayer seeks to highlight the relationship the Christian shares "with the one from whom all blessings flow."[153] Based upon this prayer relationship, "we are called into participation in the work of the One by whom all sovereign rulership is exercised."[154] As this section develops, the terms relationship and participation will become key in locating Ware's theology of prayer within hard determinism and also how his theology of prayer is differentiated from the compatibilist position.

Bruce Ware defines *divine sovereignty* as, "God exhaustively plans and meticulously carries out his perfect will as he alone knows is best, regarding all that is in heaven and on earth, and he does so without failure or defeat, accomplishing his purposes in all of creation from the smallest details to the grand purposes of his plan for the whole of the created order."[155] Ware makes it clear that his understanding of *divine sovereignty* is not to be confused with that of open theism or middle knowledge.[156] He does not

---

151. Pink, *The Sovereignty of God*, 137.
152. Ware, "Prayer and the Sovereignty of God."
153. Ibid., 143.
154. Ibid.
155. Ibid., 128.
156. Ibid., 128–29. In 2004, Ware actually argues for a "compatibilist middle knowledge." See "Robots, Royalty and Relationships?" 200. John Laing in 2004 also notes that Ware holds a Calvinistic Middle Knowledge position. See "The Compatibility of Calvinism and Middle Knowledge," 459. However, based on this definition of divine sovereignty from "Prayer and the Sovereignty of God" published in 2010, he would still hold to some version of middle knowledge. Laing helpfully asserts, " . . . this reveals the problem with the Calvinist Molinist approach, for the proponent of middle knowledge must make the further claim that the truth. . .is in no way dependent upon the will of God" ("Calvinism and Middle Knowledge," 463).

mention *middle knowledge* by name, but the commitment to reject libertarian freedom would insinuate the rejection of it.[157]

Ware defines *petitionary prayer* as

> Requesting or petitioning God, on behalf of oneself or others, to act in some specific manner in order to bring about some specific result, where the action and result are seen as brought about by God's own will and action while they are also, in certain instances, causally tied to the petition that was brought before God and requested of him.[158]

The deficiency in this definition is the phrase "in certain instances," because this leaves open the possibility that petitionary prayer is not always necessary. In addition, the Christian with finite knowledge does not know if or when his prayers are necessary. Furthermore, this is deficient as a definition of petitionary prayer, because Ware is asserting, "The action [prayer] and result are seen as brought about by God's own will and action."[159] Crump warns against such predetermined prayers, the outcome being that God would take certain actions as predestined responses to predestined prayers.[160] Similar to Ware, Pink defines petitionary prayer as "coming to God, telling Him my need (or the need of others), committing my way unto the Lord, and then leaving Him to deal with the case as seemeth Him best."[161] This definition is also deficient as it does not speak to a relationship one shares with God. Instead, for Pink, one merely calls upon God so as to notify God of the situation and then leaves him to deal with the circumstance. In this case, prayer becomes merely keeping God in the loop. However, God is already completely sovereign over the situation and knows perfectly what is taking place. There is no need to pray; God will bring about his end as he sees fit. In turn, why in those certain instances should a person offer a petitionary prayer? This question is explored next.

---

157. See also the discussion in chapter 2 concerning the relationship between Arminius and Molina. It is argued that Arminius had knowledge of Molina and was persuaded by the three-fold logical moments of natural, middle, and free knowledge.

158. Ware, "Prayer and the Sovereignty of God," 129.

159. Ware, "Prayer and the Sovereignty of God," 129.

160. Crump, *Knocking on Heaven's Door*, 293.

161. Pink, *The Sovereignty of God*, 139.

God Does Not Need Our Petitionary Prayer

For hard determinism, the idea that God does not need one's petitionary prayers is different from compatibilism discussed above. In particular, Edwards's compatibilism states that due to the sovereignty of God, he does not need our prayers, because he already knows what is needed. However, God gives the Christian "free access" to pray. Edwards even describes petitionary prayer as a necessary "privilege" believers are given and as such should be taken advantage of in their life.[162] Conversely, for hard determinism, God ordains the prayers to happen, which is similar to a parent ordaining that a child receive a cookie and so brings the child to grandma and prompts the child to request, "Can I have a cookie, grandma?" In this framework, it would seem as though the child had no choice but to make the request, and yet the child's prayer was a necessary condition for the fulfillment of the parent's will. For example, Ware asserts, "While prayer in certain instances is a necessary condition (albeit contingently necessary) for the fulfillment of God's will, by no means is prayer by itself ever sufficient to bring about the desired result."[163] In other words, he argues that the power of prayer is really the power of God so as to bring about his desired end through the ordination of prayer.[164] Also, that prayer by itself never brings about desired results contradicts Grudem's assertion above that prayer changes the way God acts.[165] This is significant as once again the question becomes why prayer is necessary if it does not ever bring about on its own a desired result. In addition to Ware, Pink argues that prayer is a human act only to the extent that God has ordained that prayer will be offered.[166] Pink argues that God has ordained the prayer, thus removing human freedom from the petition. Similar to Pink, Francis Turretin adds that a person might pray for a prolonged life; however, the terms of life have already been set.[167] For Turretin, the viability of prayer is that only God knows the terms which he has set; thus, pray. Such an act might still be labeled prayer, but surely it would be difficult to make the argument that this prayer is petitionary. For Turretin, there is hope in that one's petition aligns with God's purposes. However, the prayer itself will not change his purposes. This differentiates Grudem's explanation of compatibilism above, whereby prayer changes the way God acts, from Ware and Pink's

---

162. Edwards, "The Most High a Prayer-Hearing God," 2:114.
163. Ware, "Prayer and the Sovereignty of God," 130.
164. Ibid.
165. Grudem, *Systematic Theology*, 377.
166. Pink, *The Sovereignty of God*, 137.
167. Turretin, *Institutes of Elenctic Theology*, 1: 328.

hard determinism, which makes prayer a foregone conclusion along with its outcome irrespective of the prayer offered.

Hard determinism makes it clear that prayer does not and cannot be necessary for bringing about anything God intends to accomplish. For example, Ware writes, "God could accomplish all of the actions in human history that he plans to do totally apart from prayer. Yes, God desires our prayers; yes, God commands us to pray; but no, God does not need our prayers to 'Help' him in the execution of his perfect plans."[168] In a similar way, Pink argues that prayer does not alter God's will; rather, God brought about the petition and supplication.[169] For Ware, God does not need one's prayer, and for Pink, if God does use our prayers, it is not out of necessity but rather out of his desired plan. This is yet another example where compatibilism is set apart from hard determinism. For example, Kreider, when speaking of Jonathan Edwards, notes, "A proper understanding of prayer is that God hears and answers prayer. Further, prayer is one of the means by which the sovereign God accomplishes His will in the world."[170] For Ware, petitionary prayer is not a determining factor within God's plan for the world. For example, if prayer is offered, it is understood that God controls whether or not people pray.[171] If prayer is predetermined in such a manner, Eleonore Stump warns that one can hardly conceive "of a satisfactory justification for petitionary prayer."[172] In order to further illustrate that God controls the hearts of his people through prayer, Ware looks to the king's heart in Prov 21:1, "The king's heart is a stream of water in the hand of the Lord; he turns it wherever he will."[173] Prayer in this context is designed in such a way that the person praying really has no ability to do otherwise. This particular understanding of prayer is differentiated from compatibilism in that it put no emphasis on the mysterious dual nature of petitionary prayer as being both human and divine. For hard determinism, the mystery is revealed as God controls humans in their actions so as to bring about prayer.[174]

With regard to the relationship between God's will and prayer, Ware has argued for a divinely controlled version of prayer—one in which God uses humans at times and does not at other time. Consequently, Ware's

---

168. Ware, "Prayer and the Sovereignty of God," 130.
169. Pink, *The Sovereignty of God*, 139.
170. Kreider, "Jonathan Edwards's Theology of Prayer," 434.
171. Ware, "Prayer and the Sovereignty of God," 131.
172. Stump, "Petitionary Prayer," 81.
173. Ware, "Prayer and the Sovereignty of God," 131.
174. Lemke, "God's Relation to the World," 213.

definition of petitionary prayer reveals that the requesting or petitioning of God is not done freely. In fact, God maneuvers the human to offer such prayers. The only hint of human freedom in prayer is that in certain instances, petitionary prayers are causally linked to God's will and action. However, this is not a genuine response from the human. Rather, the human is like a stream of water that can be turned to petitionary prayer.

God Uses Prayer to Enlist Participation in His Work

One purpose for petitionary prayer is that "God has devised prayer as a means of enlisting us as participants in the work he has ordained, as part of the outworking of his sovereign rulership over all."[175] Charles Hodge similarly describes man's participation in God's work.[176] He provides the illustration of a man about to venture into what he hopes will be a great enterprise. However, the man will need to make a plan and determine his means beforehand, assigning each subordinate his part to act, even require, the subordinates to seek guidance and direction.[177] All of this, for Hodge, speaks to the efficacy of prayer. Ware goes on to describe that the Christian should marvel that God commands people to pray, "because whether they pray or not makes a difference!"[178] However, this statement about petitionary prayer making a difference contradicts what Ware previously said about God not needing "our prayers to 'help' him in the execution of his perfect plans."[179] Therefore, it seems that Ware is confused and unsure about his view on petitionary prayer.

In petitionary prayer and the divine-human relationship, a key word for Ware is *participation*. He writes,

> So because God is sovereign, he can rule the world unilaterally with no participation from anyone at all. His infinite wisdom and power, along with his uncontested authority, give him all he needs to accomplish everything he wants to do without your help or mine. His sovereignty, then, renders prayer unnecessary—in principle. But here is where the wonder and amazement at prayer increases further. Although God is fully capable of "doing it on his own," nonetheless, he enlists his people to

---

175. Ware, "Prayer and the Sovereignty of God," 138. These two points are also discussed in Ware, *God's Greater Glory*, 186–94.

176. Hodge, *Systematic Theology*, 3:699.

177. Ibid.

178. Ware, "Prayer and the Sovereignty of God," 138.

179. Ibid., 130.

join him in the work that alone is his. And one of the chief means that he employs for our participation with him in this work is prayer.[180]

This work of participation or enlistment on the part of God whereby humans through petitionary prayer make a difference, is not genuine and furthermore is contradictory. This is evident from his comments earlier in this chapter, which describe human participation and enlistment as God working within the hearts of his people in order to control them so that God can ensure that the prayers needed "for the accomplishment of his plans will be offered."[181] This form of petitionary prayer is not participation; instead, it is more appropriately described as a form of manipulation as the human does not have a choice to refrain from praying.

Hard determinism understands petitionary prayer as an essential tool, which God designs to enlist the believer toward participation in his work. For example, Ware appeals to James 5:14–15 when he writes, "God purposely designed the manner by which his ordained works would be accomplished, so that some of what he accomplishes can be brought to pass only as people pray."[182] Others have employed this passage to demonstrate that God enlists his children to participate in his work. For example, James Manton focuses upon the prayer and not oil that heals the sick person.[183] Thus human action through prayer, not a mere substance, leads the Christian to help those in need. Similarly, Luke Timothy Johnson draws a parallel between the ones praying in James with emissaries that Jesus sent out in Mark 6:13.[184] However, the difficulty with Ware's interpretation lies in the assertion that God does not need our prayers, in which case petitionary prayer ceases to be a key feature in the life of the Christian.[185] Take again the example of the mother praying for her son. One might argue that for Ware, although God does not need the mother's prayer, he has sovereignly chosen to use her prayer as a means to his good ends, which makes prayer necessary to accomplish his purposes. However, God unilaterally brings about prayer without participation from anyone.[186] Similarly, Francis Turretin argues that prayer does not change God. Rather, he uses prayer to enlist Christians to participate in the

---

180. Ibid., 139.
181. Ibid., 131.
182. Ibid., 140.
183. Manton, *James*, 337.
184. Johnson, *The Letter of James*, 331.
185. Ware, "Prayer and the Sovereignty of God," 130.
186. Ibid., 139.

work that he has already determined should come to pass.[187] For Ware and Turretin, human participation in God's work through prayer is grounded in what God has already determined to take place.

Another example of God using prayer to enlist participation in his work is through Christians' proactive responses to the prayers of another. For hard determinism, prayer for other people and their needs actually ministers the grace of God to them.[188] This work is imperative, and petitionary prayer helps accomplish this through our participation. For example, Ware writes, "God has willed to enlist our participation with him in the work he is doing, and prayer has been designed by God to get us onto the front lines, deeply involved in his work."[189] This is deficient, however, because participation for hard determinism carries the connotation that God is moving the human along in order to accomplish his ends, and in this case, God carries along the Christian to pray. This is not participation, because it removes human freedom. By contrast, a compatibilist contends that God brings about his sovereign purposes while enlisting the free actions and responses from Christians.[190] For example, Horton argues that prayer presupposes that the sovereignty of God is compatible with the affairs of free creatures.[191] Thus, prayer is much more than a therapeutic catharsis. Furthermore, Graham Redding observes that a key element in the Father's earthly work includes enlisting the free actions of Christians to participate.[192] The inspiration of Scripture provides a helpful illustration as to why hard determinism is deficient, because in order to properly define inspiration, one must explain how Scripture is the work of divine-human participation. Applying hard determinism's logic for participation in prayer to the framework of inspiration would produce a dictation view of inspiration. Dictation theory asserts that God carried along the human authors in such a way that God gave them the very words they "chose" to write. In the end, the human authors were merely writing the words God ordained them to write. Instead, inspiration is to be understood as being both a divine and human work with God remaining sovereign, because he has breathed out the Scriptures. Neither dictation theory nor hard determinism's understanding of petitionary prayer and participation stands.

Also for hard determinism, prayer enlists participation in God's kingdom work. Participation makes people more aware of what he is doing and thus gives them a greater desire to be a part of that work. He writes, "But by designing prayer, he allows us the privileged position of being insiders

---

187. Turretin, *Institutes of Elenctic Theology*, 1:319.
188. Ware, "Prayer and the Sovereignty of God," 141.
189. Ibid., 142.
190. Crump, *Knocking on Heaven's Door*, 284.
191. Horton, *The Christian Faith*, 357.
192. Redding, *Prayer and the Priesthood of Christ*, 296.

to kingdom strategy and kingdom operations."[193] The worshipful posture on behalf of the Christian while seeing the work of God unfold is worthy and essential; however, this does not give petitionary prayer any meaning, because the work "would take place with little if any notice by his people."[194] However, drawing someone to worship God is different than participating in the actual working out of the plan.

Conclusion

This book defines petitionary prayer as a genuine human behavior whereby the creature freely goes to its sovereign Creator and simply asks. In compatibilism, petitionary prayer is possible but only in the context that excludes libertarian freedom. This once again displays the difference between middle knowledge and compatibilism. The compatibilist does affirm the definition provided above; however, the creature freely going to God in prayer is understood as God working with humans who are unable to do otherwise to bring about his intended purposes. The difficulty for the compatibilist is the lack of clarity regarding the freedom of the one praying. In fact, work is done to define what freedom is not (see Feinberg, Tiessen, and Ware above), but it seems that no one has tried to define what human freedom is. If this freedom is not libertarian freedom, and therefore the option to forgo praying is removed from the human, then how can one with confidence declare that this prayer was offered freely? In particular, the doctrine of the priesthood of the believer becomes a key issue for compatibilism to resolve in petitionary prayer. These deficiencies are why middle knowledge prevails. It was important to once again separate compatibilism and hard determinism as they relate to petitionary prayer. In hard determinism, human freedom in petitionary prayer is almost impossible as God "will work in the hearts of his people to ensure that the prayers needed for the accomplishment of his plans will be offered."[195] For hard determinism, in order to fulfill such a statement, God does not need to work with humans that are free as understood by compatibilism and middle knowledge. Furthermore, if humans did possess freedom, it would not matter, because God would still work in their hearts to ensure his plan is accomplished. Ironically, this kind of petitionary prayer is described above as a participation on the part of the human in the work of God. In the end, both compatibilism and hard determinism fall short, because they do not promote the kind of communication between God and his creation that middle knowledge affords.

193. Ware, "Prayer and the Sovereignty of God," 142.
194. Ibid.
195. Ibid., 131.

4

Open Theism and Petitionary Prayer

IN THIS CHAPTER, I will examine open theism and its employment of petitionary prayer. Similar to the previous chapter on compatibilism, I will begin with the sovereignty of God. Then based upon open theism, various theological implications for petitionary prayer will be examined. This will also include systematic and pastoral theology. I will argue that open theism fails to uphold the sovereignty of God primarily due to its commitment to God self-limiting himself in order for prayer to take place in the divine-human relationship. Thus, its views concerning petitionary prayer should be rejected. This chapter supports the overall claim in this book that middle knowledge is more suitable to handle the theological question of how God can remain sovereign while humans, with libertarian freedom, offer genuine prayers of petition to God.

Introduction

For each theory of providence discussed in this book, the question is: Does prayer make a difference? For each theory, the answer is, "yes," as it is an essential discipline for the Christian, and open theism is no different.[1] Clark Pinnock notes that if a person does not believe in prayer, then he also questions the point of prayer. In response to this question, a person prays "more out of obedience than hope."[2] Furthermore, he warns that the one praying from mere obedience could be quite religious "and yet be traveling away from God."[3] For open theism, if events and circumstances do not depend on the one praying, it would make better sense to refrain from praying. However, if the one praying is able to alter the future so that God responds to prayer and changes the course of events in history, then

---

1. Pinnock, *Most Moved Mover*, 172.
2. Ibid.
3. Pinnock and Brow, *Unbounded Love*, 141.

prayer makes good sense for the open theist.[4] Pinnock uses Matt 18:18 for his rationale: "Whatever you bind on earth shall be bound in heaven, and whatever you loose on earth shall be loosed in heaven" (Matt 18:18). He also references Jas 4:2 as a scriptural foundation for divine-human interaction. Similarly, Walter Wink argues that when Christians pray, the unexpected becomes possible as heaven has been invoked which is the home of all possibilities. He concludes that the prayerful message is clear: "History belongs to the intercessors, who believe the future into being."[5] Prayer that changes the course of events in the world is not meant to elevate the human to a status greater than his humanity. Instead, this ability to affect God and the events in the world is meant to display the rich relationship that God has with his creatures.[6] For Pinnock, without this relational aspect, petitionary prayer becomes something like a pretend relationship.[7] Thus, in order for relationship to be genuine, one's prayers must exhibit a quality whereby the human is able to petition God, not out of an ordained exercise, but because the creature is dependent upon and loves the Creator.

This logic does not withstand the critique that God is then unnecessarily limiting his sovereignty as he governs the world. John Sanders emphasizes the relational aspect of the open view on prayer in that God genuinely wants to have a conversation with his creatures.[8] In other words, God has created the world with the intent of making human concerns his concerns, and prayer becomes one of the primary ways this relationship works. In this framework, God desires a relationship with people, not because he needs this relationship, but because he cares for his creatures created in his image.

Gregory Boyd argues that many Christians do not pray passionately, and, to his estimation, that makes good sense, because many Christians "don't see how [prayer] could make any significant difference."[9] Similar to Pinnock above, this means that prayer merely becomes an act of obedience on the part of the creature. Boyd understands prayer within the context of the *Imago Dei* that prior to creation, the Triune God "possessed 100 percent of all power."[10] However, when the Trinity decided to bring forth creation, which was inhabited with creatures made in the image of

---

4. Pinnock, *Most Moved Mover*, 172.

5. Wink, *Engaging the Powers*, 299.

6. See later in this chapter the discussion on human insufficiency and petitionary prayer.

7. Pinnock, *Most Moved Mover*, 174.

8. Sanders, *The God Who Risks*, 281.

9. Boyd, *God of the Possible* 95.

10. Ibid., 97.

God, these creatures were necessarily given some of the "say so" that God possessed, because they were created in God's image.[11] Concerning this creaturely influence, Boyd writes, "God's personal creations now possessed a measure of ability to influence what would occur. This was necessary if God's creations were to be personal beings who had the ability to make authentic choices."[12] For open theism, prayer is inherently linked to the doctrine of the Trinity as God gives his creatures some of their essence (say-so) in order to have a relationship with them.

The importance of petitionary prayer cannot be understated for the open theist. For example, in the "Preface" to *God of the Possible*, Gregory Boyd notes that a particular petitionary prayer in the Bible changed his perspective on divine providence and was the cause for his departure from compatibilism.[13] Prior to changing his view, Boyd would have identified himself as a compatibilist, although he uses the term *customary view*, which describes "that the future is exhaustively settled and that God knows it as such."[14] He writes, "One evening about seventeen years ago, I came upon 2 Kings 20 while reading my Bible," and in 2 Kgs 20, there is a key exchange between Isaiah, King Hezekiah, and God.[15] In this exchange, Isaiah confronts the king and proclaims that he is going to die. Hearing this terrible news, the king turns to God and offers a petitionary prayer. The Bible records this prayer: "Now, O Lord, please remember how I have walked before you in faithfulness and with a whole heart, and have done what is good in your sight" (2 Kgs 20:3). The Bible also makes it clear that non-verbally, Hezekiah communicates to God as well by turning "his face to the wall" and weeping "bitterly" (2 Kgs 20:2–3). In light of this verbal and non-verbal response, God through Isaiah declares, "Turn back, and say to Hezekiah the leader of my people, Thus says the LORD. . . and I will add fifteen years to your life. I will deliver you and this city out of the hand of the king of Assyria, and I will defend this city for my own sake and for my servant David's sake" (2 Kgs 20:5–6). Based on this passage in the Bible, Boyd writes, "I

11. Fretheim, "Prayer in the Old Testament," 57.

12. Boyd, *God of the Possible*, 97.

13. This assertion is made based upon the logic that Boyd became an open theist, which then begs the question: What did he leave in order to become an open theist? He notes, "About three years later, I became convinced that the customary view—that the future is exhaustively settled and that God knows it as such—was mistaken. I came to believe that the future is, to some degree at least, open-ended and that God knows it as such" (Boyd, *God of the Possible*, 8). This idea of coming to believe that the future is open coupled with believing that the "customary view" was mistaken, leads one to assert that Boyd left the customary view in favor of the open view.

14. Boyd, *God of the Possible*, 8.

15. Ibid., 7.

became convinced that the customary view—that the future is exhaustively settled and that God knows it as such—was mistaken. I came to believe that the future is, to some degree at least, open-ended and that God knows it as such. I began to embrace what is now generally called the 'open view' of God."[16] In the end, petitionary prayer was the key theological concept that influenced his adoption of open theism.

Sovereignty, Petitionary Prayer, and Open Theism

In the open view, the sovereignty of God is understood in general or limited terms.[17] This ensures God's dynamic relationship with the world he has created remains intact.[18] Prayer fits within God's sovereignty as, "God has sovereignly ordained that prayer be one of our central means of influencing what transpires in history."[19] However, Boyd argues, the reason for the lack of necessity is that compatibilists hold a view of divine sovereignty whereby, "the urgency of prayer simply doesn't make much sense."[20] If God's plan cannot be changed and if the future is exhaustively settled, then what is the point of prayer? The openness view instead claims that "the future is *not entirely settled and that God's plans can change*, the open view is able to render the purpose and urgency of prayer intelligible," as it declares "that some of the future *genuinely depends on prayer*."[21] David Woodruff observes that open theism must define God's sovereignty in general terms.[22] This assures for open theism that God is able to enter into a loving, reciprocal relationship with beings. Similar to Boyd, Fretheim argues that prayer demonstrates that God depends on his children in carrying out the work at hand, thus God must work in and through human frailty as well as strength.[23] For open theism, this translates into Christians that are "more inclined to pray with passion and urgency."[24] One of the primary ways that open theism achieves this is through the concept of spiritual "say-so."

16. Ibid., 8.
17. For more see chapter 2 and the relevant discussion on open theism.
18. Pinnock, "Open Theism, An Answer to My Critics," 238.
19. Boyd, *God of the Possible*, 97.
20. Ibid., 95.
21. Ibid., 95.
22. Woodruff, "Examining Problems and Assumptions," 56.
23. Fretheim, *Exodus*, 17.
24. Boyd, *God of the Possible*, 95.

Petitionary Prayer and Spiritual "Say-So"

Open theism prefers to use the language of "say-so" as a way to illustrate that God's creatures, created in his image, are able to influence how things are to transpire. Boyd defines spiritual say-so, "He [God] thus ordained that we have say-so in how things transpire. He doesn't want to relate to robots; he wants to interact with real persons. There can be no authentic personhood without some element of say-so, some degree of self-determination, some authentic power to influence things."[25] Similarly, Pinnock uses the illustration of story to add that characters must have say-so in the drama of life.[26] He rejects any theologies that deny say-so and instead are content with a character being *real enough*, even though they are merely a fictional figure with no say-so.[27] In addition to Boyd and Pinnock, Fretheim asserts that God's sovereignty seems to work in coordination with human activity.[28] Concerning prayer, Fretheim argues for something similar to spiritual say-so. He describes such work as power-sharing. Thus, in prayer the divine-human work together in a power-sharing conversation to shape the future.[29] Similar to Boyd and Fretheim, Sanders describes that prayer is rooted in God's desire for a personal relationship with his creatures, which necessitates that God chooses to make himself dependent upon humans for certain things.[30] Pinnock also adds that God takes risks. For example, through prayer God allows his will to be thwarted.[31] Action of this kind allows for the divine-human cooperation God desires. Here Sanders, Boyd, Pinnock, and Fretheim imply that the open view on prayer is that God has sovereignly chosen to create his creatures with the ability to make a significant difference. Hasker describes this risk-taking ability as a necessary element in order for the relationship between the divine-human to exist.[32] That God has self-limited himself in relationship is for the sake of love.[33]

---

25. Ibid., 96.

26. Pinnock, "Open Theism," 239.

27. Pinnock is directly referring to John Frame's use of story in *The Doctrine of God*, 156–59. This book discusses the concept of story as well in chapter 2.

28. Fretheim, *Exodus*, 16. Pinnock describes something similar but instead of *coordination*, he employs the term *cooperation*. See "Open Theism," 241.

29. Fretheim, "Prayer in the Old Testament," 60.

30. Sanders, *The God Who Risks*, 280.

31. Pinnock, "Open Theism," 241. Similarly, middle knowledge asserts that God cannot stop the sinful desires of human beings due to their libertarian freedom (MacGregor, *A Molinist Anabaptist Systematic Theology*, 116).

32. Hasker, "Response to Thomas Flint," 124.

33. Pinnock, "Open Theism," 239.

Having spiritual say-so also makes the human agent morally responsible. Pinnock argues that if one's choices are determined, then the human cannot be held morally responsible.[34] Furthermore, he asserts that libertarian freedom includes that humans will do things that God does not want them to do.[35] Similarly, Fretheim notes that humans have sufficient freedom and the power to disobey the will of God.[36] Thus, God in relationship with humans "must contend with intransigence, cruelty, and disloyalty in the human order."[37] God demonstrates the power of spiritual say-so through petitionary prayer. The divine-human interaction in petitionary prayer "displays his beautiful sovereignty by deciding *not* to always unilaterally decide matters. He enlists our input, not because he needs it, but because he desires to have an authentic, dynamic relationship with us as real, empowered persons."[38] Fretheim explains that the dynamic say-so of the believer, through prayer, represents the kind of integrity that God holds in his relationship with people.[39] Thus, for open theism, the spiritual say-so of the Christian demonstrates that a key aspect of the sovereignty of God is that he has ordained that prayer influence what transpires in history.

The term *spiritual "say-so"* is unique to Boyd; however, David Basinger articulates similar ideas concerning petitionary prayer.[40] He writes, "Freewill theists do *not* believe that God can unilaterally ensure that all and only that which he desires to come about will in fact occur in our world."[41] This implies that God has designed the world where humans work together with God in order to bring about circumstances.[42] Similar to Basinger, Fretheim asserts that God has chosen not to do everything unilaterally; rather, prayer is the means he chooses, which demonstrates that humans in conversation with God can extend or expand on God's possibilities.[43] Furthermore, in Basinger's explanation of open theism, "God voluntarily forfeits total control over earthly affairs in those cases where he allows us to exercise freedom

---

34. Ibid., 242.

35. Ibid., 237.

36. Fretheim, *Exodus*, 16.

37. Ibid.

38. Boyd, *God of the Possible*, 96.

39. Fretheim, *Exodus*, 286. Fretheim also discusses God honoring the integrity of the divine-human relationship in "Prayer in the Old Testament," 55. See also "The Repentance of God," 64–65.

40. Although, in 2005, Pinnock argues for spiritual "say-so" in "Open Theism," 239.

41. Basinger, *The Case for Freewill Theism*, 107.

42. Basinger, "Divine Control and Human Freedom," 60.

43. Fretheim, "Prayer in the Old Testament," 57.

of choice."⁴⁴ However, there is a deficiency in his claim, which then puts him in opposition to Boyd's spiritual say-so above. The deficiency goes as follows: (1) For compatibilism, the tension upheld is that God is sovereign while at the same time affirming some measure of human freedom; (2) For the open theist, the tension upheld is the affirmation of libertarian human freedom while at the same time affirming God's self-limiting intervention in earthly affairs. In order to illustrate this, Basinger writes the freewill theist denies that

> God can unilaterally control human decision-making that is truly voluntary but affirm that God can unilaterally intervene in earthly affairs, it becomes conceptually possible for freewill theists to maintain that petitionary prayer is efficacious in the sense in question—that is, to maintain that divine activity is at times dependent on our freely offered petitions.⁴⁵

Similar to Boyd, Basinger is arguing that the freewill theist must uphold that God has given the human being the ability to petition him freely, and based upon those petitions, God then intervenes in the world in such a way that he would not have otherwise done if the prayer was not offered. However, Basinger also argues that at times God intervenes unilaterally in earthly affairs to bring about a specific outcome, thus negating the need for petitionary prayer in that instance. If there are times when divine activity is not dependent upon prayer, then what is the purpose of prayer in those moments? How is the Christian to know whether (or not) prayer is necessary or if God is going to unilaterally intervene? One of the distinct characteristics of open theism is the divine-human relationship expressed in prayer, as God has imposed self-limitations upon himself in order to make it possible to respond to humanity. However, humanity does not have the confidence to know if prayer in that moment is necessary. In addition, Basinger notes that God does not possess "the ability to respond affirmatively to every request (or even to most requests) for assistance."⁴⁶ What is in view are the petitions whereby God has the ability to answer prayer but refrains from doing so, because he has given humanity the ability to thwart his will. If God does not possess the ability to respond affirmatively to most requests, then a person's motivation to pray is in jeopardy. Someone could also argue that God only cares about those things he responds to, which is shown by his unilateral intervention in the earthly affair. For example, what is the motivation of be-

---

44. Basinger, *The Case for Freewill Theism*, 108.
45. Ibid.
46. Ibid., 109.

ing persistent in prayer if God truly cannot respond affirmatively to most requests made to him? Basinger continues, "Thus there may be some (perhaps even many) prayers for assistance that God would like to answer affirmatively but simply cannot."[47] If God simply cannot in many cases answer our prayers for assistance affirmatively due to human intransigence, cruelty, disloyalty, and the overall ability to thwart God's will, then the logical conclusion is that petitionary prayer is also not necessary in many cases, because it will not change the outcome. The conclusion that God in many instances cannot answer affirmatively is troubling given the belief within open theism that God frequently responds to the prayers of his children.

Open Theism, Compatibilism, and Petitionary Prayer

Basinger believes that those that adhere to specific sovereignty, which includes compatibilism, deny that humans in their decision-making can alter God's already prescribed perfect plan. God may use human choice as a means for accomplishing his plans, but those choices never thwart or hinder God's plan.[48] Basinger argues that what distinguishes open theism from compatibilism is that open theism does not limit human freedom, so that one can either pray or refrain from praying.[49]

However, Basinger also asserts that the open view maintains "that God does retain the right to intervene unilaterally in earthly affairs. That is, we believe that God grants us freedom of choice and thus God retains the power and moral prerogative to inhibit occasionally our ability to make voluntary choices to keep things on track."[50] At this point, open theism subjects itself to the problem it is attempting to avoid in compatibilism. In other words, if compatibilism removes human ability to refrain from offering petitionary prayer, because God has ordained that the event would happen or that the petitionary prayer would be offered, then Basinger argues for similar logic as God reserves the ultimate right to intervene at any time, which includes

47. Ibid., 109.
48. Basinger, "Practical Implications," 157.
49. Ibid., 159.
50. Ibid. In addition, Basinger makes a similar contradiction in *The Case for Freewill Theism*. He writes, "Freewill theists maintain that God does retain the power to intervene unilaterally in earthly affairs. Specifically, they believe that God retains the power to suspend freedom of choice and/or modify the natural order" (Basinger, *The Case for Freewill Theism*, 108). Yet freewill theism will also affirm that God cannot "unilaterally ensure that all and only that which he desires to come about will in fact occur in our world" (Basinger, *The Case for Freewill Theism*, 107).

the possible intervention of the petitionary prayer. Basinger does qualify his remarks when he writes, "But we all agree that it is, at the very least, quite reasonable to view petitionary prayer as a means whereby we grant God the permission to influence our noncognitive states of mind and/or share with us those cognitive insights concerning ourselves and others that will help us better live out our Christian commitment in this world."[51] Still, the problem remains. If God is influencing the surroundings to intervene noncognitively in order to produce a prayer or affect a prayer, then the person offering the prayer is dangerously close to not being libertarianly free. One could argue that the lack of clarity from Basinger weakens his argument against compatibilism. In open theism, God gave up some of his sovereignty in order to ensure that humans have libertarian freedom. For example, Basinger makes the point above that humans "possess significant freedom"; however, it would appear that this freedom at times does not include the ability to refrain from acting, which is a key feature of libertarian freedom. Sanders argues, "God retains the power and moral prerogative to inhibit occasionally our ability to make voluntary choices to keep things on track."[52] In addition, Sanders doubts the compatibilist's affirmation that humans really are free under their model. He grants that humans do express freedom in the decisions they make; however, "her desires are determined by such things as genetics, upbringing, sinful nature or God so that she is not free to change her desires. In this schema [compatibilism] a person is free as long as she acts on her desires, even if her desires are determined."[53] One might also offer the same critique of the open theist position, thus demonstrating again the similarity between open theism and compatibilism. Sanders defines human freedom for the compatibilist as, "An agent is free with respect to a given action at a given time if at that time it is true that the agent can perform the action if she decides to perform and she can refrain from the action if she decides not to perform it."[54] Then, he defines libertarian freedom as "an agent is free with respect to a given action at a given time if at that time it is within the agent's power to perform the action and also in the agent's power to refrain from the action."[55] At this point, there is not a dramatic difference between the two definitions.

There is, however, a difference. In compatibilism, God is able to determine the human's desires. Thus, "a person is free as long as she acts on her

---

51. Basinger, "Practical Implications," 162.
52. Ibid., 159.
53. Sanders, *The God Who Risks*, 233.
54. Ibid. 233–34.
55. Ibid., 235.

desires, even if her desires are determined."[56] Conversely, open theism and libertarian freedom do not "ignore genetics or environmental factors that influence decisions, but they maintain that a person could have done otherwise than she did in any given situation."[57] This conflicts with Basinger's description that, "God retains the power and moral prerogative to inhibit occasionally our ability to make voluntary choices to keep things on track."[58] The lack of clarity, as to (1) the extent of human freedom, in this case libertarian freedom, and (2) the extent of God's influence in the world are examples where compatibilism and open theism might not be that far apart.

Open Theism, Petitionary Prayer, and Theology

In order to offer petitionary prayer, open theism argues that people must first have a correct understanding concerning who God is. This is a similar point made by compatibilism discussed in the previous chapter. Also the logical moments of God's knowledge and its affects upon open theism will be discussed as it relates to petitionary prayer. Finally, a key characteristic for this theory of providence is that the future is open, which deeply impacts its understanding of petitionary prayer.

Knowing God Correctly is Paramount to Prayer

Robin Collins claims that the open theist's conception of God is the most accurate account from Scripture, because it allows for prayer to affect God, which then allows the one praying to causally contribute to the event prayed for.[59] Also, Pinnock observes that open theism takes pride in how its conception of God merges the mind and the heart. He writes, "Ideally, mind and heart ought to be in agreement and theology ought not only to make intellectual sense, but have transforming effects on the lives of believers."[60] With regard to petitionary prayer, what people understand about God will deeply impact their views regarding prayer. Paul Sponheim illustrates this point by asserting that people may love their spouse, children, country, and God.[61] This activity does not single God out. However, when a person prays,

---

56. Ibid., 234.
57. Ibid., 235.
58. Basinger, "Practical Implications," 159.
59. Collins, "Prayer and Open Theism," 168.
60. Pinnock, *Most Moved Mover*, 153.
61. Sponheim, "The God of Prayer," 65.

God stands alone. Similar to Sponheim, Collins asserts that the naturalistic understanding of petitionary prayer must be rejected since God is left completely out of the picture.[62] For Sponheim and Collins, God must be at the center of Christian prayer. Collins instead offers his co-creator model of petitionary prayer, which is discussed later in this chapter. For Pinnock, open theism should be distinguished from compatibilism's apathetic view of God. He writes, "If God is apathetic to the world, why should we be committed? But, if God is solicitous of us, what a motivation!"[63] What does it mean for God to be solicitous of us? Pinnock notes, "The open view. . .upholds human significance and motivates human action. It sees human beings as God's covenant partners and co-laborers."[64] Also important is the relationship that God shares with human beings and "lets them share in shaping the open future."[65] The emphasis that one must have a right conception of God in order for prayer to make practical sense is similar to Edwards, found in chapter 3. However, the difference between compatibilism and open theism is that compatibilism focuses on the sovereignty of God and from there, builds a theology of petitionary prayer. Open theism focuses on how God is relational with humans and from there, builds a theology of petitionary prayer. What compatibilism and open theism demonstrates is that they begin at different points in their theology of prayer. For open theism, prayer depends on a highly relational God.[66]

Petitionary Prayer and the Logical Moments of God's Knowledge

A key issue for open theism is that this theory of providence focuses on the future and what knowledge God has of the future.[67] Furthermore, those that oppose open theism on the grounds that it compromises God's omniscience are simply misguided according to Boyd. He writes, "The debate between the open and classical understandings of divine foreknowledge is completely a debate over the nature of the future: it is exhaustively settled from all eternity, or is it partly open? That is the question at hand, nothing else."[68] Similar to Boyd, Hasker adds that there is simply no truth for God to

62. Collins, "Prayer and Open Theism," 163, 172.
63. Pinnock, *Most Moved Mover*, 154.
64. Ibid.
65. Ibid.
66. Sponheim, "The God of Prayer," 65.
67. Boyd, *God of the Possible*, 16.
68. Ibid., 17.

know until a particular decision is in fact made.[69] In other words, Basinger notes that the future is open, for if God is making agents respond, then it is difficult to avoid the conclusion that the agent is not free.[70] For open theism, compatibilism answers this question whereby all things concerning the future are settled and contain no possibilities.[71] In addition, Lorenzo Dow McCabe argues that if God foreknows future contingencies, then only he can modify them.[72] For open theism, this has great implications for petitionary prayer. An example might be a mother who has a son struggling with an alcohol addiction. She devoutly prays for her son to stop drinking. If God is causing the mother to respond with prayer, then the mother praying is merely a machine, and liberty is impossible. Therefore, the open theist argues that compatibilism prohibits a real relationship and that a settled future then precludes substance in the prayers. Instead, the open theist holds, "the future consists partly of settled realties and partly of unsettled realties. Some things about the future are possibly this way and possibly that way."[73] In other words, the future consists of unsettled possibilities and settled certainties, which allows for genuine possibilities as one prays.

The claim that the future includes genuine possibilities is a weakness for open theism. The weakness resides in that for open theism the content of God's knowledge of the future is grounded in God's free knowledge rather than in the logical moment of God's middle knowledge (prior to God's decree to create a world).[74] In other words, God does not know the content of the mother's prayer until she prays. One could argue that if open theism grounded the future and its "genuine possibilities" in the logical moment of God's middle knowledge, then God would no longer come to know those genuine possibilities in the actual world that he has created (i.e. free knowledge), thus eliminating the need for God to forfeit his sovereign control.[75] Thus, whether (or not) the mother will pray would be known to God prior to the creation of the world. In addition, assuming the mother prays,

69. Hasker, "A Refutation of Middle Knowledge," 546.
70. Basinger, "Middle Knowledge and Human Freedom: Some Clarifications," 331.
71. Boyd, *God of the Possible*, 16.
72. McCabe, *Divine Nescience of Future Contingencies a Necessity*, 97.
73. Boyd, *God of the Possible*, 16.
74. For a review of the logical moments of God's middle and free knowledge, see chapter 2. Also, chapter 5 discusses how middle knowledge employs petitionary prayer.
75. In response to this point by Boyd, the weakness of open theism is that they are in many ways "almost" Molinist. The open theist does not have a category for where to place God's decree to create a world within the logical moments of God's natural, middle, and free knowledge. This divide separates openness theology from middle knowledge and what ultimately gets the openness position in trouble theologically.

the content of the prayers would be known to God prior to creation. This confusion regarding the logical moments of middle and free knowledge is expressed in Boyd's statement that, "If God does not foreknow future free actions, it is not because his knowledge of the future is in any sense incomplete. It's because there is, in this view, nothing definite there for God to know!"[76] Similarly, Basinger concludes that if God does know the future, then prayer is inconsequential, because it (1) is not freely offered, and (2) will not change the outcome.[77] Thus, it is only when one prays that God comes to know when prayer occurs. The open theist concludes that God self-limited himself in order to have such knowledge of the future.[78] Otherwise human freedom is restricted, and relationship is not possible.

Instead, middle knowledge is preferred as God perfectly knows those genuine possibilities, which maintains the sovereignty of God, because his knowledge is perfect regarding the future, and yet human beings are free, because God knows what they would do (genuine possibilities) if he created them and placed them in that circumstance. For example, God knows the genuine possibilities before the mother as it relates to offering petitionary prayer. God also knows what the mother would in fact do if he were to create her and place her in that particular circumstance. Thus, Molinism does affirm that there is "nothing definite there for God to know," but only in the context of middle knowledge, because in that logical moment, God knows not only what *could* but what *would* happen if a person were instantiated in a certain circumstance. However, since the world has yet to be created in the logical moment of God's middle knowledge, there is nothing definite for God to know because there is nothing currently existing to be known.[79] Similarly, within the context of the actual world that has been created, middle knowledge rejects that there is "nothing definite there for God to know."[80] One must remember that God's free knowledge could have been different if he had chosen to create a different world (chapter 1). However, once God chose a world to create, that world became "definite" in the mind of God, thus affirming God's sovereignty and omniscience. The open theist argues instead that there is "nothing definite there for God to know" concerning this actual world, which is why, for open theism, God forfeits his sovereignty and omniscience concerning the world if he is going to participate in a relationship with human beings.

76. Boyd, *God of the Possible*, 16.
77. Basinger, "Divine Omniscience and Human Freedom," 294.
78. Pinnock, "Open Theism," 239.
79. Craig, *The Only Wise God*, 129–30.
80. Boyd, *God of the Possible*, 16.

Boyd provides Jer 7:5–7 as an example that the future must be understood as "a realm of possibilities."[81] In this text, the Lord proclaims to Israel that, "*If* you truly amend your ways and your deeds . . . *then* I will let you dwell in this place" (Jer 7:5–7, emphasis mine). Boyd focuses upon the "if. . .then" clause and asserts that it makes the most sense when understood as referring to the future being to "some extent a realm of possibilities," and thus open.[82] However, this biblical example demonstrates once again that open theism unnecessarily limits God's sovereignty and knowledge concerning the future in order to uphold realms of possibility. This conclusion is unavoidable for the open theist when the future is understood within the content of God's free knowledge of the actual world. Instead, middle knowledge is preferred, because those same possibilities are understood within the context of God's middle knowledge, which is prior to the decree to create a world. Thus, for middle knowledge the future truly is a "realm of possibilities," because God has not created the future yet.

This biblical example demonstrates that the problem for the open theist is that they process the "if . . .then" clause in God's free knowledge, which is based upon an already created world, which means where one locates petitionary prayer within the logical moments of God's knowledge will greatly affect (1) the sovereignty of God and (2) human freedom with respect to prayer. Middle knowledge is the only available option that gives the theologian the ability to affirm both.[83]

Petitionary Prayers toward an Open Future

In open theism, the belief that the future is open stems from the conviction that God has self-limited his sovereign control of the world that he has created. For Sanders, this deeply impacts the divine-human relationship. He writes that the future is open "because God elects not to decide everything apart from our input."[84] Pinnock adds to Sanders with the illustration of church government. He notes that God does not have a perfect plan, rather a detailed blueprint, thus God's plan is a general one.[85] Pinnock notes that Scripture does not offer one perfect plan for governing the church. Instead, the church is given a detailed blueprint with the expectation that humans will

---

81. Ibid., 163.
82. Ibid.
83. Hasker, "Providence and Evil: Three Theories," 97.
84. Sanders, *God Who Risks*, 281.
85. Pinnock and Brow, *Unbounded Love*, 147.

freely lead the church into the future.[86] Sanders, Pinnock, and Brow explain that God sovereignly determines an open future as he designed the world in this manner, which means that, "God has open routes into the future, and he desires that we participate with him in determining which ones to take."[87] Some open theists have taken this to mean that prayer is efficacious only when it is answered in a similar manner to the initial request.[88] Sanders offers a warning to people who pray that just because they offer petitionary prayers does not mean that they are able to get whatever they want. Robert Ellis also warns that petitionary prayer is not a human attempt to argue with God and win.[89] Sanders and Ellis posit that this amounts to prayerful manipulation and not a relationship-based prayer. In addition, Fretheim adds to Ellis's warning that it is erroneous to view success in petitionary prayer as winning an argument with God when a petition has been granted.[90] Instead, open theism argues that at times, one may "prevail with God because God genuinely takes our desires into account."[91] However, at other times, God prevails "getting us to change our minds and pursue a course of action that we did not initially think best. In this regard, prayer provides a dialogical resource for God to work in the world."[92] For open theism, when prayer is answered, it should be evidence of how seriously God takes his relationship with humanity. However, this is yet another example of the deficiency of open theism. To argue that Christians are able to prevail over God due to their petitionary prayers accords nicely with open theism; however, to then argue that God is still able to prevail over the human being to bring about his desired ends limits the efficacy of petitionary prayers because one could argue that God only answers those petitionary prayers that accord with God's intended desire for the future. And those petitionary prayers that do not accord with God's intended desires for the future are then examples whereby God prevails over the human being in order to "change our minds and pursue a course of action that we did not initially think best."[93] Even if those petitionary prayers are freely offered, it still does not necessitate the need for them because God is still bringing about his intended desires for the future in those instances. Sanders concludes, "When we turn to God in

86. Ibid., 148.
87. Sanders, *God Who Risks*, 281.
88. Collins, "Prayer and Open Theism," 163.
89. Ellis, *Answering God*, 14.
90. Fretheim, *Exodus*, 286.
91. Sanders, *God Who Risks*, 281.
92. Ibid.
93. Ibid.

prayer, we open a window of opportunity for the Spirit's work in our lives, creating new possibilities for God to carry out his project."[94] His conclusion is correct, but it does not bolster the argument that petitionary prayer is necessary. God is working with and persuading humans offering their petitionary prayers in such a way that changes their minds and thus changes their freely offered petitionary prayer so that those prayers conform to God's desired outcome for the future (that is open). Sanders defines *petitionary prayer* as "receiving something *because* one requests it."[95] What he argues thus far fulfills his definition of petitionary prayer because the people are receiving something because they requested it. However, this definition is deficient in that it does not include that what the human is requesting from God could be something that God has worked in order to change the mind of the petitioner and to get his intended desire for the future. Attention will now focus on the various implications petitionary prayer has within systematic theology as it relates to open theism.

Open Theism, Petitionary Prayer, and Systematic Theology

A thorough review of the theological evidence for open theism must include an exposition of the doctrine of the priesthood of the believer and the impact it has upon petitionary prayer. In addition, the theological concept of two-way contingency will be discussed as it relates to the manner in which God and his creation share in a relationship, which is most clearly evidenced by prayer. However, first attention will be given to the doctrine of the Trinity and how it corresponds to open theism and petitionary prayer.

The Trinity and Petitionary Prayer

The doctrine of the Trinity is foundational for open theism and its understanding of petitionary prayer. In fact, Pinnock defines open theism as "a relational and Trinitarian doctrine with an emphasis on God as personal and interactive."[96] In other words, open theism reads the meta-narrative of Scripture with the interactive social Trinity in view.[97] Also, as noted above, Boyd theologically correlates petitionary prayer with the doctrine of

---

94. Ibid.
95. Ibid., 277.
96. Pinnock, "Open Theism," 237.
97. Ibid., 239.

the Trinity.[98] Similar to Boyd, Robert Ellis contributes to the discussion of the Trinitarian implication for petitionary prayer. He writes, "The Christian experience of praying to the One God is that of stepping into a dynamic relationship whereby the Spirit catches us up into a movement with the Son to the Father."[99] Specifically, Ellis focuses upon the work of the Holy Spirit within the Trinity.[100] In addition, Pinnock and Robert Crow note that the whole Trinity is involved in prayer, which emphasizes that God is not impassive but affected by the concerns of his children.[101] Thus, Boyd and Ellis demonstrate the inherent Trinitarian nature of prayer. For open theism, the spiritual say-so of the believer helps to illustrate the relationship between petitionary prayer and the Trinity. The spiritual say-so or power-sharing view asserts that God wants to interact and relate "with real persons," which means that there has to be some "degree of self-determination, some authentic power to influence things."[102] Boyd argues that prior to creation, God possessed 100 percent of the spiritual say-so available. However, when the Trinity decided to bring forth creation, they invested "a certain percentage of their say-so" in order to assure that relationship and communication was possible.[103] Similar to Boyd, Fretheim argues that God shares his power in order to maintain the integrity of relationship.[104] God does not share his power with random creatures; rather his power is imparted to creatures made in his image.[105] The implication is that "the triune God was at this point no longer the only one that determined how things would go. God's personal creations now possessed a measure of ability to influence what would occur."[106] Thus, in order for prayer to be possible, God imparted to creatures some of their Trinitarian say-so, which validated the relationship he shares with humanity. The language strengthens as it was "necessary," ac-

---

98. Boyd, *God of the Possible*, 97.

99. Ellis, *Answering God*, 179. Sanders acknowledges Ellis's book, *Answering God*, as a key piece of literature for open theism and petitionary prayer (Sanders, *The God Who Risks*, 284).

100. Ellis, *Answering God*, 179. For more on petitionary prayer linked with the Lord's Prayer, see Stump, "Petitionary Prayer," 81–91; Goetz, "On Petitionary Prayer" 96; Kitahata and Nessan, "Give Us This Day Our Daily Bread," 48–52; Wright, "Thy Kingdom Come," 268–70.

101. Pinnock and Brow, *Unbounded Love*, 149. Louis Berkhof, not an open theist, also argues that the doctrine of the Trinity is foundational to their understanding and ability to pray. (Berkhof, *Systematic Theology*, 84.)

102. Boyd, *God of the Possible*, 96.

103. Ibid., 97.

104. Fretheim, "Prayer in the Old Testament," 57.

105. Ibid.

106. Boyd, *God of the Possible*, 97.

cording to Boyd, "If God's creations were to be personal beings who had the ability to make authentic choices, including the choice whether to enter into a loving relationship with him."[107] Due to Christians' necessity to exercise their spiritual say-so, Boyd believes that no other view captures "the power and urgency of prayer as adequately as the open view does."[108] However, a person might argue that siphoning the spiritual say-so of the believer from the Trinity is deficient. The church confesses that God eternally exists as three persons: Father, Son, and Holy Spirit, and that each person is fully God, and that there is one God.

The idea that the Trinity somehow gives up a percentage of its "say-so" in order that humans might have the ability to pray is dangerous because it calls into question the perichoresis of the Trinity, which is the idea that any essential characteristic that is shared by one of the members of the Trinity is also shared by the others as well.[109] Ellis employs the doctrine of perichoresis, which he describes as "love in movement."[110] For Ellis, because God is Father, Son, and Holy Spirit, any account of petitionary prayer must have a Trinitarian perspective.[111] However, if God is sovereignly giving to creation some of his "say-so" in order for the creature to pray, which member of the Trinity is that coming from? If some of the Trinitarian say-so is coming from just one member of the Trinity, then God is no longer three equal persons. Thus, one is not praying to a triune God. Paul Sponheim disagrees with Boyd and Fretheim on this point asserting that God does not give up his spiritual say-so in order to give it to mankind. Instead God works with humans in such a way as to give them say-so.[112] However, for Sponheim giving the creature say-so does not necessitate that God give up some of his essence.[113] This is not possible because mankind was created out of nothing. Thus, no human is made out of God but rather is made by God out of nothing. If it comes from just one member of the Trinity, one can no longer proclaim the equality of God in the Trinity. For example, if the Holy Spirit gave up a percentage of its available say-so in order to give it to humanity so that man might pray and have the ability to influence, then the Holy Spirit would no longer be equal in terms of the available say-so of the Father and Son. Thus, as a result of prayer, people could question God's Trinitarian

107. Ibid.
108. Ibid., 98.
109. McGrath, *Christian Theology*, 241.
110. Ellis, *Answering God*, 179.
111. Ibid., 180.
112. Sponheim, "The God of Prayer," 66.
113. Ibid.

equality. In addition, they could question the motivation to pray to a God that is possibly not Trinitarian in nature.

According to the theological concept of perichoresis, it would have to come from each member equally, yet Boyd never defines which member of the Trinity or if all members of the Trinity give up their say-so. If it comes from God's being, then all three members of the Trinity change, which would contradict the immutability of God and also call into question the efficacy of God's sovereignty. If the say-so comes from just one member of the Trinity, then all three members are no longer equal. In the end, for the sake of maintaining spiritual say-so as it relates to petitionary prayer, open theism has unnecessarily limited either one member of the Trinity or all members of the Trinity.

Jesus as Priest and the Priesthood of All Believers

As discussed in chapters 2 and 3, the Christian should rightly assume that genuine communication exists between the creature and Creator. As a review, one of the primary ways in which this communication is made possible is through Jesus's priesthood. Due to their standing in Christ (Rom 6:11; 8:1), Christians are given grace to share in this priesthood (1 Cor 1:2; 2 Cor 11:21; Eph 2:6).[114] The priesthood of believers relates to petitionary prayer as Christians no longer need a special intermediary. For example, Collins notes that prayer is accessible to everyone, even involving beings outside of the physical realm, like angels.[115] Thus, the Christian is encouraged from the Lord and his apostles to petition God. An important question then becomes, how does the open theist uphold the priesthood of the believer as it relates to petitionary prayer? One of the main characteristics of open theism is that God gives up some of his power and control and gives it to the believer so that the Christian is able to freely choose.[116] Giving up some of his sovereignty is God's way of bringing Christians into greater intimacy with himself.[117] For open theism, this is important because humans have say-so to influence the future with petitionary prayer.[118] However, if Christ has made it possible for human beings to freely (without a mediator) go before God in prayer,

---

114. Pinnock and Brow, *Unbounded Love*, 143.
115. Collins, "Prayer and Open Theism," 181.
116. Basinger, *The Case for Freewill Theism*, 108.
117. Pinnock and Brow, *Unbounded Love*, 143.
118. Boyd, *God of the Possible*, 96.

then it is not necessary for God to give up some of his sovereignty in order to make this a reality. Philippians 2:5–11 describes that Christ emptied himself, being born in the likeness of men. This does not mean that he forwent any of his deity in order to become a man.[119] In terms of the previous section, Christ did not give up some of his Trinitarian say-so in order to become a man. It does, however, mean that Christ gave up his position, rank, and privilege in order to incarnate himself and take on human flesh (Phil 2:5–11).[120] Jesus humbled himself for our sake; this work of Christ is termed, "Kenosis" (Phil 2:7).[121] Concerning this idea of Kenosis in light of divine accommodation and prayer, Fretheim notes that by choosing human vehicles to bring about his work, God must work in "unobtrusive, unlikely, and vulnerable ways."[122] Therefore, any definition of divine sovereignty should take into account that God does not act alone.

By affirming the priesthood of the believer, a person acknowledges that nothing is left for God to do in order to make it possible for the Christian to petition God through prayer. However, the open theist goes to great lengths to demonstrate that God "voluntarily forfeits" control in order to provide the freedom to petition God.[123] But again, the priesthood, provided by Jesus, should accomplish that freedom for the believer to pray. For open theism, it would appear that Christ's priesthood is weakened or limited because it cannot provide the necessary ability for the human to pray. Furthermore, God should not have to limit himself unless the priesthood of the believer does not remove the intermediary between God and man, thus making it imperative for God, in the interest of prayer, to self-limit himself. Perhaps due to the priesthood of the believer, the open theist unnecessarily limits God's sovereignty. Either way, the priesthood of the believer demonstrates a great weakness for the open theist conception of prayer. If he affirms the priesthood of the believer, then God unnecessarily limits his sovereignty in order to receive prayer. If the believer does not affirm her priesthood, then Christ's work as a mediational high priest is greatly limited in terms of its ability to mediate her prayer offered to God.

---

119. Melick, Jr., *Philippians, Colossians, Philemon*, 103.
120. Melick, Jr., *Philippians, Colossians, Philemon*, 103.
121. Fee, *Paul's Letter to the Philippians*, 211.
122. Fretheim, *Exodus*, 17.
123. Basinger, "Practical Implications," 159.

Petitionary Prayer, God's Immutability, and Two-Way Contingency

For open theism, petitionary prayer also involves God moving into action due to prayer. This suggests that God changes his mind in response to prayer. If so, does this contradict the immutability of God? For the Christian, what is the advantage in prayer if some of God's character changes? Brümmer argues that a person does not have to choose either God's immutability or the efficacy of petitionary prayer. He describes petitionary prayer as a "two-way contingency," which implies that God is a personal agent "who is capable of real responses to contingent events and to the free acts which human persons perform, as well as to the requests which they address to him."[124] Brümmer credits Peter Geach for the concept of two-way contingency.[125] Robert Ellis also looks to two-way contingency for a helpful account of intercession.[126] Ellis prefers two-way contingency because prayer becomes meaningful when it requires that God order events because a person petitions.[127] Brümmer goes on to describe two-way contingency in petitionary prayer as affecting the relationship between God and the person praying. Therefore, prayer in this sense has a meaningful effect on both God and the one praying. For Basinger, if prayer does not offer the potential for real change in God, then the outcome is fixed regardless of the one praying.[128] Thus, it is pointless to offer a petitionary prayer regarding what is impossible to avoid.[129] To this point, if love is inevitable, then it is not genuine. In other words, inevitable love is not "risky." Similarly, Fretheim argues that giving humans such freedom to love is fraught with negative possibilities. However, for love to be genuine, one must have the ability to refrain from love.[130] Brümmer also writes, "If the lover tries to force or oblige the beloved to return his or her love, the relationship between them is perverted, love is lost and the lover is left with an object rather than with a beloved person."[131] Pinnock also argues that if one desires mutual love, love cannot be scripted.[132]

---

124. Brümmer, *What Are We Doing When We Pray?* 34.

125. Geach, *God and the Soul*, 89–99.

126. Ellis, *Answering God*, 175.

127. Ibid.

128. Basinger, "Why Petition an Omnipotent, Omniscient, Wholly Good God?" 25–41. See also Brümmer, *What Are We Doing When We Pray?* 44.

129. Brümmer, *What Are We Doing When We Pray?*, 34.

130. Fretheim, *Exodus*, 17. Fretheim similarly discusses the risk God manages in the divine-human relationship, see, "Prayer in the Old Testament," 54.

131. Brümmer, *What Are We Doing When We Pray?*, 36.

132. Pinnock, "Open Theism," 243.

For this reason, God "has created us as personal agents who freely initiate their own actions."[133] Similar to Fretheim, Pinnock, and Brümmer, Rice adds that open theism acknowledges that there are genuine wrongs in the world.[134] This includes the various ways that creatures work against God and bring harm to themselves and others. Thus, in two-way contingency, people have been created as personal agents that can freely initiate their own prayer. Also, God is able to respond to those petitions.

If petitionary prayer "entails that God does things he would not have done if we had not prayed," then God has changed his mind in response to human prayer.[135] Brümmer does not want to adopt the view that all temporal events are inevitable since they have been determined from eternity by the immutable will of God.[136] The fear is that prayer would then become meaningless. Instead, Brümmer offers what Geach has termed the Cambridge criterion as a possible way to uphold God's immutability and petitionary prayer.[137] In addition, T. P. Smith argues for a similar criterion to Geach.[138] For Geach and Smith, the Cambridge criterion argues that God's nature is unchanging and yet compatible with God's changing relationship to the temporal world.[139] Brümmer notes that "armed with this criterion," the immutability of God is formulated as such: "God is immutable in the sense that (a) he cannot change with respect to non-relational predicates and (b) he can change with respect to relation predicates, but in that case the change in him is a mere Cambridge change and the real change takes place in whatever he is related to."[140] In this case, what God is related to is the one offering petitionary prayer. The implication is that the prayer affected a real change in the one praying and his circumstances and not in the "immutable intention of God."[141] The advantage to such a view of petitionary prayer is that "it does not entail a deterministic view of the universe. Real changes are possible in the world, and these both have two-way contingency and can result from the free decisions of human persons."[142] However, with regard to the immutability of God, Brümmer rejects Geach's proposal for two rea-

---

133. Brümmer, *What Are We Doing When We Pray?*, 36.
134. Rice, "The Final Form of Love," 214.
135. Brümmer, *What Are We Doing When We Pray?*, 39.
136. Ibid., 40.
137. Geach, *God and the Soul*, 71.
138. Smith, "On the Applicability of a Criterion of Change," 325.
139. Geach, *God and the Soul*, 99.
140. Brümmer, *What Are We Doing When We Pray?*, 41–42.
141. Ibid., 42.
142. Ibid.

sons. First, there is not enough clarity regarding what non-relational predicates are, which then makes "the whole distinction between real change and 'mere' Cambridge change" problematic.[143] Also, if the change only takes place with the one praying so that God merely changes in a Cambridge way, then Brümmer questions the true relational qualities in the divine-human relationship. For open theism, relationship entails change from both in the divine-human.[144] Similarly, Paul Sponheim argues that prayer affects God, the world, and the one praying.[145]

The grounds for such powerful prayers are found in the relationship God shares with the one praying. Thus, if petitionary prayer and the divine-human relationship is meaningful activity, then "God is a personal agent who is capable of *real* responses to contingent events and to the free acts which human persons perform, as well as to the requests which they address to him."[146] Open theism understands God's immutability in a similar way to its understanding of God's sovereignty discussed above. For example, God has settled certain things about the future while he has also left open other outcomes to be determined by libertarian human freedom. In a similar way, God is immutable concerning some things, like his nature. However, he is open to change regarding his relationship to his children.[147] For Fretheim, God will move from a decision made and change course midstream due to his interaction with the world. However, God will also remain consistent in his steadfastness, faithfulness, and knowledge of the truth.[148] With respect to petitionary prayer, the advantage for open theism is that God responds to and even changes his course of action due to prayer. This emphasizes the genuine divine-human relationship the open theist desires. However, if God changes some of his character in response to prayer, what other aspects of his character is he willing to change? The human being changing God's course of action is finite and sinful in nature. What in the two-way contingency prevents the sinful human being from causing God to alter his course of action which pleases the sinful desires of the one praying? For example, a person cannot argue that God's goodness would be a prevention because if God changes his mind due to prayer, he would also be able to change his goodness as a result of prayer. Furthermore, for open theism, a relation-

---

143. Ibid., 43.

144. Boyd, *God of the Possible*, 95. For more on this change in both God and human, see also the section on Dynamic Relationships in Petitionary Prayer below.

145. Sponheim, "The God of Prayer," 73.

146. Brümmer, *What Are We Doing When We Pray?*, 44.

147. Ibid., 45.

148. Fretheim, "The Repentance of God," 63.

ship is characterized by a change in God and the one praying. However, what if God cannot change because it would affect his goodness? Therefore, it seems that the divine-human relationship is not genuine because God is unable to change. For open theism, the act of God whereby he is able to change some of his character is a deficiency in petitionary prayer. For example, in petitionary prayer one could potentially be praying to a God that is not good due to his ability to change. Moreover, God could also be responsible for answering in an evil way as a result of petitionary prayer. Or if God cannot change, then open theism loses one of its main features in the divine-human relationship, which is a God that alters his course of action in response to prayer. Thus, the one praying does not have confidence that God will alter his course of action. The preservation of God's immutable character is essential in the attempt to unfold the relationship shared between God and his creatures in prayer.

This section has called into question some of the views of open theism as it pertains to petitionary prayer in the doctrines of the Trinity and the priesthood of the believer. Also, it was important to describe how open theism employs two-way contingency and the deficiency this presents in petitionary prayer as it relates to the immutability of God. Next, attention will turn to those ways in which petitionary prayer relates to open theism and pastoral theology.

Open Theism, Petitionary Prayer, and Pastoral Theology

This section is an examination of pastoral theology as it relates to petitionary prayer. This will include a discussion concerning the spiritual disciplines of confession and repentance. Exercising these spiritual disciplines is important as it signifies a Christian turning away from sin and restoring one's relationship with God.

When the divine-human relationship is damaged due to sin, the human being is able to confess their sin to God without an intermediary, and the Bible promises that he is faithful and just to forgive them for their sin and to cleanse them from all unrighteousness (1 John 1:9). For Fretheim, God serves as a model of repentance for the human.[149] God never repents from sin; however he does repent from evil (change his mind), and this is clearly evidenced in the exchange between God and Moses in Exod 32:7–14.[150] Similar to Fretheim, Knight describes the exchange between

149. Fretheim, *Exodus*, 286.
150. Fretheim, "Prayer in the Old Testament," 58.

God and Moses as the human petitioning God with temerity, calling upon him to repent.[151] In this instance, God repents as he stands ready to back away from the impending destruction of the people due to Moses' prayer.[152] The important link for open theism is repentance and relationship. God has chosen to enter into a genuine relationship, which includes his repentance.[153] Brümmer says that confession is a form of petitionary prayer. He writes "expressing our change of heart," which "enables God's forgiveness to restore our fellowship with him. The believer will also claim that, since divine forgiveness, unlike human forgiveness, blots out my sins, knowing that I am forgiven by God restores my life to meaningfulness."[154] Similar to Brümmer, Fretheim argues that prayer is the bond, which holds God's presence and forgiveness together.[155] Thus, prayers of confession offer the needed restoration in fellowship between God and his creatures.

For open theism, the divine-human interchange of confession has three characteristics. The first is that the love of God is perfect, and there is never any doubt that he will withhold forgiveness to those who are truly penitent.[156] Rice adds to this first claim by emphasizing that God's response is characterized by patience, hope, love, and grace.[157] Second, God knows what has been done, which means one is unable to hide it.[158] Similarly, Rice asserts that an important factor for forgiveness is that the Christian recognize that a wrong has been done.[159] Thus, in order for Christians to be reconciled with God, they must acknowledge the sin committed. And third, only God can remove sin as far as the east is from the west (Ps 103:12), which means that a Christian's understanding that sin has been forgiven is grounded in the belief that God accepts her, thus it would "be meaningless for [her] not to accept [herself]."[160] For the open theist, God forgives the Christian when he freely confesses and repents from sin. Also, the future is not blocked so as to remove the ability of humans to confess their sin and receive forgiveness. This demonstrates that the future is open.[161]

---

151. Knight, *Theology as Narration*, 187.
152. Fretheim, "The Repentance of God," 54.
153. Ibid., 59.
154. Brümmer, *What Are We Doing When We Pray?*, 104.
155. Fretheim, *Exodus*, 303.
156. Brümmer, *What Are We Doing When We Pray?*, 101.
157. Rice, "The Final Form of Love," 214.
158. Brümmer, *What Are We Doing When We Pray?*, 102.
159. Rice, "The Final Form of Love," 213.
160. Brümmer, *What Are We Doing When We Pray?*, 104.
161. Fretheim, "The Repentance of God," 65.

Open theism and middle knowledge both affirm that the one petitioning for forgiveness from sin must be libertarianly free. God cannot hold people accountable for sin that they had no choice to refrain from. Also, the authenticity of confession is grounded in the humans' response to confess or refrain from confessing. The difference between middle knowledge and open theism on this account is that open theism does not affirm that God knows people's sin until it is committed, which is a problem because it unnecessarily limits the sovereignty of God so that a person can remain libertarianly free with respect to sin and confession.[162] Also, middle knowledge is preferred because God knew prior to creation what sin a person would commit in addition to the would-be response of confession in light of sin. Thus, middle knowledge upholds the authenticity of confession through libertarian freedom while also maintaining God's complete sovereignty.

Conclusion

This book defines petitionary prayer as a genuine human behavior whereby the creature freely goes to its sovereign Creator and simply asks (chapter 2). Thus far, it might appear that open theism would have the easiest time affirming this definition because (1) of the two-way contingency and spiritual say-so of the believer, and (2) there is a strong emphasis on petitionary prayer within open theism. For example, in the case of Boyd and 2 Kgs 20, petitionary prayer causes him to rethink his theory of providence and adopt open theism. However, a key deficiency of an open theist's view is that it fails to differentiate libertarian freedom from compatibilist freedom with respect to petitionary prayer. Briefly, while writing on petitionary prayer, Basinger argues that what distinguishes open theism from compatibilism is that open theism does not limit human freedom.[163] However, Basinger also asserts that the open view maintains "that God does retain the right to intervene unilaterally in earthly affairs. That is, we believe that freedom of choice is a gift granted to us by God and thus that God retains the power and moral prerogative to inhibit occasionally our ability to make voluntary choices to keep things on track."[164] One example of how God keeps "things on track" is through prayer. Another way things are kept on track is through God's right to "retain the power" over the human's voluntary choice to pray. This lack of consistency within the openness position questions the motivating force to

---

162. A middle knowledge account of confession and repentance occurs in the following chapter.
163. Basinger, "Practical Implications," 159.
164. Basinger, "Practical Implications," 159.

pray as it would appear that God's intended desire prevails regardless of the human desire to pray.

Also a key deficiency concerning petitionary prayer for open theists is the view that the Trinity self-emptied itself of spiritual say-so in order to give it to humans. This was necessary in order for communication between God and humans to take place as they co-create the future together. The intent is to uphold the relationship God shares with his creatures; however, the cost is great as the Trinity must divest of some of its nature in order to maintain the relationship. Thus, as a result of prayer one could question God's Trinitarian equality as open theism is not entirely clear as to which member of the Trinity divests of their say-so, or if it comes from each member of the Trinity. One might also question the motivation to pray to a God that is possibly not Trinitarian in nature. In either case, the nature of God changes, which conflicts with the doctrine of immutability. It also questions the doctrine of the priesthood of the believer, which is another deficiency discussed next.

Another perceived weakness is that God forfeits his sovereignty in order to bring about the freedom necessary in petitionary prayer. However, based on the discussion above, this is not the case. The priesthood of the believer makes it possible for the Christian to go before God and without a mediator offer petitionary prayers to God. In that case, the sovereignty of God should not have to be limited even if it is self-limiting by God in order to make petitionary prayer a free response by the human being. Thus, the deficiency is that petitionary prayer is not compatible with either the priesthood of the believer or the sovereignty of God or both. If the open theist affirms the priesthood of the believer, then God does not need to self-limit himself in order to give his spiritual say-so (sovereignty) to the believer so that God may receive prayer. Christ's work as High Priest should have secured the means for believers to pray. If open theism contends that God had to give up some of his sovereignty (spiritual say-so) in order for Christians to influence how things transpire in the world through prayer, then open theism has unnecessarily limited Christ's work as a mediational high priest. In other words, the priesthood of the believer provides the Christian access to God though prayer, without the need for God to divest of any of his sovereignty.

In the end, open theism does not accomplish its goal. Understanding and articulating the genuine relationship that the creature shares with its Creator is a worthy pursuit. However, in so doing, open theists have for example emphasized the divine-human relationship in prayer at the cost of the doctrines of the Trinity and the Priesthood of the Believer. At a minimum, the result is a diminished motivation to pray as the Christian must question whether (or not) Jesus' mediation on behalf of the prayer offered is efficacious. In addition, it is important to question the motivation in praying to a God that potentially is not equal in essence. One might also question the wisdom in praying to a God that self-limits his essence in order to receive prayer. This chapter continues to support the thesis of this book that middle knowledge makes the best sense of petitionary prayer as it reveals the inherent weaknesses of emphasizing the influence of the human at the cost of the divine in the divine-human interaction.

5

Middle Knowledge and Petitionary Prayer

Introduction

IN THIS CHAPTER, I will examine petitionary prayer as understood by middle knowledge. I believe that middle knowledge is the most suitable answer to the theological question as to how God can remain sovereign while humans freely offer prayers of petition to God. John David Laing proposes that the doctrine of middle knowledge asserts that God "has knowledge not only of metaphysically necessary states of affairs via natural knowledge, and of what he intends to do via free knowledge, but also of what free creatures would do if they were created."[1] As a result, middle knowledge argues that God's sovereignty is such that it includes both his omniscience and libertarian human freedom in prayer. Middle knowledge is the only theological system that desires to make such a claim.[2] The key nuance between compatibilism and middle knowledge rests in compatibilism's rejection of libertarian freedom in prayer. The key difference between open theism and middle knowledge is in the affirmation of God's complete sovereignty and foreknowledge by middle knowledge. This question has also been extended to compatibilism, hard determinism, and open theism in earlier chapters (3–4), which included an examination of the strengths and deficiencies of each theory of providence. In this chapter, attention is given to the sovereignty of God and its function within petitionary prayer for middle knowledge. Also, I will provide a brief discussion as to why middle knowledge is preferred over compatibilism. Then, consideration is given to the various theological implications that middle knowledge has upon petitionary prayer. This will include both systematic and pastoral theology.

---

1. Laing, "The Compatibility of Calvinism and Middle Knowledge," 457.
2. Hasker, "Response to Thomas Flint," 118.

Sovereignty, Petitionary Prayer, Middle Knowledge

As defined in chapter 1, God's sovereignty through his middle knowledge includes both (1) God's omniscience and (2) libertarian freedom. Each of these components of middle knowledge speak directly to one's relationship with God through petitionary prayer. Middle knowledge asserts that God knows exactly what he will be petitioned for in prayer. Also, the people praying are freely offering their petitions before God. This includes the human's ability to refrain from praying in the same circumstance. In what follows, God's omniscience and libertarian freedom will be discussed as it relates to petitionary prayer.

Omniscience

The sovereignty of God is an essential component of middle knowledge. Traditionally, other theological words describe God's sovereignty, such as: the decree of God, foreknowledge, omnipotence, omniscience, and providence. These terms describe to some degree or another that God is in control and has perfect knowledge concerning all matters because he is the Creator. The middle knowledge position argues that God makes use of creaturely (libertarian) freedom to bring about his plan.[3] This means that middle knowledge includes human freedom within the scope and under the authority of God's sovereignty because God's middle knowledge includes not only that a human could pray, but also what that human would in fact pray if they were created and placed in a certain circumstance. Furthermore, God's middle knowledge is prior to God's decree to create a world.[4]

---

3. MacGregor, *Luis de Molina*, 118.

4. William Lane Craig addresses the key objection that those attempting to dismiss middle knowledge give: the grounding objection (Craig, "Middle Knowledge, Truth-Makers, and the Grounding Objection," 337–38). Scott Davison wrote an article in response to Craig's critique of the grounding objection. Davison admits he is partaking in "friendly fire" as a fellow Molinist and is writing "on behalf of the grounding objector" (Davison, "Craig on the Grounding Objection to Middle Knowledge," 367). Davison sees the real issue as this: "Logically prior to creation, what explains why a given true counterfactual of creaturely freedom is true, and what explains why a given false counterfactual of creaturely freedom is false?" (Davison, "Craig on the Grounding Objection to Middle Knowledge," 367). In the end, the answer might be that no answer exists and there is "no explanation at all for these truths (Davison, "Craig on the Grounding Objection to Middle Knowledge," 368). Furthermore, he writes, "Craig's appeal to counterfactuals confirms the suspicion that Molinists must simply accept the truth of counterfactuals of creaturely freedom logically prior to creation as a brute, unexplained fact" (Davison, "Craig on the Grounding Objection to Middle Knowledge," 368).

If the content of God's middle knowledge were logically posterior to God's decree to create a world, then it would not be possible under God's sovereignty for humans to be libertarianly free in prayer, because once a world is actualized (i.e. free knowledge), the content of God's knowledge concerning what humans would pray for is actualized.[5] Herman Hoeksema, for example, offers a critique of middle knowledge in his *Reformed Dogmatics*.[6] However, he gets middle knowledge wrong in that he locates the content of God's knowledge in the logical moment after creation and before God's free knowledge.[7] He illustrates this with God's reaction to the fall of Adam within the framework of middle knowledge, which left God to confront the contingent possibility that Adam would fall after Adam was created. Thus, God stands ready to act, leaving God's middle knowledge to a kind of magical foresight.[8] Similarly, Charles Hodge argues that for God, human free acts remain uncertain until their occurrence.[9] Thus, Hoeksema and Hodge reject middle knowledge because it denies God's omniscience and therefore God's sovereignty. This critique from Hoeksema and Hodge is valid; however, it is more appropriately describing open theism than middle knowledge, because open theism rejects that God has middle knowledge.[10] If you place the content of God's knowledge after the creation event, one is essentially left with open theism whereby God's knowledge is dependent upon his reaction to human free acts.[11] Instead,

---

5. MacGregor, *Luis de Molina*, 90.
6. Hoeksema, *Reformed Dogmatics*, 1:126–31.
7. Ibid., 1:127.
8. Ibid., 1:128.
9. Hodge, *Systematic Theology*, 1:399–400.

10. Bruce Ware sought to conflate Molinism and open theism into one view based upon Boyd's neo-Molinism (Ware, "Robots, Royalty and Relationships?," 192–203). Boyd defines neo-Molinism as, "God knows what agents might do insofar as agents possess libertarian freedom. And God knows what agents would do insofar as they have received from God and through circumstances or acquired for themselves determinate characters. God knows both categories of counterfactuals as they pertain to every possible subject in every possible world throughout eternity (Boyd, *Satan and the Problem of Evil*, 425). For another perspective on possible words. See Leftow, "No Best World," 269–85.

11. Pinnock, "Open Theism," 242. Both middle knowledge and open theism affirm libertarian freedom, but the open theist has to limit God's sovereignty in order to uphold libertarian freedom (Sanders, *The God Who Risks*, 281). This is because open theism situates libertarian freedom after God's decree to create the world. Thus, God needs to observe and respond to an open future in which these libertarianly free humans are acting. However, when placed prior to the creation of the world, God can have perfect knowledge of what humans would do if he were to create them. In turn, God's sovereignty then includes his omniscience but also human freedom. This sets

middle knowledge argues that God's knowledge of what a creature would do is logically prior to his creating work. For example, Craig argues that middle knowledge is the intervening moment between God's natural knowledge and the creation event.[12] In addition to Craig, MacGregor argues that middle knowledge is rendered impossible if it is located logically posterior to the divine decree to create.[13] Thus, middle knowledge must be understood as logically prior to the creation event if God's omniscience is to be upheld.[14] Furthermore, as God's middle knowledge is prior to his decree to create a world, God has within his sovereignty the ability to know what a creature would do if that creature were instantiated in a certain circumstance.[15] As it relates to petitionary prayer, God knew if he instantiated someone in a given situation whether or not they would pray.[16] If in fact they would pray, God knew this. This does not mean that prayer in the actual world becomes flippant. Instead, it should reveal all the more the intimacy the human being shares with God. For example, God knows all the times that a person will pray throughout a lifetime. The believer does not know this. Instead, he comes to realize how much God knows concerning how much he prays as he prays.[17] This is to demonstrate a man's finitude, not God's. God does not have to wait until believers pray to realize they have prayed. God does not have to wait until the believer's life is over to realize how much he prayed throughout his life.

Consequently, as it relates to petitionary prayer, God's omniscience within the framework of middle knowledge argues that in God's natural knowledge, he knows what a creature *could* pray for were the creature instantiated in a certain circumstance. In God's middle knowledge, he knows what the same creature *would* pray for if the creature were instantiated in that circumstance. Craig posits that God has complete and perfect knowledge

---

middle knowledge apart theologically, because it not only says that God's sovereignty has room for his knowledge of what a creature could do but also would do in a certain circumstance.

12. Craig, "'No Other Name,'" 178. Terrance Tiessen, not a proponent of middle knowledge makes a similar point that middle knowledge should be located between God's natural knowledge and the creation event, "Why Calvinists Should Believe in Divine Middle Knowledge, Although They Reject Molinism," 354. Once a proponent of middle knowledge, Tiessen later rejects middle knowledge, and in 2009, he cites Helm as contributing to this change in his theology (Helm and Tiessen, "Does Calvinism Have Room For Middle Knowledge? A Conversation," 454).

13. MacGregor, *Luis de Molina*, 86.
14. Davison, "Craig on the Grounding Objection to Middle Knowledge," 365.
15. Craig, *The Only Wise God*, 130.
16. MacGregor, *A Molinist Anabaptist Systematic Theology*, 96.
17. Flint, "'A Death He Freely Accepted,'" 8.

regarding all circumstances in a human's life as God knew prior to the creation of the world not only what the creature could do but would do in any given circumstance.[18] Theologically, this is significant because those passages that detail God's perfect knowledge concerning a certain circumstance, coupled with libertarian human freedom, now both fall under God's sovereignty.[19] MacGregor adds that there is nothing wrong with expanding God's sovereignty; the problem arises when God's sovereignty is limited.[20]

Libertarian Freedom as Expressed through Love

Along with God's sovereignty, libertarian human love directed towards God is an essential component for middle knowledge and petitionary prayer. Eleonore Stump notes, "Judeo-Christian concepts of God commonly represent God as loving mankind and wanting to be loved by men in return."[21] Stump asserts that biblically this loving relationship is given as a type represented by various images. For example, she uses the illustration of a loving relationship between a husband and wife, a father and child, or a relationship between true friends.[22] Brümmer says something similar as he uses love as his illustration that the human possesses libertarian freedom. Brümmer is arguing for a two-way contingency, and if the human is not libertarianly free in his response to God, then he questions whether or not he is really free.[23] Also, if God is not free in his response to human freedom, then Brümmer accuses God of being merely deterministic.[24] Clark Pinnock and Robert Brow add to Brümmer in that the one praying must be free in a libertarian sense in his prayers. Otherwise, God is participating in a uneven relationship.[25] There is a sense in which an uneven relationship is to be expected in any relationship with God. However, Pinnock and Brow are attempting to safeguard the divine-human relationship from the understanding that God is merely ruling in a deterministic way. The adherence to libertarian freedom demonstrates a key similarity between open theism

---

18. Craig, *The Only Wise God*, 130–31.

19. For examples where God (1) knows what one will pray when placed in a given situation and (2) the individual is freely beseeching upon the lord, see, 1 Sam 23:1–14; Jonah, Luke 1:5–17.

20. MacGregor, *Luis de Molina*, 118.

21. Stump, "Petitionary Prayer," 86.

22. Ibid.

23. See chapter 4 for a review of Brümmer's two-way contingency.

24. Brümmer, *What Are We Doing When We Pray?*, 43–44.

25. Pinnock and Brow, *Unbounded Love*, 142–43.

and middle knowledge.[26] However, what differentiates middle knowledge is its adherence to God's omniscience, particularly of the future, in addition to libertarian human freedom. In addition, the previous chapter noted that a key deficiency for the relational two-way contingency of open theism was God's necessary self-limitation of his essence in order to provide the freedom for the human to respond to God.

The book of Deuteronomy provides a theological foundation for such love, which demonstrates God's sovereignty along with libertarian human freedom at work in the divine-human relationship.[27] Patrick Miller argues that the term *love* used to define the divine-human relationship is essentially the result of Deuteronomic theology.[28] Similarly, Eugene Merrill argues that Deuteronomy outlines what God expects within his covenant relationship.[29] Starting in Deut 4, God through Moses calls the Israelites to be obedient to the laws and statutes that they have heard. This call culminates in the giving of the Ten Commandments (Deut 5). Deuteronomy 4:1, 5:1, and 6:4 all share in the same admonition of, "Hear, O Israel," or "Obey, O Israel."[30] In Deut 4:1 and 5:1, the admonition is in reference to the Ten Commandments. Deuteronomy 6:4 still references the law and statutes; however, the emphasis is now on a person's love for God, thus producing an obedience to the law and statutes.[31] Miller notes, "The oneness of the Lord your God is matched by the oneness and totality of your devotion."[32] In other words, obedience means loving God, so that, if humans were to love God with all their heart, soul, and might, they would in turn be fulfilling the charge of obedience to the Lord.[33]

This has Christological implications as well.[34] In Matt 22:34–40, Jesus argues for the greatest commandment and summarizes all the law and prophets with the directive of loving God, which reaffirms Deut 6:4–6.[35] Jesus' second commandment, which was like the first, to "love your neighbor

---

26. See also the imagery of a dynamic relationship between true friends in chapter 4 as it is very similar to middle knowledge. Both affirm libertarian freedom, the difference is that for middle knowledge, God perceives this freedom prior to the creation event.

27. Miller, *Deuteronomy*, 98.

28. Ibid., 101.

29. Merrill, *Deuteronomy*, 162.

30. Miller, *Deuteronomy*, 66.

31. Work, *Deuteronomy*, 95.

32. Miller, *Deuteronomy*, 103.

33. Merrill, *Deuteronomy*, 163.

34. Work, *Deuteronomy*, 94.

35. Merrill, *Deuteronomy*, 164.

as yourself" (Matt 22:39), is also a reaffirmation of Deut 10:19.[36] Deuteronomy 10:12–18 talks about the importance of loving God. Deuteronomy 10:19 goes on to admonish the Israelites to "love your neighbor": "*Love the sojourner*, therefore, for you were sojourners in the land of Egypt" (Deut 10:19, emphasis mine).[37] These verses demonstrate that love of God and neighbor still remains true as it did in Deut 6:4–8. Deuteronomy 11:18–21 restates 6:4–8. This restatement emphasizes human responsibility: if they love God and teach these things to their children, their lives may be enhanced, and they will have longevity of life (Deut 11:21).[38] Deuteronomy 11:26–28 further emphasizes human responsibility by way of a blessing and a curse.[39] This means that a blessing awaits those who obey the command to love God and neighbor, and a curse is for those who do not obey the same command. That this blessing and curse is wrapped around one's love for God and neighbor is most clearly evidenced in Deut 11:26–28.[40]

Furthermore, Paul in Galatians urges the church to live out their freedom as an expression of love and not as an opportunity for the flesh (Gal 5:13–15). James Dunn notes that love and not the law serves as the key corollary to grace and faith. In addition, Douglas Moo argues that Christians are to freely enslave themselves to love, which then fulfills the law.[41] Both Dunn and Moo add to the discussion above, concerning Deuteronomy's emphasis on loving God and one's neighbor.[42] Rooted in Paul's words is the call to love freely. In fact, God through Jesus Christ, is the source of this freedom (1 John 4:19).[43]

Love is an essential element to middle knowledge because it affirms that God's sovereignty includes both his omniscience *and* libertarian human freedom. For the former, the call to love God and others is a powerful example of God's sovereignty and omniscience as the command to love comes from a sovereign Lord (Deut 4:1, 29–31, 39–40).[44] God sovereignly gave the Ten Commandments (Deut 4:13–14; 5:4–6). Also, he sovereignly chose the people of Israel that they might love him (Deut 7:6–8; 9:6–7; 10:15). Matthew 22:34–40 displays the sovereignty of God as Christ com-

---

36. Ibid., 204.
37. Brueggemann, *Deuteronomy*, 131.
38. Merrill, *Deuteronomy*, 211–12.
39. Miller, *Deuteronomy*, 127.
40. Merrill, *Deuteronomy*, 213–14.
41. Moo, *Galatians*, 45.
42. Dunn, *The Epistle to the Galatians*, 288. See also, Moo, *Galatians*, 345–8.
43. Marshall, *The Epistles of John*, 225.
44. Miller, *Deuteronomy*, 103.

mands people to love God and neighbor. Thus, this summary of the law and prophets down to the one word, *love*, directed towards God and neighbor is consistent throughout the Bible.

For the latter, libertarian freedom also plays an imperative role in that humans are called to love God with all their capacity (Deut 4:29–31; 5:6–22; 6:4–9; 11:26–28; 30:11–20).[45] Dunn notes that freedom is a human responsibility and dangerous commodity.[46] Open theism similarly warns that libertarian freedom makes it possible for the human to work with or against God's will.[47] Merrill also argues that Deut 6:4, which is a prayer of obedience, encompasses the idea that if people hear God, then they will manifest what they have heard through obedience to his command.[48] Similarly, Miller notes that one's love for the Lord is made visible through obedience to the law.[49] Thus, God holds people responsible for their actions by bestowing a curse or blessing, which they are responsible for (Deut 11:26–28).[50] Merrill argues that God demands unqualified obedience, which supports the claim that humans are free in a libertarian sense as God can only hold humans accountable if they are libertarianly free in their actions.[51] How could God bless or curse humans based on an action (love) they never had a chance to refrain from? Thus, humans respond freely to the proposition to love God and neighbor. Matthew further emphasizes Jesus and the greatest commandment, and Paul affirms this teaching of the Lord in Galatians as he appeals to the behavior of Christians in light of their freedom. For middle knowledge, the decision to love God includes "a freedom of choice that is self-determined and not caused by events outside the control of the agent."[52] Therefore, the choice to love God also includes the possibility that the agent could have chosen otherwise. In addition, God knew that if he were to instantiate a human in a particular situation whether (or not) the human would respond in love, and because he knew this prior to his decision to create a world, God's sovereignty includes both his omniscience and libertarian human freedom. Conversely, for open theism, if God's knowledge of how a human would respond in a particular situation were posterior to the human acting, then God's sovereignty is limited in such a way that he would have

---

45. Ibid., 102–3.
46. Dunn, *The Epistle to the Galatians*, 287.
47. Pinnock, *Most Moved Mover*, 4.
48. Merrill, *Deuteronomy*, 162.
49. Miller, *Deuteronomy*, 102.
50. Ibid., 127.
51. Merrill, *Deuteronomy*, 164.
52. Laing, "The Compatibility of Calvinism and Middle Knowledge," 455.

to wait and observe how the human will act in order to execute a blessing or curse.[53] In other words, the human's libertarian freedom to love is upheld at the unnecessary cost of God's sovereignty. One might also argue that in order to maintain God's sovereignty for the compatibilist, he would have to assure the outcome of either a blessing or curse, which would be dependent upon God's will as he causally determines events outside the control of the agent. For example, if the human agent chooses to love God, the human agent did not have the ability to refrain from loving God. Instead, love understood by middle knowledge is preferred as it is the only theory of providence that can affirm that God's sovereignty includes both his omniscience *and* libertarian human freedom. In light of petitionary prayer, this assures that humanity's communication with God is a loving dialogue as petitions are freely offered to God while God remains sovereign throughout the entire exchange.

Compatibilism or Middle Knowledge?

It might seem that middle knowledge is similar to compatibilism because they both affirm the sovereignty of God and human freedom. Using Jonathan Edwards's theology of prayer, Glenn Kreider provides a helpful illustration for the close parallel between compatibilism and middle knowledge. He observes that for Edwards,

> God's knowledge of human decisions stands prior to the exercise of the human will, that God's knowledge extends to the choices that creatures have not yet made. God's knowledge extends not only to the entire realm of possible choices humans might make, but even extends to the actual choices they will make. God's knowledge of the past, present, and future is comprehensive.[54]

The idea that God's knowledge stands prior to the actual execution of the human action is similar to middle knowledge in that God knows what a human would do prior to the creation of the world. In addition, that God's knowledge includes not only the realm of possible choices that people might make but even the choices they will make is similar to middle knowledge in that God knows in his natural knowledge what humans could do as well as would do (middle knowledge) prior to the creation of the world. Thus, one that subscribes to middle knowledge could interpret from Kreider that God's knowledge of human prayer and his ability to answer prayer took place in his middle knowledge while at

53. Hasker, "Providence and Evil: Three Theories," 95.
54. Kreider, "Jonathan Edwards's Theology of Prayer," 442.

the same time interpreting that an individual with libertarian freedom offered those prayers. In addition, Paul Helm describes that the advantage of compatibilism is that humans are not constrained or compelled in their actions, and that their actions flow from their wants, desires, and preferences.[55] Similar to Helm, Terrance Tiessen asserts that a key characteristic for compatibilism is the belief that human actions have not been coerced by anything outside of the human, thus maintaining that the actor does them voluntarily.[56] Kreider, Helm, and Tiessen all demonstrate that compatibilism has a strong semblance with middle knowledge.

In 2004, Laing wrote an article which sought to determine the compatibility of Calvinism and middle knowledge. In the end for Laing, this attempt must be rejected as "an ultimately untenable position."[57] The real problem concerning the compatibility between Calvinism and middle knowledge is that the truth of the counterfactual of creaturely freedom "is in no way dependent upon the will of God" due to libertarian freedom.[58] Affirming such a statement is difficult for the compatibilist.[59]

---

55. Helm, *The Providence of God,* 67. When Helm uses "no-risk," that is in direct response to open theism and its "risky" view of divine providence.

56. Tiessen, *Providence and Prayer,* 365.

57. Laing, "The Compatibility of Calvinism and Middle Knowledge," 457. Thomas Flint, a proponent of middle knowledge defended theological compatibilism in 1991; however, that compatibilism includes libertarian freedom is due to Flint's employment of the term *compatibilism* in the philosophical sense. See "In Defense of Theological Compatibilism," *Faith and Philosophy* 8 (1991): 242.

58. Laing, "The Compatibility of Calvinism and Middle Knowledge," 463.

59. Laing's article joins a larger discussion in the early part of the new millennium, which seeks the viability of merging middle knowledge with Calvinism. For discussion of this merging, see Tiessen, *Providence and Prayer*; Bruce A. Ware, "Robots, Royalty and Relationships?, 192–203. Tiessen wrote an article in 2007, which poses the possibilities that Calvinists can and should employ middle knowledge theologically (Tiessen, "Why Calvinists Should Believe in Divine Middle Knowledge," 345–66). At the heart of Tiessen's argument is that human freedom should be understood compatibilistically and not in a libertarian sense. To accomplish this, Tiessen distances middle knowledge from Molinism. In 2009, Paul Helm and Tiessen wrote an article together in which Helm offers his rejoinder to Tiessen. At the conclusion of this article, Tiessen surprisingly rejects his earlier claims. He writes, "Clearly, Professor Helm's critique has been helpful to me. It has led me finally to abandon the attempt to incorporate divine middle knowledge into my Calvinist understanding of Gods eternal purposing of the history of the universe, in all its detail" (Helm and Tiessen, "Does Calvinism Have Room For Middle Knowledge?" 437–54). This marks a key transition for middle knowledge since Tiessen was a formidable contributor to the contemporary middle knowledge discussion. In 2006, Travis J. Campbell wrote an article where he strongly criticizes middle knowledge to the extent that it might be an over-simplification (Campbell, "Middle Knowledge," 1–22). He questions the ability of one to maintain their Christianity and still subscribe to middle knowledge. He writes, "More importantly, middle knowledge

The question is, why not argue for compatibilism instead of middle knowledge when trying to understand petitionary prayer? This book argues the rejection of libertarian freedom from compatibilism presents the most serious problem. Libertarian freedom only works within the context of middle knowledge because this theory of providence also argues for God's complete knowledge of the future, something the open theist is unable to do. Tiessen defines libertarian freedom as having the choice "to have done something other than one actually did in exactly the same circumstances. Everything else being equal, one has the ability to choose at least two courses of action."[60] In middle knowledge, God knows what a human would libertarianly freely do in a given circumstance prior to creation. This knowledge does not take place after the creation of the world because then God would merely be responding to humanity and its actions, which minimizes the sovereignty of God.[61] In addition, if God is going to uphold his sovereignty over libertarian freedom, then God becomes so controlling that the human does not have the ability to choose to do otherwise, leaving God responsible for whatever the action is.[62] Instead, libertarian freedom must be understood in God's middle knowledge. In the case of petitionary prayer, the human is freely acting on the motivation to pray in that given circumstance; nothing is coercing him to pray. Thomas Oden asserts that it is a misjudgment to view God as routinely coercing free wills.[63] However, God perfectly knew that he would pray once before the world began and then again in the actual moment the prayer occurs in creation.[64]

The freedom of the human being in the actual world is compatibilistic as God is sovereign in his knowledge of the prayer to be offered, and the human is free in his actions. The freedom whereby God knew, in his middle knowledge, that the human being would pray before the world began is libertarian freedom. This is due to the possibility that the human being could have chosen not to pray instead. In this case, God is sovereign as he knows perfectly what the human would do, and the human is libertarianly free as he could pray or not pray. Assuming for example that the human being chose

---

seems to compromise the very nature of the God described in the Bible. Therefore, not only a consistent Calvinist, but a consistent Christian must reject the doctrine of middle knowledge" (Campbell, "Middle Knowledge: A Reformed Critique," 22).

60. Tiessen, *Providence and Prayer*, 367.
61. Hoeksema, *Reformed Dogmatics*, 1:129.
62. Brümmer, *What Are We Doing When We Pray?*, 43–44.
63. Oden, *Classical Christianity*, 163–64.
64. MacGregor, "Hubmaier's Concord of Predestination with Free Will," 283–86, accessed October 9, 2015, http://www.directionjournal.org/35/2/hubmaiers-concord-of-predestination-with.html.

to pray and assuming that God chose to create that world in which he knew that the human would pray, then in creation, God's sovereign plan determined that he *will* pray. In other words, God's choice to actualize the world where the human will pray ensures that he will pray. However, the desires which determine that the human will pray does not come from somewhere in the chain of causation, which can be traced back to God. Middle knowledge helps us understand petitionary prayer as we have the confidence that God knew prior to the creation of the world that we would pray, thus we are praying to a God that governs the world with meticulous sovereignty. Also important is that the person take advantage of the circumstance and pray when faced with the proposition to refrain from praying because the person's choice to pray is a real decision that God has known for all eternity, yet now is the moment for him or her to carry out the prayer.

While compatibilism and middle knowledge share similarities in terms of God's sovereignty, middle knowledge is preferred as it also argues for human freedom in prayer whereby nothing is causing the person to pray. A further exposition of middle knowledge as it relates to various areas of theology is discussed below.

Middle Knowledge, Petitionary Prayer, and Theology

A thorough review of the theological evidence of middle knowledge will include a discussion concerning the logical moments of God's knowledge and how they affect petitionary prayer. In addition, discussion will include the manner in which petitionary prayer is meant to change the person praying. Also, for middle knowledge, petitionary prayer focuses on a divine-human friendship. However, attention will first be given to the importance of humility in prayer.

Middle Knowledge, Humility, and Petitionary Prayer

God uses Christians as instruments to carry out his plans through petitionary prayer.[65] God accomplishes this cooperation through libertarian free creatures. MacGregor notes that God gives humans the ability to act causally on their own in the fulfillment of his plans.[66] For middle knowledge, this is not meant to foster a prideful human attitude in the unfolding of God's

---

65. Stump, "Petititonary Prayer," 90.
66. MacGregor, *Luis de Molina*, 199.

plan in the world.[67] Instead, due to people's continual dependence on God, he has given them the privilege to participate based upon his sovereignty.[68] By petitioning God, people with libertarian freedom demonstrate that they are not capable to fulfill the request on their own. In addition, as Christians pray for one another, it is yet another sign of humility as they acknowledge not only the need for help from God, but from other Christians as well. Conversely, those unwilling to petition God or another Christian exhibit pride and self-assurance. Paul, the ecclesia, and Jehoshaphat will provide helpful illustrations of the humility necessary for petitionary prayer.[69]

One example of humility in petitionary prayer comes from those that offer prayer on behalf of others. Murray calls this "other-directed prayer."[70] Using Paul in Colossians and 2 Corinthians as an example, he notes, "We find him not only giving explicit teaching about the efficacy of corporate prayer, but also requesting the prayers of his audience."[71] Colossians 4:3 states, "At the same time, pray also for us, that God may open to us a door for the word, to declare the mystery of Christ, on account of which I am in prison," and 2 Cor 1:11 asserts, "You also must help us by prayer, so that many will give thanks on our behalf for the blessing granted us through the prayers of many." Murray explains that the implication is that the "more people petitioning for a particular outcome makes it more likely that it will be granted."[72] This demonstrates humility as Paul is not isolated but rather dependent upon the church for prayer. The model that Paul exhibits is that one should humbly be dependent upon another in prayer. Also, Paul and all those involved are dependent upon God. In other words, Paul is not looking to the Church as the one to petition, rather collectively the church is petitioning God. Theologically, it would appear that as many humble themselves before God in prayer and with unity petition him, it is more likely that he will grant the petition. Similar to Murray, MacGregor identifies

---

67. Petitionary prayer protects the one praying from becoming prideful or spoiled. Murray writes, "Praying helps safeguard against spoiling in that the petitioner is forced to acknowledge her need, and further acknowledge a dependence on God for fulfillment of that need" (Murray, "Does God Respond to Petitionary Prayer?", 248). See also Stump, "Petitionary Prayer," 143; Brümmer, *What Are We Doing When We Pray?* 47. In response to Murray, Stump, and Brümmer, see Collins, "Prayer and Open Theism," in *God in an Open Universe*, 170.

68. MacGregor, *Luis de Molina*, 199.

69. Murray, "Does God Respond to Petitionary Prayer?" 242–67. For more on this corporate aspect of prayer, see Murray and Meyers, "Ask and it Will Be Given You," 325–30.

70. Murray, "Does God Respond to Petitionary Prayer?" 246.

71. Ibid., 250.

72. Ibid.

petitionary prayer as a kind of social action whereby Christians enter into a self-sacrificial service toward other human beings.[73]

Another example of humility in petitionary prayer is illustrated through the ecclesia. The Bible describes the church as a physical body, as the church is made up of many members with Christ as the head (1 Cor 12:12–31). This diversity of members is called to be united without division (1 Cor 12:24–26). Additionally, if one member suffers, all suffer together; if one member is honored, all rejoice together. Built into the body of Christ is the necessity that each become dependent on the other. For Murray, petitionary prayer follows this same logic. As Christians pray for one another, it demonstrates the kind of interdependence God has designed through prayer as the people praying are dependent upon God.[74] In addition, as people participate in other-directed prayer, this illustrates the church's dependency upon one another as they are dependent upon God. Collins argues for a co-creator model of prayer, which enlists prayer as a way that a person can contribute to the wellbeing of another.[75] Similarly, Pinnock and Brow assert that when a person genuinely loves others, this will naturally lead the person to pray for them.[76] This demonstrates a similarity between open theism and middle knowledge as they both affirm that humans with libertarian freedom offer their prayers to God on behalf of others. However, open theism differs with regard to the nature of change as it relates to petitionary prayer. The open theist stresses that God's mind and intentions are altered due to petitionary prayer. In middle knowledge, the focus is on one's dependency upon God to meet the needs of the community.[77]

In addition to unity, another result from other-directed prayer is that the church becomes aware of the needs of the people and from there is able to meet those needs. Murray notes that when the church is confronted with another's petitionary prayer, the church is "moved not only to intercede for them but to provide for them themselves."[78] Similar to Murray, Graham Redding asserts that prayer is an ecclesiastical event rather than a mere private one.[79] In addition to Murray and Redding, open theism also asserts that prayer for one another is an important way in which the mission of God

---

73. MacGregor, *A Molinist Anabaptist Systematic Theology*, 285.

74. Murray, "Does God Respond to Petitionary Prayer?" 251.

75. Collins, "Prayer and Open Theism," 181. See chapter 4 for more on the co-creator model.

76. Pinnock and Brow, *Unbounded Love*, 148–49.

77. Murray, "Does God Respond to Petitionary Prayer?" 251.

78. Murray, "Does God Respond to Petitionary Prayer?" 251. See also Buttrick, *Prayer*.

79. Redding, *Prayer and the Priesthood of Christ in the Reformed Tradition*, 294.

is furthered.[80] Also, Charles Hodge asserts that prayer must be a social act of worship and fellowship in the church.[81] One could then ask, why pray? Instead, just ask the church, and it will meet your needs. However, by asking people to pray, a person is assuming that God can use them to answer the prayer. Similarly, God could also be using the one praying on their behalf to answer the prayer as well. For example, a doctor is able to pray for the healing of his patient, and God can heal this patient in a miraculous way, or God could use the doctor himself to bring about the healing. Murray concludes, "Thus, praying for one another develops a pathos among the members of the community that again disposes them towards interdependence and away from independent self-reliance."[82]

Murray adheres to middle knowledge and interprets such other-directive prayers as yet another way that God sovereignly provides for his children. In the case of praying for another, Murray assumes that if God had "perfect middle knowledge," that he would then know that the human being in need would *not* pray for the necessary provision created in that particular circumstance.[83] However, God would also know that in the same circumstance, others would pray for their fellow Christian so that his needs would be met. Thus, God in his goodness, by the body of Christ, meets the needs of the one that would not pray. For open theism, the needs of the Christian can still be met, however God's sovereignty would not include what the needs are until the church prayed since the human chose not to pray for the needed provision. An open theist might argue that God's present knowledge affords him that information since the moment the need is actualized God would have perfect knowledge of that need. However, if God's desire were to provide in response to prayer, then God would have to wait until a prayer was offered. While the result is beneficial to the Christian because his needs are met, theologically God does not retain his meticulous sovereignty as to who will pray. One might argue that this is unnecessary as middle knowledge maintains that God perfectly knew what the individual would need before the world began. In the same fashion, God knew who would and would not petition him for the provision needed. Furthermore, the one that refrained from petitioning and the church's prayers were both actions resulting from libertarian freedom. In compatibilism, the needs of the Christian are met, and the factors involved, such as the non-praying Christian and the praying church, were both intended in God's will and plan

80. Fretheim, "Prayer in the Old Testament," 62.
81. Hodge, *Systematic Theology*, 3:706.
82. Murray, "Does God Respond to Petitionary Prayer?" 252.
83. Ibid., 254.

because they were causally determined by events outside of their control. Once again the needs of the Christian are met; however, God has casually determined the Christian's lack of praying in addition to the prayers of the church. One could argue that the one which refrained from praying should do more of the same because his desired needs were met. Also, God causally determined for one of his children to not petition him. Furthermore, one could argue that even though the people of the church prayed, they could not have chosen otherwise. This questions the motivation to hold the church as a positive example of how to love one another as they could not have done otherwise. Instead, middle knowledge is preferred over compatibilism as (1) the human being in need libertarianly freely *chose not* to pray, (2) the other member of the body of Christ libertarianly freely *chose to* pray, and (3) God has perfect knowledge concerning the circumstance and creates the world in which people's needs are met.

Christians have confidence in their prayers because of the biblical narrative, which portrays individuals altering God's original reactions to various circumstances.[84] For example, in 2 Chr 20:1–23, Jehoshaphat learns that the Moabites, Ammonites, and Meunites are going to come against Jehoshaphat for battle (2 Chr 20:1). Upon learning this he "was afraid and set his face to seek the Lord, and proclaimed a fast throughout all Judah. And Judah assembled to seek help from the Lord; from all the cities of Judah they came to seek the Lord" (2 Chr 20:3–4). Next, from vv. 5–12, Jehoshaphat offers a petitionary prayer to the Lord seeking protection proclaiming, "We do not know what to do, but our eyes are on you" (2 Chr 20:12). Then from vv. 13–17, the Lord offers comfort that their salvation will prevail, and they will not be harmed (2 Chr 20:17). Upon hearing this in response to his prayer, "Jehoshaphat bowed his head with his face to the ground, and all Judah and the inhabitants of Jerusalem fell down before the Lord, worshiping the Lord" (2 Chr 20:18). Earlier in this book, God proclaims the importance of being humble when offering prayer. God is concerned about and promises to hear a humble heart (2 Chr 7:14). Humility is an essential component to petitionary prayer, and Jehoshaphat is a helpful example. Humility cannot be forced upon humans so as to work against their will.

This insinuates that human beings are libertarianly free with respect to humility, because if God has coerced them to be humble or worked within their surroundings to bring about their humility, then God has achieved the humility and not the humans performing the action. As noted with Jehoshaphat, humility was a necessary condition in order for God to answer his prayer; however, God cannot proclaim that he is humble in heart

---

84. MacGregor, *A Molinist Anabaptist Systematic Theology*, 286.

if Jehoshaphat lacks the ability to choose otherwise. In this case, middle knowledge is more suitable to handle the genuine humility required in petitionary prayer, because God knew whether or not Jehoshaphat would act humbly before creation. This includes the possibility that he would not act humbly. He also knew whether or not Jehoshaphat would pray. Thus, the action from Jehoshaphat to act humbly was a libertarianly free action, which made his petitionary prayer efficacious in that God hears his prayer.

Coupled with the libertarian freedom in Jehoshaphat's prayer is that God is completely sovereign over the circumstance at hand. The biblical text proclaims that the "battle is not yours but God's" (2 Chr 20:15), and then God tells them what to do "tomorrow" (2 Chr 20:16–17), implying that God's knowledge is not such that he needs to wait until tomorrow to see what the humans will do and then respond. At this point open theism differs from middle knowledge because in open theism, God comes to know the future as it happens. Middle knowledge also differs from compatibilism in that God telling them what to do tomorrow does not mean that he is coercing the people to act so that they have no choice in the matter tomorrow. Instead, God knew in his middle knowledge how they would act prior to creation. The text states, "Tomorrow go down against them. Behold, they will come up by the ascent of Ziz. You will find them at the end of the valley, east of the wilderness of Jeruel. You will not need to fight in this battle. Stand firm, hold your position, and see the salvation of the Lord on your behalf, O Judah and Jerusalem" (2 Chr 20:16–17). What the biblical text does not say is that tomorrow they will go down, or that they will stand firm, or that they will hold their position. Instead, the Lord tells them what they should do. The Lord also tells them what the enemy will do, not because God has coerced them into such an action, but because God has sovereign knowledge over the circumstance and knows what they will freely do tomorrow. This knowledge is best understood by God's middle knowledge, as God knew what they would freely do tomorrow before the world was created. Unlike open theism, God does not have to wait until tomorrow to come to this knowledge. Instead, God's knowledge concerning tomorrow is quite detailed. Also, opposed to compatibilism, the individuals involved appear to have the kind of freedom that allows them to refrain from acting. Also, opposed to compatibilism, the individuals involved appear to have the kind of freedom that allows them to refrain from acting, which includes not going down, standing firm, or holding their position (2 Chr 20:16–17). Thus, in petitionary prayer, (1) God is sovereign, and (2) the human beings involved are free. In other words, humans change the world through prayer. For Murray and MacGregor, it becomes a Christian duty to cry out to God on behalf of our neighbors.

Logical Moments of God's Knowledge and Petitionary Prayer

The sovereignty of God must be maintained in order for middle knowledge to work in petitionary prayer. Preserving this right of God to control all things fuels middle knowledge. God's sovereignty includes not just his omniscience but libertarian human freedom—and prayer is no different.[85] Concerning prayer, middle knowledge argues that God does not force humans to pray or give them what to pray, thus relegating human prayer to an advanced robotic automation.[86] Instead, the interaction between the Creator and creature is genuine and relational. Similarly, as it relates to moral evils, MacGregor adds that God does not violate libertarian human freedom in the outworking of human actions.[87] In addition, open theism argues that due to God's desire to preserve his relationship with humanity, he does not override libertarian freedom.[88] Even compatibilism, which rejects libertarian freedom, acknowledges the impact such freedom would have upon God and the one praying.[89] For the one that employs middle knowledge to the theological genre of prayer, the end results are the revealed (in part) interworking of the relationship between Creator and creature—both prior to and posterior to the creation of the world.

One example of the relationship between God's logical moments and petitionary prayer in middle knowledge is found in Exod 32. It seems that middle knowledge provides the best interpretation of this text. The narrative begins with the people lacking patience due to the long absence of Moses on the mountain (v. 1). The people request from Aaron that gods be made so that they might go before them. Aaron obliges and takes their gold jewelry from the people and fashions a golden calf (vv. 2–6). While this is taking place at the base of the mountain, God speaks with Moses about their actions and the creation of this calf being worshiped. God tells Moses that he is going to bring about a great wrath so as to consume the Israelites (vv. 7–10). But Moses quickly requests on behalf of the people to relent from his wrath. He asks

---

85. Barry Bryant identifies individuals throughout Christian history who have dealt with the problem that the doctrine of free will creates for Theology Proper and particularly God's omniscience. He argues that Molina, Arminius, Plaifere, Goad, and Wesley have a shared feature of middle knowledge in their framework. Bryant, "Molina, Arminius, Plaifere, Goad, and Wesley on Human Free-Will, Divine Omniscience, and Middle Knowledge," 93–103.

86. Tiessen, "Can God be Responsive if the Future is Not Open?" 106.

87. MacGregor, *A Molinist Anabaptist Systematic Theology*, 116.

88. Basinger, "Middle Knowledge and Human Freedom," 331; Pinnock, "Open Theism," 239.

89. Feinberg, *No One Like Him*, 704–5.

God to remember the promise made to Abraham, Isaac, and Israel, which is to multiply their offspring as the stars of heaven. The narrative reveals that because Moses prays, God relents from his wrath (vv. 11–14). Middle knowledge contends that God's sovereignty is displayed because he had complete knowledge of the circumstances at hand. This is unlike open theism, which affirms that God comes to know about the creation of the golden calf only after it was created. Compatibilism interprets such acts in a way that Aaron and the people could not have chosen to act differently, thus assuring the action will take place. Instead, middle knowledge asserts that God knew before the world was created that if this circumstance were instantiated, then the people of Israel would ask Aaron to build them a god that they might worship. God also knew that Aaron would in fact build the golden calf.

Not only is God's sovereignty displayed through his omniscience, but it is also displayed in that the Israelites, Aaron, and Moses all act freely in a libertarian sense. God knew that if he were to instantiate Moses in this circumstance, then Moses would freely offer a petitionary prayer that God would relent of his wrath. In one way, this prayer is answered already prior to the creation of the world because God knew that Moses will pray this prayer. However, this does not make the communication between Moses and God contrived because once the world is created, the course of events known to God prior to the creation of the world begin to be realized. Once petitionary prayer has become a part of God's decree, it does not detract from the genuine agency or personal relationship the human shares with God. No longer is God's knowledge merely of those pre-instantiated possibilities; now they are in fact reality. Time is set in motion. God knew about this conversation prior to the creation of the world, and now it is time to have that conversation. Both Moses and God interact in a real way. Moses needs to freely pray so that the wrath of God will be averted; however, God knows with certainty how this will all transpire. Kirk MacGregor puts it this way: "Accommodating himself to our space-time limitations, God has graciously chosen to act with us in many cases (namely, those which would benefit us) according to his original reactions to feasible circumstances rather than always acting with us according to the full scope of his knowledge gleaned from the entirety of his *scientia media* and mediated through *scientia libera*."[90] This emotive language one encounters in Scripture is based on God's original reaction and emotions in his natural knowledge as he holds that knowledge of what "could" happen.[91] This quote from MacGregor is helpful because it sheds light on where this emotive language comes from: that God knows

---

90. MacGregor, *A Molinist-Anabaptist Systematic Theology*, 107.
91. Craig, "No Other Name," 177.

what creatures "could" and "would" do if he were to instantiate them in a given circumstance. God must know that creatures will do some things that will bring sorrow to him. After all, the creatures are acting freely. At this logical moment of God's natural and middle knowledge, he has not chosen a world to create, which means that time is in fact non-existent.[92] Once he makes a decision to actualize a world and thus ushers in the beginning of time, those particular circumstances and their outcomes begin to work themselves out. Thus, when God is sorrowful regarding a circumstance, it is actually an expression of an emotion known by God before the world began. It is also a real emotion in time because before, it was a pre-instantiated emotion; however, now that it has been instantiated, it does not change God's emotions towards that tragedy.

For middle knowledge, God's love for his creatures far exceeds time and the creation of this world.[93] Psalm 139 demonstrates this. This means that God's love and the emotions that go along with this love far exceed time as well. The result is that when people experience God's love today, it is not like some galaxy far off in the distance that they can see even though it is light years away.[94] Instead, the experience of God's love is the same love from before the foundations of the world (Ps 139), except now it is immediate as it is occurring within time.

An example of petitionary prayer might be a mother who has a son that struggles with an alcohol addiction. She prays earnestly for her son to stop drinking.[95] Middle knowledge argues that God knew prior to the creation of the world that if he were to create this son, he would in fact struggle with this addiction. God also knew that this mother would pray earnestly for her son. God is grieved as he knows what will happen if he creates this world. God then acts and creates the world, and time is set in motion. This circumstance then becomes a human reality as the son is addicted to alcohol, and the mother is begging the Lord that the son would stop. The self-limitation of God's sovereignty found in open theism is a weakness as the mother is left to pray and find comfort in a God that comes to know the plight of her family as it unfolds. For the compatibilist, even though there is human freedom, God knew prior to creation that the son could not have chosen otherwise. Thus, the mother is to petition God concerning her son that she knows had no other choice but to act out the alcohol addiction. However, she also believes that her prayers may be the very God-ordained means by

---

92. MacGregor, "Hubmaier's Concord of Predestination with Free Will," 283–86.
93. Flint, "Divine Providence," 284. See also Flint, *Divine Providence*, 37, 174–76.
94. Kraus, *Psalms 60-150*, 517.
95. See also Stump, "Petitionary Prayer," 84.

which her son is rescued. Furthermore, she knows that she is supposed to pray and believes that God is wholly loving and good. In middle knowledge, God cares for his creation. In particular, his relationship with his children is such that he knew and was grieved prior to the creation of the world over this circumstance, and yet God experiences this emotion again as the circumstance is instantiated in time. However, God cannot override the freedom of this son to make him stop.[96] He must decide on his own to do that, and God will remain patient with him through that process (2 Pet 3:9). Compatibilism and middle knowledge both agree that God knows if the son will stop; however, in compatibilism, the son has no choice to refrain from acting. Thus, the mother prays to God that he will change his son. For middle knowledge, until this son has libertarianly freely chosen to stop or tragically dies, the mother can remain hopeful and prayerful that the son will change his life. In addition, the mother prays and seeks comfort from God through this trial. God comforts the mother, which does not mean that God will fix the problem, but rather in the midst of the turmoil, God will not leave her nor forsake her.[97] If there is any doubt of whether or not God cares, believers can look to these logical moments of God's knowledge and know that God has experienced this grief and prayer twice—once prior to the creation of the world and then again in actual time.

Petitionary Prayer Is Meant to Change Us

In middle knowledge, the unity of the church, dependency upon God, and Christian action within the community are specific ways in which petitionary prayer changes the one praying. Thomas Flint discusses in *Divine Providence* that petitionary prayer affects the person praying. He writes, "Prayer may make no difference to *God*, but it makes a big difference to *us*. Properly understood, the aim of our prayer should be not to elicit a response from God, but to elicit a response from us."[98] Brümmer similarly argues that petitionary prayer has a great effect upon the person praying.[99] For example, employing the imagery of the body of Christ, it is not surprising that for Flint, as the members of church pray for one another, it builds up and unites the church.[100] Flint writes, "Prayer, one might argue, helps us to

96. MacGregor, *A Molinist Anabaptist Systematic Theology*, 116.
97. Crump, *Knocking on Heaven's Door*, 292.
98. Flint, *Divine Providence*, 221.
99. Brümmer, *What Are We Doing When We Pray?*, 52.
100. Here Flint is speaking to the unity brought upon the church as they pray for one another and together towards a common end.

recognize more clearly our needs and the needs of others. It strengthens in us a feeling of gratitude when those needs are met, a recognition that God is taking care of us."[101] In addition, Tiessen agrees that as the church prays towards a common end, this corporate prayer has the potential to expose the desired will of God in that given circumstance.[102] Nevertheless, Tiessen is not saying that just because the church shares in common a similar prayer, it is the prompting of the Spirit of God.

Murray also explains that petitionary prayer changes the people praying as they become dependent upon God for their needs. He begins by describing modern day atheism as an "urban phenomenon," as the humans distance themselves from the growth and development of the natural resources that they are dependent on.[103] In order to illustrate this, he uses the imagery of a farmer, noting that when things go wrong, "we tend to look for human agents" to blame, and conversely, "when we are in need, we tend to look to the appropriate human benefactors for their provision."[104] In doing so, "we tend to put creatures in the position reserved for God as the giver of 'every good, and perfect gift' (James 1:17), as he is described in the Christian Scriptures; thus we are at risk of committing idolatry."[105] However, petitionary prayer can "short-circuit this tendency by forcing the believer to realize that the goods she receives have their source beyond human agency."[106] David Basinger responds to Murray's claim by asserting that if God withholds what he would like people to receive until they ask for it, then they are reminded that they are dependent on God as the ultimate source of all good.[107] Basinger rejects this forceful action within the divine-human relationship because God is merely using the prayers to get what he has already prescribed for the people as good.[108] This critique lacks the appropriate location of petitionary prayer within the logical moments of God's knowledge. For example, as with compatibilism, if the content of the people's prayer is located within God's free knowledge, then Basinger is correct. God is forcefully using prayer to get what he has already prescribed for the world he has created. However, that is not the case for middle knowledge. Instead, God knew prior to the

---

101. Flint, *Divine Providence*, 221.

102. Tiessen, *Providence and Prayer*, 349.

103. Murray, "Does God Respond to Petitionary Prayer?" 246. See Thomas Morris for the idea that atheism is an urban phenomenon in *Making Sense of It All*.

104. Murray, "Does God Respond to Petitionary Prayer?" 246.

105. Ibid., 246.

106. Ibid. Similarly, idolatry is discussed here: Murray and Meyers, "Ask and It Will Be Given to You," 313–18.

107. Basinger, "Petitionary Prayer," 480.

108. Ibid.

creation of the world that they would petition God, and he chose to answer their requests. That God would know prior to the creation of the world that people would, based upon their libertarian freedom, pray does not mean that he has forcefully brought about the action of prayer. In addition, God did not have to wait until the creation of the world to determine that prayer was offered. In addition, using the example of farming, Murray notes, "It is still God who brings the rain, provides the chemist with the intellect required to thwart white-fly infestations, and give the physical strength to the assembly-line worker who construct the tractors which harvest the wheat."[109] Through petitionary prayer, the believer is made aware "that she is directly dependent on God for her provisions in life."[110]

Another way petitionary prayer changes people is that it provides a way for the members of the church to love one another, which leads the body of Christ to action.[111] However, Flint does not want to build an argument that prayer only affects the one praying, or that it only affects God but that prayer also has the ability to affect both God and people. This is due to the inherent relational qualities within the divine-human relationship. Flint writes, "It should make a difference to God; it should be at least a factor in his decisions as to how he will act; and sometimes, his actions can and should be seen as responses to our prayers. Petitionary prayer is more than individualistic meditative therapy; it is the act of speaking to another person who can help us."[112] Although Crump is not a proponent of middle knowledge, he similarly argues while looking at the New Testament that both God and the one praying are affected (or changed) through the interaction of prayerful dialogue.[113] Tiessen also asserts that petitionary prayer changes the one praying. In fact, he rejects any model of providence that argues for prayer not having an effect on the way in which the world goes.[114] For Tiessen, prayer changes the one praying as God changes his circumstances in response to prayer.[115] Thomas Constable adds that prayer changes the person, the situation, and even God himself occasionally.[116] In addition to

---

109. Murray, "Does God Respond to Petitionary Prayer?" 246.
110. Ibid.
111. Flint, *Divine Providence*, 221.
112. Ibid., 222.
113. Crump, *Knocking on Heaven's Door*, 297.
114. Tiessen, *Providence and Prayer*, 342.
115. Ibid., 342.
116. Constable, "What Prayer Will and Will Not Change," 105.

Crump, Constable, and Tiessen, Grudem argues that prayer changes not only the one praying but also the way God acts.[117]

This draws a parallel between compatibilism and middle knowledge concerning petitionary prayer as both God and the one praying are affected. In compatibilism, the one affected by prayer experiences change that God has causally determined outside of the control of the agent. Thus any change in the human due to prayer was such that the agent could not have chosen to do otherwise as it relates to the prayer offered and the ensuing change as a result of the prayer. If God also changes occasionally in response to prayer, it is only a change in relation to what he has already planned in light of the circumstance or agent involved. Thus it is only a change in appearance to the human and not a real change in God's plan as a response to prayer. One might question at this point the genuineness of change from both God and the human in response to prayer in this theory of providence. While close in comparison, middle knowledge better captures the divine-human relationship in petitionary prayer as it "makes a big difference to us" both individually and as a church.[118] For example, the one praying is offering a prayer that the agent could have chosen to refrain from, thus God is responding relationally to a genuine prayer. Also, any change in God as a result of the prayer in the divine-human relationship is genuine as God knew prior to the creation of the world that a person would libertarianly freely pray and based upon this knowledge God makes a decision to respond. In middle knowledge, God is more responsive as the prayer God desires to answer came from a human that chose to pray even though she could have refrained from praying. Thus, God did not merely create a person with the desire to pray and then respond to that prayer when it is uttered. Instead, now that the world is created, God is responding to a prayer that will occur based upon his knowledge of what a creature would do, which assures that God is sovereign over the situation and petitionary prayer. Thus, God, not prayer, changes things even though God is responding by answering prayer.

In conclusion, middle knowledge believes that through petitionary prayer, the Christian is changed from ecclesiastical disunity to unity, from inaction to action, and away from self-dependency to dependency upon God. Attention now turns to the divine-human relationship shared in petitionary prayer. This relationship is another instance where middle knowledge is preferred over compatibilism and open theism because middle knowledge argues that man's relationship with God is expressed through his libertarian freedom. In the case of prayer, this means that in addition to offering prayer,

---

117. Grudem, *Systematic Theology*, 377.
118. Flint, *Divine Providence*, 221.

the human is able to refrain from praying in the same instance. Also, by affirming libertarian freedom, or in spite of its affirmation of libertarian freedom, middle knowledge does not give up God's sovereignty.

Divine-Human Friendship

God has designed prayer to enrich his relationship with humanity, and this section will in part discuss how this transpires. The divine-human relationship shapes the future in such a way that is unknown to the human. Humility is a key element in this prayerful relationship. One that is willing to go to another for help demonstrates humility from within. God requires such a humility if one is to have a relationship with him. For example, Craig argues that Christians who are unaware about middle knowledge assume that God has such knowledge as they pray. He notes that as a Christian prays for guidance, she assumes that God knows which of the two paths before her would be better to take.[119] He uses the illustration of a girl praying concerning two marriage proposals. In prayer, she assumes that God knows if she were to marry one of the men, the marriage would end in divorce, whereas if she were to marry the other, their love would endure.[120] Compatibilism offers a similar prayer; however, the thrust of the prayer is to determine who God has chosen for her, which entails that God's plan concerning who she will marry is definite irrespective of the prayer offered. However, out of obedience and desire to know the will of God, she earnestly prays. For middle knowledge, prayer concerning which man to marry is genuine as she has the ability to refrain from petitioning God. Thus, she could withhold the prayer and make the decision independent from the possible answer from God as to whom she should marry if she would have prayed. As a result, if she were to get a divorce, perhaps God would have answered her prayer as to the right choice in marriage, which demonstrates that petitionary prayer as it relates to the divine-human friendship makes it possible to adjudicate such knowledge.

In addition, Murray describes an aspect of the divine-human friendship. He uses the illustration of a teacher observing a student struggling in class and falling behind. The teacher could call the student at home and provide a helpful course schedule for the student to follow, which would alleviate the burden of falling behind. However, the student could reasonably respond with, "Stay out of my business."[121] Another response from the stu-

---

119. Craig, *The Only Wise God*, 137.
120. Ibid., 137.
121. Murray, "Does God Respond to Petitionary Prayer?" 248. This illustration of

dent could be to ask the teacher for help, which "the teacher could provide the student with the needed instruction without the danger of overwhelming him."[122] Murray concludes, "If humans were led to docile acceptance of God's unrequested provision, it would infringe on their autonomy. Only if believers ask for those things they are given can the necessary condition for true friendship between God and his human creature be met."[123] Stump argues for something similar, asserting that God is willing to bring certain good about because someone has prayed.[124] Stump believes that God allowing prayer to influence his actions assures his genuine friendship with human beings.[125] One could argue that it is not genuine friendship if God is causally determining outside the control of the agent that a request be made. For middle knowledge, an important element in the divine-human relationship is that the human agent is able to reject requesting the provision. However, when a request is made, it makes the needed provision all the more important to God when the human freely petitions him. Conversely, non-prayer regarding a specific need speaks volumes as to what is important to the human. One might also argue, for example, that with compatibilism it is unnecessary to offer petitionary prayer if God gives unrequested provision. Or if prayer is necessary, that God will causally determine that the prayer be offered. The one praying might be confused as to whether (or not) God has ordained the provision irrespective of the prayer offered.

Through this involvement, Christians grow in their knowledge of God and love for him through relationship.[126] Also, when Christians are involved in God's kingdom work, "we learn to desire above all else the coming of God's kingdom and the doing of his will in the world." Thus, Christian prayer "for daily needs and for forgiveness is subsumed under the overall quest for God's glory."[127] The divine-human relationship, brought about through prayer, is characterized by a dependence upon God as Christians participate in the institution of God's will. Next attention is given to the priesthood of the believer and its implications for petitionary prayer as it relates to middle knowledge.

---

the teacher is borrowed from Stump, "Petitionary Prayer," 81–91.

122. Ibid. See also the emphasis on relationship in: Murray and Meyers, "Ask and It Will Be Given to You," 322–25.

123. Murray, "Does God Respond to Petitionary Prayer?" 248.

124. Stump, "Hoffman on Petitionary Prayer," 36–37.

125. Ibid.

126. Tiessen, *Providence and Prayer*, 348.

127. Ibid.

Middle Knowledge, Petitionary Prayer, and Systematic Theology

The following is an examination of the priesthood of the believer. This book has also treated the way in which compatibilism (chapter 3) and open theism (chapter 4) employ this doctrine within petitionary prayer. However, middle knowledge has the unique ability of affirming libertarian human freedom without limiting divine sovereignty, which sets middle knowledge apart and should be the preferred choice when employing petitionary prayer.

The priesthood of the believer relates to petitionary prayer in that the Christian no longer needs a special intermediary to go before the Father and pray.[128] Instead, the Christian is encouraged from the Lord and his apostles to petition God. Middle knowledge is preferred over compatibilism and open theism, because it takes full advantage of what the priesthood of the believer offers in petitionary prayer, which is (1) that God is omniscient concerning the prayer being offered and (2) the human is free in a libertarian sense as he prays. For example, a key deficiency with compatibilism is that it unnecessarily reduces what the human is able to offer in prayer down to those things that God has ordained he would pray. Therefore, prayer is causally determined by circumstances and events outside his control. As a result, it is not necessary for the priesthood of the believer to provide the Christian access to God concerning limitless possibilities in prayer. Rather, the priesthood of the believer only needs to provide access to the Father concerning those prayers that God has planned. In other words, the priesthood of the believer only requires that it provide access to the extent that the human being is free.

The human can petition God for or about anything. Richard Rice illustrates this with the concept of forgiveness. He points out that from the perspective of open theism, "there are no limits to forgiveness. There is no situation that lies beyond the reach of God's creative providence, so there is no situation where forgiveness would not apply."[129] If the priesthood of the believer removes any intermediary between the divine-human, it only makes sense that the human is then provided the ability to offer, without any limitation, their petitionary prayers. This does not mean that the human being will receive everything they ask for.[130] That is not what

---

128. MacGregor, *A Molinist Anabaptist Systematic Theology*, 280.

129. Rice, "The Final Form of Love," 216.

130. See the discussion in chapter 4, specifically open theism's reaction to Collins definition of prayer as he correlates answered prayer to the very thing prayed for in, "Prayer and Open theism," 163.

petitionary prayer is arguing for. Instead, petitionary prayer understood within the context of libertarian freedom simply affirms that humans can petition God without any limitation, and those petitions are offered freely as demonstrated by their ability to not pray as well. The ability for the human being in a specific circumstance to either pray or refrain from praying displays libertarian freedom. For middle knowledge, such freedom does not limit God's sovereignty. With regard to petitionary prayer, God knew that if he instantiated someone in a given situation whether (or not) they would pray.[131] If in fact they would pray, God knew this. The believer does not know this. Instead, the believer comes to realize how much God knows concerning how much they pray as they pray.

Chapter 4 notes that both open theism and middle knowledge subscribe to libertarian freedom. The difference for middle knowledge is that by affirming libertarian freedom in petitionary prayer as occurring prior to God's decree to create the world, God does not forego or self-limit his sovereignty. For the open theist, however, God must limit his sovereignty in order to maintain libertarian freedom. This assures that the divine-human relationship is understood as a co-creator model.[132]

Similar to open theism, middle knowledge argues that humans participate as co-creators of the world.[133] What differentiates open theism from middle knowledge concerning the co-creator model is that middle knowledge affirms the complete sovereignty of God in addition to libertarian human freedom. MacGregor notes that this is only made possible through the priesthood of all believers.[134] Thus, concerning prayer, God perfectly knew in his middle knowledge if the human being would pray, and if he would pray, God knew perfectly what he would pray for. This means that the human being was libertarianly free in their prayers and that God is omniscient concerning those prayers. This also exposes a key difference between open theism and middle knowledge with regard to petitionary prayer as the open theist asserts that God willingly forfeits some of his sovereignty in order to maintain libertarian human freedom. Thus, concerning the doctrine of the priesthood of the believer, middle knowledge is preferred over compatibilism and open theism, as it is the only theory of providence able to claim the sovereignty of God with respect to his omniscient knowledge about the content of human prayer while also arguing that humans are libertarianly free as they pray.

131. MacGregor, *A Molinist Anabaptist Systematic Theology*, 96.
132. Collins, "Prayer and Open Theism," 171.
133. MacGregor, *Luis de Molina*, 180.
134. Ibid.

Middle Knowledge, Petitionary Prayer, and Pastoral Theology

This section exposes various areas of pastoral theology that relate to middle knowledge and petitionary prayer. This will include a discussion concerning confession and repentance, which demonstrates the intimate nature of the divine-human relationship as the human is able to go before God with sin. This spiritual practice is not meant to produce shame but rather confidence as God promises to forgive and cleanse the one that confesses. Also, this section will discuss the reality of unanswered prayer and employ middle knowledge as a possible solution to why some petitions are left unanswered.

Petitionary Prayer as Confession and Repentance

When the divine-human relationship is damaged due to sin (1 John 1:8), the human being is able to confess his sin to God, and the Bible promises that God is faithful and just to forgive them and to cleanse them from all unrighteousness (1 John 1:9). This act of confession is a form of petitionary prayer as Christians go before God, confess their sin, and ask for forgiveness.[135] Middle knowledge is preferred over compatibilism and open theism as it asserts that God perfectly knows what sins the Christian has committed and will commit (1 John 3:19).[136] In addition, middle knowledge asserts that the sins committed are due to the libertarian freewill of the human being. Middle knowledge is the only theory of providence that can argue for God's complete sovereignty and libertarian human freedom concerning the sin committed and the act of confession on the part of the transgressor.[137]

---

135. The focus in this chapter is upon a post-conversion confession. Elsewhere soteriology is discussed. For example, Craig, "'No other name,'" 172–88. Hasker wrote an article in response to Craig's soteriological problem of evil (Hasker, "Middle Knowledge and the Damnation of the Heathen," 380–89). Also, David B. Myers will write a helpful and clear response to Craig in 2003. Myers clearly rejects soteriological exclusivism and begs the question: "The eternal punishment of all non-Christians simply because they are non-believers, regardless of the reasons for their non-belief, seems arbitrary and ultimately unjust" (Myers, "Exclusivism, Eternal Damnation, and the Problem of Evil," 407–8). In addition, *Salvation and Sovereignty* by Kenneth Keathley sought to provide a Molinist account to soteriology, namely, to make the case that God's sovereignty and soft libertarian human choice are not mutually exclusive (Keathley, *Salvation and Sovereignty*). Keathley employs the acronym, ROSES, first developed by Timothy George in order to make his case even though George does not hold to Molinism (George, *Amazing Grace*, 71–83).

136. See chapters 4 and 5 respectively for more discussion of confession and repentance.

137. Hasker, "Response to Thomas Flint," 118.

The Bible affirms that God sovereignly knows what sins the Christian commits. For example, Ps 69:5 states, "O God, you know my folly; the wrongs I have done are not hidden from you." Psalm 44:20–21 states, "If we had forgotten the name of our God or spread out our hands to a foreign god, would not God discover this? For he knows the secrets of the heart." In addition, Ps 90:8 asserts, "You have set our iniquities before you, our secret sins in the light of your presence," and Jer 16:17 states, "For my eyes are on all their ways. They are not hidden from me." Hebrews 4:12–13 describes the condition of man before God: "And no creature is hidden from his sight, but all are naked and exposed to the eyes of him to whom we must give account." For middle knowledge, these verses demonstrate that God perfectly knows our condition and the sins we commit. Compatibilism argues for something similar and places great emphasis on God's sovereignty and the need to confess sin.[138] Furthermore, as Berkhof notes, Christians should daily petition God for the forgiveness of sin.[139] However, if humans are not free in a libertarian sense, then who is responsible for the sin committed?[140] If the human being is not responsible, then God would be held responsible.[141] However, God cannot be responsible for sin. Or to say it another way, how can God morally justify condemning humans for their sin if they did not have a choice to refrain from that sin? In addition, due to the lack of libertarian freedom possessed in compatibilism, people do not have the ability to refrain from petitions for forgiveness. This leaves God in the position to forgive someone that never had a choice to do otherwise, which is not genuine contrition.

Open theism argues that God gave up some of his spiritual say-so in order to give it to humans so that the relationship between the divine-human is secured.[142] However, with regard to the sovereignty of God, how can open theism proclaim that God is sovereign if he is learning about sin as we commit it?[143] In addition to the verses above, Ps 139:1–7 proclaims that God knows before one sits down when they will sit down. He knows when one will rise up before they actually rise up. He knows thoughts while they are still far away. He knows the words that one will produce before they reach

---

138. Crump, *Knocking on Heaven's Door*, 297.
139. Berkhof, *Systematic Theology*, 514, 540.
140. Craig, "No Other Name," 176.
141. See chapter 3, which discusses at length compatibilism's view concerning confession and repentance.
142. Pinnock, "Open Theism," 239.
143. Pinnock, et al., *The Openness of God*, 16.

the tongue.[144] That would also include that God knows those sinful actions, thoughts, and speech before they are committed.

Middle knowledge argues that God knows these committed sins prior to the creation of the world, which is one reason why this theory of providence is preferred over open theism. In the logical moment of God's middle knowledge, God knows that the human being would sin if they were created and placed in that particular circumstance. MacGregor notes that God's knowledge is not in a general sense so that he knows the essence of humanity only. Rather God knows all individuals, with all their unique patterns, which includes sinful patterns.[145] In addition, Craig asserts that this knowledge of God includes sinful behavior, which assures that the human is responsible and not God.[146] Tiessen adds that God's knowledge is comprehensive so that he knows who would and would not repent from their sins within his middle knowledge.[147] Thus God's knowledge is not of a general sinfulness on the part of humanity. It is a detailed knowledge of the sin committed by each individual as well as their response to sin in repentance. One might argue that middle knowledge holds a position similar to hard determinism or compatibilism with respect to divine culpability as God brings about a world with sin and evil.[148] However, Craig and MacGregor demonstrate that for middle knowledge, God knows prior to creation what sin would be committed. Then God creates a world in which that human being lives the reality of that circumstance and sins in that moment. The human was free in the libertarian sense because he could have chosen to do otherwise, thus God is culpable in that he creates the world, which includes many evils and sinful circumstances for humanity. However, he does not create the evil and sinful circumstances whereby humans involved were causally determined outside of their control to perform those actions. In other words, without libertarian freedom, the human had only one prescribed choice to make. Therefore, God's divine culpability is different from the theological compatibilist due to God's middle

144. Kraus, *Psalms 60–150*, 517.

145. MacGregor, *Luis De Molina*, 48.

146. Craig, "No Other Name," 184.

147. Tiessen, "Why Calvinists Should Believe in Divine Middle Knowledge, Although They Reject Molinism," 364.

148. Hasker notes that if God has middle knowledge, he still had to create a world, and that world possessed evil, which presents a problem for in maneuvering God away from being the author of evil [Hasker, "Response to Thomas Flint," 124–25]. Hasker's point here is in response to Flint, "Hasker's 'God, Time, and Knowledge," 103–15. For more on this problem for middle knowledge, see Basinger, "Middle Knowledge and Divine Control," 131. See also Hasker, "A Refutation of Middle Knowledge," 545–57. Basinger offers further response in "Middle Knowledge and Human Freedom: Some Clarifications," 330–36.

knowledge concerning those libertarianly free sinful actions he knew the human being would make.[149] For middle knowledge, God is sovereign in that he knows (1) prior to the creation of the world what the human being would do, and he also knows (2) when the event takes place in the actual world what the creature would do.[150] This is evidenced in Ps 139:16 where God has this kind of knowledge of an "unformed" substance.

Thus far, attention has been given to those sinful actions on the part of the human being and the necessity that the human involved in those actions be libertarianly free. In terms of libertarian freedom, it is also important that the human is free in the act of confession, so that the human could have chosen to do otherwise. If people are free in their sinful actions, so as not to accuse God of being responsible for their sin, then it would also make sense that the human being has libertarian freedom in their confession of that sin.

If the human does not have libertarian freedom, then one could argue that the confession was not genuine. The Psalmist writes, "If I had cherished iniquity in my heart, the Lord would not have listened. But truly God has listened; he has attended to the voice of my prayer" (Ps 66:18–19). How can God refuse to hear the Christian's prayer due to sin if the Christian is not free to commit the sin?[151] A key aspect of confession is that Christians confess their sin to God, which also includes the possibility that Christians would refrain from confession as well. If God only requires a measure of freedom whereby he causally determines that the human would confess, then one might argue that when a person forgoes confession, God did not want to receive confession in that moment, which is troubling because the Christian would be left in a state of unrighteousness.[152] Thus, how can God promise to listen to the voice of prayer from the people that have confessed their sin if their confession was not genuine? The Apostle John describes confession in a libertarian manner. He writes, "*If* we confess our sins, he is faithful and just to forgive us our sins and to cleanse us from all unrighteousness" (1 John 1:9, emphasis mine). The idea is that Christians have the spiritual opportunity to bring a cleansing from all unrighteousness "if" they confess their sins. There is also the reality that if Christians refrain

---

149. Jerry L. Walls and Joseph R. Dongell also note that Molinism is not exempt from the sort of moral problems that compatibilism and hard determinism struggles with (*Why I am Not A Calvinist*, 141). For Walls and Dongell, middle knowledge is better off in resolving this problem. See also Walls, "Is Molinism as Bad as Calvinism?" 85–98.

150. Flint, "Hasker's 'God, Time, and Knowledge,'" 104.

151. Smilansky, "Free Will and Moral Responsibility," 226–27.

152. Marshall, *The Epistles of John*, 114.

from confessing sins, then cleansing is forbidden.[153] In this instance, middle knowledge makes the best sense of confession and repentance, because it upholds that God sovereignly knows the sins that are committed while at the same time the human being has the libertarian freedom to commit the sin and also to confess the sin.

Unanswered Petitionary Prayer

Middle knowledge accepts the reality that sometimes people go before God and ask for something and never receive it. This section will address that for middle knowledge, God knows how a person will respond to the answer he gives and the variety of human responses to the situations that will arise, which could account for God not answering the prayer. For example, a prayer might go unanswered because God is primarily concerned with what is good for the one praying. Within the framework of middle knowledge, this means that God middle-knows that answering the prayer in the manner requested would not be advantageous to the individual or people group. Also, prayer may go unanswered if the prayer is offered with sinful intentions or perhaps because of specific sin in the Christian's life. In addition, for middle knowledge, God withholds answering prayer if that prayer requires God to override the libertarian freedom of the individual or of other people involved in the request.

Concerning unanswered prayer, Stump notes, "Christian writings are full of examples of prayers which are not answered, and there are painful cases of unanswered prayer in which the one praying must be tempted more to the belief that God is his implacable enemy than to the sentimental-seeming belief that God is his friend."[154] What does the Christian do in those instances? Does unanswered prayer nullify the importance of petitionary prayer? Middle knowledge looks to Matt 7:7–11 for answers. For example, Flint primarily focuses upon the idea that the Father, who is in heaven, will give *good* things to those who ask (Matt 7:11). Flint observes that the comfort in this passage is not that Christians can ask, or that they will receive; instead, the focus should remain on God's output of good things.[155] Similar to Flint, MacGregor notes that for middle knowledge, the attention must fall upon Jesus' claim that the Father will give good gifts to those who ask.[156] Thus, for MacGregor, "Molina argued that God actually gives us *everything* we ask for

---

153. Flint, "In Defense of Theological Compatibilism," 238.
154. Stump, "Petitionary Prayer," 90.
155. Flint, *Divine Providence*, 217.
156. MacGregor, *Luis de Molina*, 129.

that is objectively good."[157] However, it is also rightly understood as good, in those instances, where God does not give according to the request. For middle knowledge, answered prayer is not linked only to the specifics of the prayer requested. Thus, it is a viable option for God to respond with "no," and such a response does not warrant that prayer was unanswered.

When one prays and the prayer goes unanswered, Flint concludes that God in his middle knowledge knows the entire possible *could be* and *would be* outcomes, so that if the answer is "no," there is a good reason for this reply. The same occurs when the reply is "yes," but in those instances, what is good for God matches the request made.[158] Open theism cannot make this claim because God comes to know the future as it happens. Open theism can say with some confidence that it will be good due to God being endlessly resourceful.[159] However, it cannot say that God knows with certainty it will be good for the one praying in the future. Thus, if God were to allow a petition to go unanswered, it would not be due to his knowledge of the future and what would be best for the human. Within the framework of compatibilism, the divine-human relationship is such that the human did not have the choice to refrain from petitioning God. Thus, in the case of unanswered prayer, God brings about a prayer that he intends not to answer, and the human could not have chosen other than to offer the unanswered prayer. With unanswered prayers, middle knowledge offers the assurance that God hears their prayers due to the priesthood of the believer. However, just because a prayer is heard does not mean that it must be answered in the manner in which it is prayed for in order to prove that God has heard it. Stump writes, "Asking God for something is not in itself a sufficient condition for God's doing what he is asked."[160] Instead, God may withhold an answer due to his knowledge of the future, as he knows this is the best thing for the one praying. The open theist can affirm that God's answer is good at the present moment. However, God cannot promise that it will be good into the future because God lacks the knowledge which would afford him the ability to know the future. Compatibilism affirms something similar to middle knowledge but credits unanswered prayer to the nature of the petition. For example, Kreider rightfully notes that prayers for selfish reasons will not be answered.[161] In addition to Kreider, David Crump warns that prayers only focused upon the petitioner's purposes will likely

---

157. Ibid.
158. Flint, *Divine Providence*, 227–8.
159. Pinnock, *Most Moved Mover*, 4.
160. Stump, "Petitionary Prayer," 90.
161. Kreider, "Jonathan Edwards's Theology of Prayer," 454.

result in missing God's purposes.[162] In other words, if answered prayer only looks like one receiving exactly what is being prayed for, then it is understandably possible to miss God's response.[163]

Middle knowledge also argues that as long as humans freely offer petitionary prayer, it should not be surprising that some of those prayers are made in vain.[164] Those prayers offered in vain assure that some prayers will go unanswered due to sinful intentions. Also, God may be withholding an affirmative answer due to other sin.[165] The idea that God withholds an answer to prayer due to sin correlates with the previous section and the importance of confession. Similar to Stump above, MacGregor asserts that God may not answer a prayer in the exact manner in which it is prayed for because God middle-knows that answering the prayer in that manner would not be advantageous to an individual, people, or the world at large.[166] Thus, for middle knowledge, God not answering a prayer in the manner in which it is petitioned is due to his ultimate wisdom given God's knowledge of would-be circumstances as a result of the prayer.

Another possible explanation for unanswered prayer is that the petition is logically impossible for God to answer. MacGregor notes that this kind of prayer for middle knowledge will assuredly lead to an unanswered prayer.[167] For example, he notes that it is impossible for God to answer the prayer that a person's enemy was never born, or that the Holocaust never happened, or that God would commit evil in order to get revenge on someone.[168]

Middle knowledge also asserts that God may withhold answering a prayer if that prayer requires God to override the libertarian freedom of the individual or people group.[169] This means that God may reject answering a prayer even though it is logically feasible for God. For example, Flint argues that prayers, which involve another individual, may go unanswered because it is not solely up to God whether the prayer is answered.[170] Take again, for example, the mother with a son struggling with an alcohol addiction. She prays earnestly for her son to stop drinking, and the outcome that

---

162. Crump, *Knocking on Heaven's Door*, 14.
163. Ibid., 281.
164. Flint, *Divine Providence*, 216.
165. Crump, *Knocking on Heaven's Door*, 285.
166. MacGregor, *Luis de Molina*, 127-8.
167. Ibid., 127.
168. Ibid.
169. Ibid.
170. Flint, *Divine Providence*, 216.

he would stop drinking is a good thing for all parties involved. However, after months and months of prayer, the son is still drinking. Does God not care? Is he teaching the family how to draw closer to God by causing the son to drink, which fosters a spiritual dependence upon God that otherwise would not be possible? For example, the response from open theism is that God would not know the future and whether (or not) the son will stop drinking. Thus, the mother could persistently pray but God could not override the libertarian freedom of the son. In addition, the mother must find comfort in the Lord, which comes from God completely knowing the circumstance at hand; however, God could not offer the same comfort as middle knowledge due to the lack of knowledge concerning the future. God is in a responsive position similar to the mother he is receiving prayer from. With compatibilism, the mother is praying for her son to stop drinking, yet God already knows the outcome. In fact, God has causally determined the outcome, such that the son (alcoholism) and mother (prayer) could not have done otherwise in terms of their freedom to act. The mother petitioning God has to come to terms with (1) praying to God, and (2) her son is free in his action, which means the son could not have done otherwise as he freely (compatibilistically) chose to drink. According to middle knowledge, God knew prior to the creation of the world that if he were to create this child under any and all circumstances, he would become an alcoholic. God also knew that this mother would pray earnestly for her son. Due to the sovereignty of God, the world is created, which includes this son that would become an alcoholic. In addition, this mother is created, and she is praying earnestly. Middle knowledge asserts that God is responding in light of these prayers that this son would change his life; however, God cannot override the freedom of his creatures and their actions. Instead, God's promise to this mother is that he will not leave her, nor the son, and will not forsake them. Thus, prayer becomes an opportunity for the mother to continue in praying that the son would change his ways but also to request God for a peace, which surpasses understanding (Phil 4:7) and for a comfort that God can only give (Matt 5:4; 2 Cor 1:4).[171] Still creatures are not given access to all hope of the future, but we know that God is patient with his children (Rom 12:12; 1 Cor 13:4; 1 Thess 5:14; Jas 5:7–8), even those that have not trusted in God for salvation (2 Pet 3:9).

---

171. See Wells, "A Different Way to Pray," 51.

Conclusion

This book defines petitionary prayer as a genuine human behavior whereby the creature freely goes to its sovereign Creator and simply asks. Middle knowledge fulfills this definition as it maintains that God knew prior to the creation of the world whether (or not) the human would pray. God also knew what the human would pray for. In other words, God did not have to wait until the human prayed in order to determine that prayer was offered. Open theism cannot make this claim as God's sovereignty is self-limited in nature, which restricts God's knowledge of the future as he responds to humanity. In addition, for middle knowledge the human praying is free in a libertarian sense as there is nothing outside the control of the human causing his desire to pray. Compatibilism finds this claim difficult as it rejects libertarian freedom and the result is that the human could not have chosen to do otherwise. Open theism and middle knowledge both affirm libertarian freedom; however, it was argued in this chapter that the logical moments of God's knowledge as it relates to petitionary prayer demonstrate that middle knowledge includes God's meticulous sovereignty into its theological framework.

In addition, this chapter provided various ways in which middle knowledge had a clear advantage over open theism and compatibilism. For example, it was argued that middle knowledge provides the best account for the necessary humility required in prayer. For compatibilism, it was difficult to determine how genuinely humble the human is in prayer when the action of humility was causally determined in such a way so as to assure that the human could not have acted otherwise. Open theism encountered its own difficulties as God does not know of the human's humility until he acted humbly. It was argued that God lacked the necessary knowledge of the future in his omniscience in order to uphold human libertarian freedom. Without God's knowledge of the future and the humility of the one praying, God is not able to determine if the human is genuinely humble or if this is an attempt to manipulate God because the person knows the desired behavior is humility in that moment. Middle knowledge asserts that God knew prior to the creation of the world whether (or not) the human would be humble in heart, and based upon his knowledge, he can make a decision as to answering the petitionary prayer.

Unanswered prayer is another example whereby middle knowledge has an advantage over compatibilism and open theism. For example, middle knowledge argues that God knows how a person will respond to the answer he gives and to a variety of situations that will arise in light of the human's response, which could result in God not answering the prayer. In compatibilism, the human did not have the choice to refrain from offering the prayer that would go unanswered. As a result, God is understood to bring about an unanswered prayer that the human could not have chosen otherwise but to offer. Also, in the framework of open theism, as God comes to know the future as it happens, God does not allow a prayer to go unanswered due to his wisdom and sovereign knowledge of the future and what is best for the one praying.

That middle knowledge is able to affirm God's sovereignty in petitionary prayer without having to forfeit the libertarian freedom of the one praying sets this theory of providence apart. Middle knowledge best captures the divine-human relationship evidenced in petitionary prayer as the human is genuinely offering prayers of petition. In addition, God is sovereign concerning the needs and content of the prayer as he knew the human would offer the prayer prior to the creation of the world.

6

Conclusion

THE TENSION BETWEEN GOD'S sovereignty and human freedom in petitionary prayer is palpable, and each of the theories of divine providence discussed in this book has humbly handled this tension. At points throughout the book, each scholar has argued with confidence while at other times willing to subject his understanding of petitionary prayer to mystery. While each scholar believes that his theory of providence handles the divine-human interaction in prayer the best, not one scholar noted in this book is antagonistic towards the sovereignty of God or human freedom. It is just the opposite. These scholars are trying to love God with all their heart, soul, and mind. With that attempt, I want this book to reside. However, what each theory demonstrates is that one's view of providence affects the behavior and how motivated one is to offer petitionary prayer.

Speaking to this tension, Glenn Kreider writes, "Perhaps the most that humans can affirm is that God hears and responds to prayer and He also remains the Sovereign of His universe. Perhaps a solution to this difficulty will remain forever outside the grasp of humans."[1] For Kreider, this ambiguity is both intentional and appropriate. Similarly, Clark Pinnock writes, "The Bible seems to be pretheoretical in its approach to the relationship between divine sovereignty and human freedom. Some passages can be read to support God's determining all things. Others, with equal strength, stress the significant freedom of human beings. A tension is allowed to stand in the biblical text; a definitive resolution is nowhere attempted."[2] Thus, the work for each of these chapters was to explain petitionary prayer with the reality of this tension in view, and for finite creatures, this is a difficult undertaking. In addition to Pinnock, William Hasker writes, "Then it is up to us to construct a consistent position on the question, and to do it on the basis of biblical data without claiming that the

---

1. Kreider, "Jonathan Edwards's Theology of Prayer," 455.
2. Pinnock, "God Limits His Knowledge," 143.

text clearly or unambiguously supports the conclusion we have reached."[3] Since finite creatures are taking upon themselves this difficult task, Hasker is right to conclude that one must exhibit a great measure of humility as the construction of a consistent position regarding petitionary prayer is built. Each of the theories of divine providence discussed in this book share a desire to construct a view concerning petitionary prayer that would propel the Christian toward God in relationship and then lead the body of Christ to pray without ceasing (1 Thess 5:17).

In the end, middle knowledge is preferred over compatibilism, hard determinism, and open theism with respect to petitionary prayer. According to Hasker, *middle knowledge* is "the only game in town" claiming that the sovereignty of God includes both his omniscience and libertarian human freedom.[4] The ability to support this claim provides relational conditions in petitionary prayer that sets middle knowledge apart as the preferred theory of providence. Thus, petitionary prayer is a genuine human behavior whereby the creature goes before its sovereign Creator and simply asks. Within the framework of middle knowledge, there is an extensive and beautiful expansion of God's sovereignty.[5] This is a sovereignty that I believe the compatibilist and hard determinist could find helpful as human freedom is not at odds with the sovereignty of God but instead, is under the authority of God when understood in God's middle knowledge. In other words, concerns are genuine and so are the accompanied prayers that go along with those concerns as one could have chosen to refrain from prayer. Therefore, God is not forcing or manufacturing petitionary prayer so that he can prove himself just or holy. Additionally, prayers offered are not unknown to God until they are prayed. God is sovereign in his knowledge concerning those petitionary prayers. Furthermore, one of the key characteristics of middle knowledge is that it defines human freedom as libertarian, thus providing the needed clarity for the compatibilist as it relates to the extent of human freedom. Similar to middle knowledge, open theism argues for libertarian freedom. The difference is that open theists limit some of God's sovereignty in order to uphold libertarian freedom, something middle knowledge avoids. In petitionary prayer, middle knowledge provides a way to maintain both instead of giving up one in order to affirm the other. Thus, middle knowledge assures that the divine-human interaction in petitionary prayer is characterized by God's sovereign knowledge, prior to the creation of the world, concerning whether (or not) the human will pray and also God's

---

3. Hasker, *God, Time, and Knowledge*, 190–91.
4. Hasker, "Response to Thomas Flint," 117–18.
5. MacGregor, *Luis de Molina*, 118.

knowledge with respect to the needs of the one praying. In addition, the human offering petitionary prayer was free in a libertarian sense as he could have chosen not to pray.

This book does not presume to be the last word on the divine-human relationship in petitionary prayer. Instead, this work serves as a springboard for future study. In addition to petitionary prayer, one could also employ the same theories of providence discussed in this book as it relates to the divine-human relationship in prophecy, tongues, and the doctrine of the inspiration of Scripture. Also important to each of the theories of divine providence is their appeal to mystery as it relates to divine-human interaction. There is further study needed which would demonstrate at what point(s) the various theories of providence rely on mystery as it relates to the divine-human interaction in petitionary prayer. Another area for further study pertains to theological determinism as each of the theories of divine providence discussed in this book is at some level deterministic in nature. Thus, one could demonstrate at what point, for example in petitionary prayer, each of the theories of providence are deterministic.

In conclusion, this book hopes to persuade its readers to adopt the middle knowledge position as their own with regard to petitionary prayer. In so doing, the one praying will have confidence that prayer makes a difference, if for no other reason but because the one praying could have chosen to change the course of events by not praying. In other words, the Christian should always be motivated to pray. Also, the one praying does so with confidence that the one to whom they are offering petitionary prayer to is sovereign concerning the future. Moreover, God sovereignly knows the needs before they are requested and is sovereign in his knowledge as to whether (or not) the human will petition him. However, if one does not adopt middle knowledge over its primary competitors as it relates to petitionary prayer, perhaps one might acknowledge that middle knowledge helps strengthen their positions where they are weak. In addition, it provides an irenic position between open theism and compatibilism as it affirms at points both the open theist and compatibilist positions regarding petitionary prayer.

Bibliography

Adams, Robert. "Middle Knowledge and the Problem of Evil." *American Philosophical Quarterly* 14, no. 2 (1977): 109–17.

———. "An Anti-Molinist Argument," *Philosophical Perspectives* 5 (1991): 343–53.

Allen, Leslie C. *Jeremiah.* Old Testament Library. Louisville: Westminster John Knox, 2008.

Alston, William P. "Divine-Human Dialogue and the Nature of God." *Faith and Philosophy* 2 (1985): 5–20.

———. *Divine Nature and Human Language: Essays in Philosophical Theology*. Ithaca: Cornell University Press, 1989.

Arminius, James. *The Writings of James Arminius*. Translated by James Nichols and W. R. Bagnall, vol. 1. Grand Rapids: Baker, 1977. Accessed October 13, 2015. http://wesley.nnu.edu/arminianism/the-works-of-james-arminius-volume-1/public-disputations/disputation-4-on-the-nature-of-god/.

Augustine. *Homilies on the First Epistle of John.* Edited by Daniel E. Doyle and Thomas Marting. Works of Saint Augustine: A Translation for the 21st Century. Edited and translated by Boniface Ramsey, vol. III/14. Hyde Park, NY: New City, 2008.

Basinger, David. *The Case for Freewill Theism: A Philosophical Assessment*. Downers Grove, IL: InterVarsity, 1996.

———. "Divine Control and Human Freedom: Is Middle Knowledge the Answer?" *Journal of the Evangelical Theological Society* 36, no. 1 (1993): 55–64.

———. "Divine Omniscience and Human Freedom: A 'Middle Knowledge' Perspective." *Faith and Philosophy* 1, no. 3 (1984): 291–302.

———. "Middle Knowledge and Classical Christian Thought." *Religious Studies* 22, no. 3/4 (1986): 407–22.

———. "Middle Knowledge and Divine Control: Some Clarifications." *International Journal for Philosophy of Religion* 30, no. 3 (1991): 131.

———. "Middle Knowledge and Human Freedom: Some Clarifications." *Faith and Philosophy* 4, no. 3 (1987): 330–36.

———. "Petitionary Prayer: A Response to Murray and Meyers." *Religious Studies* 31 (1995): 475–84.

———. "Practical Implications." In *The Openness of God,* 155–176. Downers Grove, IL: InterVarsity, 1994.

———. "Why Petition an Omnipotent, Omniscient, Wholly Good God?" *Religious Studies* 19 (1983): 25–41.

Bavinck, Herman. *Reformed Dogmatics.* Vol. 2, *God and Creation.* Grand Rapids: Baker, 2004.

Beck, Peter. *The Voice of Faith: Jonathan Edward's Theology of Prayer*. Ontario, Canada: Joshua, 2010.

Beeke, Joel R. *Living for God's Glory*. Orlando: Reformation Trust, 2008.

Berkhof, Louis. *Systematic Theology*. N.p.: n.p., 1938. Reprint, East Periora, IL: Banner of Truth Trust, 2012.

Berkouwer, G. C. *The Providence of God*. Studies in Dogmatics. Grand Rapids: Eerdmans, 1952. Reprint, Grand Rapids: Eerdmans, 1983.

Bertolet, Rod. "Hasker on Middle Knowledge." *Faith and Philosophy* 10 (1993): 3–17.

Bloesch, Donald G. *God the Almighty: Power, Wisdom, Holiness, Love*. Christian Foundations. Downers Grove, IL: InterVarsity, 1995.

Bovon, François. *Luke 1: A Commentary on the Gospel of Luke 1:1–9:50*. Hermeneia: A Critical and Historical Commentary on the Bible. Minneapolis: Fortress, 2002.

———. *Luke 2: A Commentary on the Gospel of Luke 9:51–19:27*. Hermeneia: A Critical and Historical Commentary on the Bible. Minneapolis: Fortress, 2013.

Boyd, Gregory A. *God of the Possible: A Biblical Introduction to the Open View of God*. Grand Rapids: Baker, 2000.

———. *Satan and the Problem of Evil: Constructing a Trinitarian Warfare Theodicy*. Downers Grove, IL: InterVarsity, 2001.

Brown, Colin. *From the Ancient World to the Age of Enlightenment*. Christianity and Western Thought: A History of Philosophers, Ideas and Movements 1. Downers Grove: InterVarsity, 1990.

Brümmer, Vincent. *What Are We Doing When We Pray? On Prayer and the Nature of Faith*. London: Ashgate, 2008.

Bruce, F. F. *The Epistles to the Colossians, to Philemon, and to the Ephesians*. New International Commentary on the New Testament. Grand Rapids: Eerdmans, 1984.

Brueggemann, Walter. *Deuteronomy*. Abingdon Old Testament Commentaries. Nashville: Abingdon, 2001.

Bryant, Barry E. "Molina, Arminius, Plaifere, Goad, and Wesley on Human Free-Will, Divine Omniscience, and Middle Knowledge." *Wesleyan Theological Journal* 27, no. 1–2 (1992): 93–103.

Buttrick, George A. *Prayer*. New York: Abingdon-Cokesbury, 1942.

Calvin, John. *Institutes of the Christian Religion*. Edited by John T. McNeill. Translated by Ford Lewis Battles, Library of Christian Classics, vol. 20–21. Philadelphia, PA: Westminster, 1960. Reprint, Louisville, KY: Westminster John Knox, 2006.

———. *1, 2, and 3 John*. Crossway Classic Commentaries, ed. Alister McGrath and J. I. Packer. Wheaton: Crossway, 1998.

Campbell, Travis James. "Middle Knowledge: A Reformed Critique." *Westminster Theological Journal* 68, no. 1 (2006): 1–22.

Canfield, John V. "The Compatibility of Free Will and Determinism." *The Philosophical Review* 71 (1962): 352–68.

Carson, D. A. *Praying with Paul: A Call To Spiritual Reformation*. 2nd ed. Grand Rapids: Baker, 2014.

———. *How Long, O Lord? Reflections on Suffering and Evil*. Grand Rapids: Baker, 2006.

Childs, Brevard S. *The Book of Exodus*. Old Testament Library. Philadelphia: Westminster, 1974.

Clements-Jewery, Philip. *Intercessory Prayer: Modern Theology, Biblical Teaching and Philosophical Thought*. London: Ashgate, 2005.

Collins, Robin. "Prayer and Open Theism." In *God in an Open Universe: Science, Metaphysics, and Open Theism*. Edited by William Hasker, Thomas Jay Oord and Dean Zimmerman, 161–185. Eugene, OR: Pickwick, 2011.

Constable, Thomas L. "What Prayer Will and Will Not Change." In *Essays in Honor of J. Dwight Pentecost*. Edited by Stanley D. Toussaint and Charles Dyer, 99–113. Chicago: Moody, 1986.

Cosby, Brian H. *A Christian's Pocket Guide to Suffering: How God Shapes Us Through Pain and Tragedy*. Fearn, Scotland: Christian Focus, 2015.

———. *Suffering and Sovereignty: John Flavel and the Puritans on Afflictive Providence*. Grand Rapids: Reformation Heritage Books, 2012.

Craig, William Lane. "Hasker on Divine Knowledge." *Philosophical Studies: An International Journal for Philosophy in the Analytic Tradition* 67, no. 2 (1992): 89–110.

———. "Middle Knowledge, Truth-Makers, and the Grounding Objection." *Faith and Philosophy* 18 (2001): 337–38.

———. "'No Other Name': A Middle Knowledge Perspective on the Exclusivity of Salvation through Christ." *Faith and Philosophy* 6, no. 2 (1989): 172–88.

———. *The Only Wise God: The Compatibility of Divine Foreknowledge*. Eugene, OR: Wipf and Stock, 1999.

Crump, David. *Knocking on Heaven's Door: A New Testament Theology of Petitionary Prayer*. Grand Rapids: Baker, 2006.

Crosby, Brian H. *A Christian's Pocket Guide to Suffering: How God Shapes Us through Pain and Tragedy*. Ross Shire, Scotland: Christian Focus, 2015.

Daane, James. *The Freedom of God: A Study of Election and Pulpit*. Grand Rapids: Eerdmans, 1973.

Davison, Scott A. "Craig on the Grounding Objection to Middle Knowledge." *Faith and Philosophy* 21, no. 3 (2004): 365–69.

de Molina, Luis. *On Divine Foreknowledge: Part 4 of the Concordia*. Translated by Alfred J. Freddoso. New York: Cornell University, 1988.

Dekker, Eef. "Was Arminius a Molinist?" *Sixteenth Century Journal* 27, no. 2 (1996): 337–52.

Doran, Robert. "The Pharisee and the Tax Collector: An Agonistic Story." *Catholic Biblical Quarterly* 69 (2007): 259–70.

Dunn, James D. G. *The Epistles to the Colossians and to Philemon*. New International Greek Testament Commentary. Grand Rapids: Eerdmans, 1996.

———. *The Epistle to the Galatians*. Black's New Testament Commentary. Grand Rapids: Baker, 1993.

Edwards, Jonathan. "The Most High a Prayer-Hearing God." In *The Complete Works of Jonathan Edwards*, vol. 2, 113–18. N.p.: n.p., 1834. Reprint. Peabody, MA: Hendrickson, 2011.

———. "The Terms of Prayer." In *Sermons and Discourses: 1734–1738*. Edited by M. X. Lesser, vol. 19, 768–791. The Works of Jonathan Edwards. New Haven, CT: Yale University Press, 2001.

———. "The Free and Voluntary Suffering and Death of Christ." In *Sermons and Discourses: 1734–1738*, edited by M. X. Lesser, vol. 19, 491–514. The Works of Jonathan Edwards. New Haven, CT: Yale University Press, 2001.

———. *Freedom of the Will*. The Works of Jonathan Edwards. Ed. Paul Ramsey, vol. 1. New Haven, CT: Yale University Press, 2009.

Ellis, Robert. *Answering God: Towards a Theology of Intercession*. Waynesboro, GA: Paternoster, 2005.

Erickson, Millard J. *Christian Theology*. 3rd ed. Grand Rapids: Baker, 2013.

———. *Introducing Christian Doctrine*, Edited by L. Arnold Hustad, 3rd ed. Grand Rapids: Baker, 2015.

Fee, Gordon D. *Paul's Letter to the Philippians*. New International Commentary of the New Testament. Grand Rapids: Eerdmans, 1995.

Feinberg, John. "God Ordains All Things." In *Predestination and Free Will: Four Views of Divine Sovereignty and Human Freedom*. Edited by David Basinger and Randall Basinger, 17–43. Downers Grove, IL: InterVarsity, 1986.

———. *No One Like Him: The Doctrine of God*. Foundations of Evangelical Theology. Edited by John S. Feinberg. Wheaton, IL: Crossway, 2001.

Ferguson, Sinclair. *In Christ Alone: Living the Gospel Centered Life*. Orlando: Reformation Trust, 2007.

Fretheim, Terence E. *Exodus*. Interpretation: A Biblical Commentary for Teaching and Preaching. Edited by James Luther Mays and Patrick D. Miller Jr. Louisville: John Knox, 1991.

Flavel, John. *The Works of John Flavel*. 6 vols. Paternoster Row, London: W. Baynes and Son, 1820. Reprint, Carlisle, PA: The Banner of Truth Trust, 2015.

Flint, Thomas P. "'A Death He Freely Accepted': Molinist Reflections on the Incarnation." *Faith and Philosophy* 18 (2001): 3–20.

———. *Divine Providence: The Molinist Account*. Ithaca, NY: Cornell University Press, 1998.

———. "Hasker's 'God, Time, and Knowledge.'" *Philosophical Studies* 60 (1990): 103–15.

———. "In Defense of Theological Compatibilism." *Faith and Philosophy* 8 (1991): 237–43.

———. "The Multiple Muddles of Maverick Molinism." *Faith and Philosophy* 20, no. 1 (2003): 91–100.

———. "The Possibilities of Incarnation: Some Radical Molinist Suggestions." *Religious Studies* 37 (2001): 308.

Flint, Thomas P., and Michael C. Rea, eds. *The Oxford Handbook of Philosophical Theology*. Oxford: Oxford University Press, 2009. Reprint, Oxford: Oxford University Press, 2013.

Frame, John M. *The Doctrine of God: A Theology of Lordship*. Phillipsburg, NJ: P&R, 2002.

Fretheim, Terence E. *Exodus*. Interpretation: A Bible Commentary for Teaching and Preaching. Edited by James Luther Mays and Patrick D. Miller Jr. Louisville: Westminster John Knox, 1991.

———. "Prayer in the Old Testament: Creating Space in the World for God." In *A Primer on Prayer*. Edited by Paul R. Sponheim, 51–62. Philadelphia: Fortress, 1988.

———. "The Repentance of God: A Key to Evaluating Old Testament God-Talk." *Horizons in Biblical Theology* 10 (1988): 47–70.

Garrett, Duane A. *A Commentary on Exodus*. Kregel Exegetical Library. Grand Rapids: Kregel, 2014.

Gaskin, Richard. "Conditionals of Freedom and Middle Knowledge." *Philosophical Quarterly* 43, no. 173 (1993): 412–30.
Geach, Peter. *God and the Soul*. New York: Schocken, 1969.
George, Timothy. *Amazing Grace: God's Initiative—Our Response*. Nashville: Lifeway, 2000.
Goetz, Ronald G. "Jesus Loves Everybody." *Christian Century* 109 (1992): 274–77.
———. "On Petitionary Prayer: Pleading with the Unjust Judge?" *Christian Century* (1997): 96–98
———. "The Suffering God: The Rise of a New Orthodoxy." *Christian Century* 103 (1986): 385–89.
Goodwin, Thomas. *The Works of Thomas Goodwin*. Vol 3. Edinburgh: James Nochol, 1890.
Green, Joel B. *The Gospel of Luke*. New International Commentary of the New Testament. Grand Rapids: Eerdmans, 1997.
Grudem, Wayne. *Systematic Theology: An Introduction to Biblical Doctrine*. Grand Rapids: Zondervan, 1994.
Hasker, William. *God, Time, and Knowledge*. Ithaca, NY: Cornell University Press, 1989.
Hasker, William. "Middle Knowledge and the Damnation of the Heathen: A Response to William Craig," *Faith and Philosophy* 8 (1991): 380–89.
———. "Providence and Evil: Three Theories." *Religious Studies* 28, no. 1 (1992): 91–105.
———. "A Refutation of Middle Knowledge." *Nous* 20, no. 4 (1986): 545–57.
———. "Response to Thomas Flint." *Philosophical Studies: An International Journal for Philosophy in the Analytic Tradition* 60 (1990): 117–26.
Helm, Paul. *The Providence of God*. Contours of Christian Theology. Downers Grove, IL: InterVarsity, 1993.
Helm, Paul, and Terrance L. Tiessen. "Does Calvinism Have Room for Middle Knowledge? A Conversation." *Westminster Theological Journal* 71, no. 2 (2009): 437–54.
Hendry, George S. "The Life Line of Theology." *The Princeton Seminary Bulletin* 65, no. 2 (1972): 24–26.
Hodge, Charles. *Systematic Theology*. 3 vols. N.p.: n.p., 1872. Reprint, Peabody, MA: Hendrickson, 1999.
Hoeksema, Herman. *Reformed Dogmatics*. 2 vols. Grandville, MI: Reformed Free Publishing Association, 2004.
Hoffman, Joshua. "On Petitionary Prayer." *Faith and Philosophy* 2 (1985): 21–29.
Holloman, Henry W. "Lecture Notes on Theology of Prayer." Class notes, Talbot School of Theology, June 28, 2010.
Holmgren, Fredrick. "The Pharisee and the Tax Collector: Luke 18:9–14 and Deuteronomy 26:1–15." *Interpretation: A Journal of Bible and Theology* 48 (1994): 252–61.
Horton, Michael. *The Christian Faith: A Systematic Theology for Pilgrims on the Way*. Grand Rapids: Zondervan, 2011.
Hunter, W. Bingham. *The God Who Hears*. Downers Grove, IL: InterVarsity Press, 1986.
Japhet, Sara. *1 & 2 Chronicles*. Old Testament Library. Louisville: Westminster John Knox, 1993.

Johnson, Luke Timothy. *The Letter of James: A New Translation with Introduction and Commentary by Luke Timothy Johnson*. Anchor Bible. Edited by D. N. Freedman, vol. 37A. New Haven: Yale University Press, 1995.

Keathley, Kenneth. *Salvation and Sovereignty: A Molinist Approach*. Nashville, TN: B&H, 2010.

Kelly, Douglas F. "Prayer and Union With Christ." *Scottish Bulletin of Evangelical Theology* 8, no. 2 (1990): 109–27.

Kitahata, Stacy and Craig L. Nessan. "Give Us This Day Our Daily Bread." *Currents in Theology and Mission* 38 (2011): 48–52.

Klein, Ralph W. *2 Chronicles*. Hermenia: A Critical and Historical Commentary of the Bible. Minneapolis: Fortress, 2012.

Knight, George A. F. *Theology as Narration: A Commentary on the Book of Exodus*. Grand Rapids: Eerdmans, 1976.

Koons, Jeremy Randel. "Is Hard Determinism a Form of Compatibilism?" *The Philosophical Forum* 33 (2002): 81–99.

Kraus, Hans-Joachim. *Psalms 60–150*. Continental Commentary. Minneapolis: Fortress, 1993.

Kreider, Glenn R. "God Never Begrutches His People Anything They Desire." *Reformation and Revival Journal* 12 (2003): 71–91.

———. *God With Us: Exploring God's Personal Interactions with His People throughout the Bible*. Phillipsburg, NJ: P & R, 2014.

———. "Jonathan Edwards's Theology of Prayer." *Bibliotheca Sacra* 160 (2003): 434–56.

Kvanvig, Jonathan L. "On Behalf of Maverick Molinism." *Faith and Philosophy* 19, no. 3 (2002): 348–57.

Laing, John D. "The Compatibility of Calvinism and Middle Knowledge." *Journal of the Evangelical Theological Society* 47, no. 3 (2004): 455–67.

Leftow, Brian. "No Best World: Creaturely Freedom." *Religious Studies* 41 (2005): 269–85.

Lemke, Steve W. "God's Relation to the World: Terrance Tiessen's Proposal on Providence and Prayer." *Criswell Theological Review* 1, no. 2 (2004): 205–13.

Letham, Robert. *The Holy Trinity in Scripture, History, Theology, and Worship*. Phillipsburg, NJ: P & R, 2004.

Lundbom, Jack R. *Jeremiah 1–20*. Anchor Bible. Edited by D.N. Freedman, vol. 21A. New York: Doubleday, 1999.

MacGregor, Kirk R. "Hubmaier's Concord of Predestination with Free Will." *Direction: A Mennonite Brethren Forum* 35, no. 2 (2006): 279–99. Accessed October 9, 2015. http://www.directionjournal.org/35/2/hubmaiers-concord-of-predestination-with.html.

———. *Luis De Molina: The Life and Theology of the Founder of Middle Knowledge*. Grand Rapids: Zondervan, 2015.

———. *A Molinist-Anabaptist Systematic Theology*. Lanham, MD: University Press of America, 2007.

Manton, Thomas. *James*. Crossway Classic Commentaries. Edited by Alister McGrath and J. I. Packer. Wheaton: Crossway, 1995.

Marshall, I. Howard. *The Gospel of Luke*. New International Greek Testament Commentary. Grand Rapids: Eerdmans, 1978.

———. *The Epistles of John*. New International Commentary on the New Testament. Grand Rapids: Eerdmans, 1978.

McCabe, Lorenzo Dow. *Divine Nescience of Future Contingencies a Necessity: Being an Introduction to "The Foreknowledge of God, and Cognate Themes."* New York: Phillips and Hung, 1882.

McGrath, Alister E. *Christian Theology: An Introduction*, 5th Edition. West Sussex: John Wiley and Sons, 2011.

Melick, Richard R. Jr. *Philippians, Colossians, Philemon*. Vol. 32 of *New American Commentary: An Exegetical and Theological Exposition of Holy Scripture*. Nashville: B&H, 1991.

Merrill, Eugene H. *A Commentary on 1 and 2 Chronicles*. Kregel Exegetical Library. Grand Rapids: Kregel, 2015.

———. *Deuteronomy*. New American Commentary, vol. 4. Nashville: B&H, 1994.

Miller, Patrick D. *Deuteronomy*. Interpretation: A Bible Commentary for Teaching and Preaching. Louisville: John Knox, 2012.

Moo, Douglas J. *Galatians*. Baker Exegetical Commentary on the New Testament. Grand Rapids: Baker, 2013.

Morris, Thomas V. *Making Sense of It All*. Grand Rapids: Eerdmans, 1992.

Morriston, Wes. "Explanatory Priority and the 'Counterfactuals of Freedom.'" *Faith and Philosophy* 18, no. 1 (2001): 21–35.

Murray, Michael J. "Does God Respond to Petitionary Prayer?" In *Contemporary Debates in Philosophy of Religion*. Edited by Michael L. Peterson and Raymond J. VanArragon, 242–67. Malden, MA: Blackwell, 2004.

Murray, Michael J. and Kurt Meyers. "Ask and it Will Be Given You." *Religious Studies* 30 (1994): 311–30.

Myers, David B. "Exclusivism, Eternal Damnation, and the Problem of Evil: A Critique of Craig's Molinist Soteriological Theodicy." *Religious Studies* 39 (2003): 407–8.

Nagel, Norman. "Luther and the Priesthood of All Believers." *Concordia Theological Quarterly* 61 (1997): 277–98.

Nesbitt, Winston, and Stewart Candlish. "Determinism and the Ability to do Otherwise." *Mind* 87 (1978): 415–520.

———. "On Not Being Able to do Otherwise." *Mind* 82 (1973): 321–30.

Oden, Thomas C. *Class Christianity: A Systematic Theology*. New York: Harper Collins, 1992.

Okorie, A. M. "The Characterization of the Tax Collectors in the Gospel of Luke." *Currents in Theology and Mission* 22 (1995): 27–32.

Oord, Thomas Jay, ed. *Creation Made Free: Open Theology Engaging Science*. Eugene, OR: Pickwick, 2009.

———. *The Uncontrolling Love of God: An Open and Relational Account of Providence*. Downers Grove, IL: InterVarsity, 2015.

Ostrander, Rick. *The Life of Prayer in a World of Science: Protestants, Prayer, and American Culture, 1870–1930*. Oxford: Oxford University Press, 2000.

Owen, H. P. *The Basics of Christian Prayer*. Vancouver, British Columbia: Regent College, 2006.

Owen, John. *The Priesthood of Christ: Its Necessity and Nature*. Kirby Street, London: Christian Heritage, 2010.

Packer, J. I. "When Prayer Doesn't 'Work.'" *Christianity Today*, January 6, 1997.

Perszyk, Kenneth J. "Free Will Defense With and Without Molinism." *International Journal for Philosophy of Religion* 43, no. 1 (1998): 29–64.

———. "Molinism and Compatibilism." *International Journal for Philosophy of Religion* 48, no. 1 (2000): 11–33.

Phillips, Richard. "Prayer and the Sovereignty of God." In *Let Us Pray: A Symposium on Prayer by Leading Preachers and Theologians*. Edited by Don Kistler, 86–101. Orlando: Northampton, 2011.

Pink, Arthur W. *The Sovereignty of God*. Blacksburg, VA: Wilder, 2008.

Pinnock, Clark H. *The Doctrine of God*. Phillipsburg, NJ: P. & P., 2002.

———. *Most Moved Mover: A Theology of God's Openness*. Grand Rapids: Baker, 2001.

———. "God Limits His Knowledge." In *Predestination and Free will: Four Views of Divine Sovereignty and Human Freedom*. Edited by David Basinger and Randall Basinger, 141–162. Downers Grove, IL: InterVarsity, 1986.

———. "Open Theism: An Answer to My Critics." *Dialog: A Journal of Theology* 44 (2005): 237–45.

Pinnock, Clark, Richard Rice, John Sanders, William Hasker, and David Basinger. *The Openness of God: A Biblical Challenge to the Traditional Understanding of God*. Downers Grove, IL: InterVarsity, 1994.

Pinnock, Clark H., and Robert C. Brow. *Unbounded Love: A Good News Theology for the Twenty-First Century*. Downers Grove, IL: InterVarsity, 1994. Reprint, Eugene: Wipf and Stock, 2000.

Piper, John. "Cancer Is a Parable About Sin." *Desiring God* (2015): 1. Accessed June 2, 2015. http://www.desiringgod.org/articles/cancer-is-a-parable-about-sin.

Piper, John. *Doctrine Matters: Ten Theological Trademarks from a Lifetime of Preaching*. Minneapolis, MN: Desiring God, 2014.

———. *Don't Waste Your Cancer*. Wheaton, IL: Crossway, 2011.

———. "Has God Predetermined Every Tiny Detail in the Universe, Including Sin?" *Desiring God* (2010). Accessed June 2, 2015. http://www.desiringgod.org/interviews/has-god-predetermined-every-tiny-detail-in-the-universe-including-sin.

———. "Let Your Requests Be Made Known to God." *Desiring God* (2003): 1. Accessed May 5, 2015. http://www.desiringgod.org/sermons/let-your-requests-be-made-known-to-god.

———. *The Pleasures of God: Meditations on God's Delight in Being God*. Sisters, OR: Multnomah, 2000.

———. "The Sovereignty of God: My Counsel Shall Stand, and I Will Accomplish All My Purpose." *Desiring God* (2012). Accessed March 30, 2015. http://www.desiringgod.org/sermons/the-sovereignty-of-god-my-counsel-shall-stand-and-i-will-accomplish-all-my-purpose.

———. *Spectacular Sins and Their Global Purpose in the Glory of Christ*. Wheaton, IL: Crossway, 2008.

Piper, John, and Justin Taylor, eds. *Suffering and the Sovereignty of God*. Wheaton, IL: Crossway, 2006.

Ratzinger, Joseph. *Catechism of the Catholic Church*. New York: Doubleday, 1995.

Redding, Graham. *Prayer and the Priesthood of Christ in the Reformed Tradition*. London: T. & T. Clark, 2003.

Rice, John R. "Biblical Support for a New Perspective," in *The Openness of God*, 11–58. Downers Grove, IL: InterVarsity, 1994.

———. *Whosoever and Whatsoever: When You Pray*. Murfreesboro, TN: Sword of the Lord Publishers, 1970.

Rice, Richard. "The Final Form of Love: The Science of Forgiveness and the Openness of God." In *Creation Made Free: Open Theology Engaging Science*. Edited by Thomas Jay Oord, 195–218. Eugene, OR: Pickwick, 2009.
Ryrie, Charles C. *Basic Theology*. Chicago: Moody, 1999.
Sanders, John. *The God Who Risks: A Theology of Divine Providence*. Downers Grove, IL: InterVarsity, 2007.
Sasson, Jack M. *Jonah*. Anchor Bible. Edited by D. N. Freedman, vol. 24B. New York: Doubleday, 1990.
Smilansky, Saul. "Free Will and Moral Responsibility: The Trap, the Appreciation of Agency, and the Bubble." *Journal of Ethics* 16 (2012): 211–39.
Smith, T. P. "On the Applicability of a Criterion of Change." *Ratio* 15 (1973): 325–33.
Sponheim, Paul R. "The God of Prayer." In *A Primer on Prayer*. Edited by Paul R. Sponheim, 63–76. Philadelphia, PA: Fortress, 1988.
Stuart, Douglas K. *Exodus: An Exegetical and Theological Exposition of Holy Scripture*. New American Commentary. Nashville: B&H, 2006.
Stump, Eleonore. "Hoffman on Petitionary Prayer." *Faith and Philosophy* 2 (1985): 30–37.
———. "Petitionary Prayer." *American Philosophical Quarterly* 16, no. 2 (1979): 81–91.
Suchocki, Marjorie Hewitt. *Theological Reflections on Prayer: In God's Presence*. Atlanta: Chalice, 1996.
Sumney, Jerry L. *Colossians: A Commentary*. New Testament Library. Louisville: Westminster John Knox, 2008.
Talbot, Mark R. "'All the Good That Is Ours in Christ': Seeing God's Gracious Hand in the Hurts Other Do to Us." In *Suffering and the Sovereignty of God*. Edited by John Piper and Justin Taylor, 31–77 (Wheaton: Crossway, 2006).
Thompson, J. A. *The Book of Jeremiah*. New International Commentary of the Old Testament. Grand Rapids: Eerdmans, 1980.
Tiessen, Terrance L. "Can God be Responsive if the Future is Not Open?" In *Semper Reformandum: Studies in Honour of Clark H. Pinnock*. Edited by Stanley E. Porter and Anthony R. Cross, 94–110. Carlisle, Cumbria: Paternoster, 2003.
———. "Is God's Knowledge of Counterfactuals Necessary, Middle or Free? A Calvinist Proposal." A Paper Presented at the Annual Meeting of the Evangelical Theological Society. Valley Forge, PA, November 17, 2005.
———. *Providence and Prayer: How Does God Work in the World?* Downers Grove, IL: InterVarsity, 2000.
———. "Why Calvinists Should Believe in Divine Middle Knowledge, Although They Reject Molinism." *Westminster Theological Journal* 69, no. 2 (2007): 345–66.
Turretin, Francis. *Institutes of Elenctic Theology*. Edited by James T. Dennison, Jr., Translated by George Musgrave Giger. 3 vols. Phillipsburg, NJ: P&R, 1992.
Ulanov, Ann Belford. "What Do We Think People Are Doing When They Pray?" *Anglican Theological Review* 60 (1978): 387–98.
Van Horn, Luke. "On Incorporating Middle Knowledge into Calvinism: A Theological/Metaphysical Muddle?" *Journal of the Evangelical Theological Society* 55, no. 4 (2012): 807–27.
Van Inwagen, Peter. *An Essay on Free Will*. Oxford: Oxford University Press, 1983. Reprint, New York: Oxford University Press, 2002.
Vilhauer, Ben. "Hard Determinism, Humeanism, and Virtue Ethics." *Southern Journal of Philosophy* 46 (2008): 121–44.

Voak, Nigel. "English Molinism in the Late 1590s: Richard Hooker on Free Will, Predestination, and Divine Foreknowledge." *Journal of Theological Studies* 60, no. 1 (2009): 130–77.

Walls, Jerry L. "Is Molinism as Bad as Calvinism?" *Faith and Philosophy* 7 (1990): 85–98

Walls, Jerry L., and Joseph R. Dongell. *Why I am Not A Calvinist*. Downers Grove, IL: InterVarsity, 2004.

Ware, Bruce. *God's Greater Glory: The Exalted God of Scripture and the Christian Faith*. Wheaton, IL: Crossway, 2004.

———. "Prayer and the Sovereignty of God." In *For the Fame of God's Name: Essays in Honor of John Piper*. Edited by Sam Storms and Justin Taylor, 126–143. Wheaton, IL: Crossway, 2010.

———. "Robots, Royalty, and Relationships? Toward a Clarified Understanding of Real Human Relations with the God Who Knows and Decrees All That Is." *Criswell Theological Review* 1, no. 2 (2004): 191–203.

Warrington, Keith. "James 5:14–18: Healing Then and Now." *International Review of Mission* 93 (2004): 348–67.

Wells, Samuel. "A Different Way to Pray." *Christian Century* (2014): 51.

Wink, Walter. *Engaging the Powers: Discerning and Resistance in a World of Domination*. Minneapolis: Fortress, 1992.

Woodruff, David W. "Examining Problems and Assumptions: An Update on Criticisms of Open Theism." *Dialog* 47, no. 1 (2008): 53–63.

Work, Telford. *Deuteronomy*. Brazos Theological Commentary on the Bible. Grand Rapids: Brazos, 2009.

Wright, N. T. "Thy Kingdom Come: Living the Lord's Prayer." *Christian Century* (1997): 268–70.

Young, J. Terry. "Baptists and the Priesthood of Believers." *Theological Educator* 53 (1996): 19–29.

Young, Robert. "Petitioning God." *American Philosophical Quarterly* 11 (1974): 193–201.

Youngblood, Kevin J. *Jonah: God's Scandalous Mercy*. Hearing the Message of Scripture Commentary. Grand Rapids: Zondervan, 2013.

www.ingramcontent.com/pod-product-compliance
Lightning Source LLC
Chambersburg PA
CBHW062041220426
43662CB00010B/1596